SUSTAINABLE DEVELOPMENT AND THE FUTURE OF CITIES

SUSTAINABLE DEVELOPMENT
AND
THE FUTURE OF CITIES

Edited by

Bernd Hamm / Pandurang K. Muttagi

Jean-Monnet-Chair
in European Studies

UNESCO-Chair
Europe in an International Perspective

Zentrum für europäische Studien
Centre for European Studies
Centre d' études européennes

PUBLISHING

Published by ITDG Publishing
103–105 Southampton Row, London WC1B 4HL, UK
www.itdgpublishing.org.uk

© Centre for European Studies 1998
Published with the support of UNESCO

First published in 1998
Reprinted 2001

ISBN 1 85339 425 1

A catalogue record for this book is available from the British Library.

ITDG Publishing is the publishing arm of the Intermediate Technology
Development Group. Our mission is to build the skills and capacity of people in
developing countries through the dissemination of information in all forms,
enabling them to improve the quality of their lives and that of future generations.

Printed in India

Contents

Part II
Regional Perspectives

Part III
Local Answers

Ecological Urban Development: An Experiment in Active Learning

The Authors

Alex Brillantes is director of the Local Government Academy, Department of the Interior and Local Government, Manila, Philippines.

Marina Fischer-Kowalski teaches sociology at the Inter-University Institute for Interdisciplinary Research and Continuing Education, Vienna, Austria.

Nikolai Genov is professor of sociology and head of the Department of Global and Regional Development in the Institute of Sociology, Bulgarian Academy of Sciences, Sofia, Bulgaria.

Miroslav Grochowski teaches geography at the European Institute for Regional and Local Development, University of Warsaw, Poland.

Helmut Haberl, Inter-University Institute for Interdisciplinary Research and Continuing Education, Vienna, Austria.

Bernd Hamm is professor of sociology and director of the Centre for European Studies, University of Trier, Germany.

Lorenz Hilty is assistant professor of informatics, University of Hamburg, Germany.

Irena Jedrzejczyk is asisstant professor of ecological economics at the Economic Academy of Katowice, Poland.

On-kwok Lai is professor with the Department of Political Science and Public Policy, University of Waikato, Hamilton, New Zealand.

Peter Marcuse is a lawyer who teaches urban planning at Columbia University, New York, USA.

Charles Middleton is professor at the Department of Architectural Science and Landscape Architecture, Ryerson Polytechnic University, Toronto, Canada.

Pandurang K. Muttagi was, before retirement, professor of sociology and head of the Urban Research Unit at the Tata Institute for Social Sciences, Bombay, India.

Inge Osthoff is a doctoral student at the University of Paderborn, Germany.

Ljubinko Pusic teaches sociology and futures studies at the University of Novi Sad, Yugoslavia.

William E. Rees, a biologist and ecological economist, is director of the School of Community and Regional Planning, University of British Columbia, Vancouver, Canada.

Mark Roseland is a Ph.D. Candidate in the School of Community and Reguional Planning, University of British Columbia, Vancouver, Canada.

Salah El-Shakhs is professor with the Department of Urban Planning and Policy Development, Rutgers University, New Brunswick NJ, USA.

Arne Tarumaa is professor at the Department of Architecture, University of Oulu, Finnland.

Jadranka Veselic-Bruvo is an architect and advisor to the Bureau for Development Planning and Protection of the Environment, City of Zagreb, Croatia.

Ulrike Weiland is associate professor, Institute of Management in Environmental Planning, Berlin Technical University, Germany.

Asghar Zarrabi is professor and vice-chancellor of the University of Isfahan, Iran.

Introduction

Bernd Hamm and Pandurang K. Muttagi

The Stockholm Environmental Conference of the United Nations (1972) was the first major meeting of the international community to express grave concern over the deteriorating environment. Since then, innumerable workshops and seminars have been held in different parts of the world and thousands of recommendations made to improve the situation. The Earth Summit held in Brazil in June 1992 was an important landmark in global efforts. Academics, planners, policy-makers and administrators continue to discuss the intricacies of development. This is necessary in view of the fact that as globalization accelerates, the global society is getting more and more urban and its problems more complex and interrelated. Despite dozens of meetings and conferences, of manifestos and declarations, of conventions and protocols signed for the sake of sustainable cities, despite even the daily increasing number of cities around the world committing themselves to the Local Agenda 21—there is not one city hall which would meet rigorous ecological standards. We have heard the plenary speeches of heads of state at the Rio summit and its several follow-ups, including at HABITAT 2, and there is clear evidence that almost none of the promised actions has followed. It is especially the affluent West which carries the responsibility of causing a hindrance in the process of global sustainability.

Urban areas are by far the most serious pollutants of our environment. Urban areas have become the functional entities by which humanity organizes its metabolism with nature. The material throughput of the human species is being transformed mostly in cities. Having no natural resources of their own, they import into the urban areas raw materials, capital, and information, which are transformed to emit wastes of all sorts, attitudes, orientations, decisions. They have to absorb new technologies, the changing demographic composition of populations, and new and massive migration streams. In the past, the hinterland from where these urban areas received their inputs and to where they expelled their outputs was relatively limited and in close proximity. The hinterland of the urban areas of today is the entire globe. Every urban supermarket gives easy proof to this consequence of modern transportation technology. This is why the old mechanisms to restrict urban growth and to regulate urban problems no longer work. The development of even small towns can no longer be understood and analysed without taking into account the supralocal, which in most cases means the national, and often international, conditions. Being at the receiving end of supralocal developments on which they have hardly any influence, urban institutions are extremely overburdened. Moreover, urban policies have to cope with missionaries and mafiosi, with ambition and parochialism, with dedication and incompetence, and above all, with short terms of office. The margins for manoeuvre are tight, and city budgets even tighter.

The idea of a sustainable society composed of sustainable cities carries a heavy load of hopes and expectations. Sustainability is not a concept referring to some static paradise, but rather a capacity of human beings to continuously adapt to their nonhuman environments by means of social organization. This is why sustainable development is essentially not about the environment but rather about the capacity of human society to enact permanent reform in order to safeguard the delicate balance between humans and their natural life support system. The emergence of the concept of sustainable development marks an end of the industrial civilization, of fordist production, of the logics of economies of scale. But it also signals that societies based on a vulgar Darwinistic principle of survival of the fittest, of ruthless egoism of the few who mercilessly and thoughtlessly exploit their fellow-humans as they exploit nature, will not survive. Either humanity will eventually succeed in establishing the truly humane principles, or it will vanish from Planet Earth. The African drama is a clear warning. Sustainability indicates the end of the affluent industrial society and points, at the same time, to a future which is not yet clear. It is, however, clear that the basic problem lies in social organizations, in social institutions, in the way how decisions are made, to whose profit and at whose cost. Sustainable development is a complex concept and needs a clearer understanding from various perspectives for effective implementation. But its essence is easy to understand, despite all the efforts presently made to obscure and inflate the concept with different and even contradictory meanings. The bottom-line is that humanity can not and will not survive beyond the limits set by the reproductive abilities of nature. Above all, humanity will have to reduce its total consumption of natural resources.

The obvious inequalities in the consumption of natural resources demand for differentiation. While the countries of the capitalist West, with something like fifteen per cent of the global population (OECD countries), appropriate three-quarters of the earth's natural resources, their wealth is largely based on wasteful consumption. The totally inefficient use of materials and energy goes together with every new fashion, a bizarre multitude of media hardly transporting serious information, or an advertising industry which lacks in value added to the consumable product. Thus, a sharp reduction in natural resource consumption is not only possible but must not necessarily, at least for some time, mean a reduction in welfare. This is what proponents of ecological modernization have in mind when asking for an "efficiency revolution", and this is how they try to make their position politically acceptable. They, however, carefully avoid questions like: Where does this overconsumption of Western societies come from? How and at whose cost is it appropriated? What would the social consequences be if we really would make serious attempts to follow the reduction imperatives? How could a society be imagined which is based on the principle of minimum natural resource consumption? How could an efficiency revolution be introduced, and with what social consequences? How could we proceed towards a sufficiency revolution? While increasing the efficiency in the use of natural resources is a formula pretending that there are technical solutions to the problem, sufficiency is totally contrasting the capitalist way of life, and implies a quest for social solutions. Is it possible to avoid the cynical way of development according to which the broad majority becomes deprived down to the subsistence level, while a small minority indulges in luxury? While it would not be too difficult to imagine a hypothetical sustainable society with not more than one billion global population, we are rapidly approaching six billion: How can social justice be realized in a sustainable society? The basic problem of the capitalist West is that necessary contribution to global sustainability will result in further unemployment. There is no social, political, or economic coalition visible for conserving natural resources without the problem of unemployment being solved.

The former socialist countries had a recent history of relative economic security with full employment, although on a modest welfare level. Environmental concerns were of less than secondary importance. The silent revolutions of 1989/90 were directed against political suppression and mobility restrictions, but first of all they were motivated by the promise of material well-being extended by the Western media. After eight years it is clear that the shock therapy dictated by Chicago boy advisors and their political backing will not only result in temporary adjustment problems but in long-term poverty for major parts of the population and, what is more problematic, in sharp increasing socio-economic polarization. The result, as foreseeable to every social scientist, is social conflict and tension, increasing corruption and crime, political extremism, violence and racism, where mere survival will by far outweigh any idea of long-term environmental protection and sustainability. By all possible means investment by Western companies is attracted, including low wages, minimum environmental restrictions, minimum influence of trade unions, cheap land, and subventions of any kind. The situation is desperate—riots, poverty revolts and civil war are realistic possibilities. At the same time, a small group of profiteers mercilessly exploits the situation backed by vulgar Darwinism which is already the prominent ideology of supply-side economics in the West.

Much more depressing is the situation in many countries of the Third World. Strangled by structural adjustment programmes imposed by the International Monetary Fund and the related cutbacks in social infrastructure and public expenditures, majority of the populations are at risk of sheer existence. Globalization helps the winners to take refuge on the islands of wealth which still exist in the increasingly large oceans of poverty and misery. The globalizing economy marginalizes large proportions of the so-called developing world. The iron law of wages is claiming validity not only here but all over the world. There is of course increasing foreign direct investment in the Third World which seems to support the globalization hypothesis. But a closer look at available statistics clearly reveals that by far most of that goes into the free enterprise zones in China. Most parts of the Third World simply have no room for sustainability considerations of any kind.

There is no more independent, or autonomous, development in any part of the world. All developments are interrelated and interdependent. A vicious paradox arises: While in the West mass purchasing power is deliberately eroded, production capacities have been sharply increased. Export is the only remaining source of economic growth. But this can only work under condition that the export receiving societies have no realistic chance to develop their own production capacities and, thus, remain "underdeveloped". With large populations striving for at least some material well-being, and the desperate necessity to lower ecological standards, global ecological harakiri is well under way. We are caught in a trap, and the only way out would be global solidarity. This is far out of sight.

Analytically, ecological, economic, and social sustainability are inseparable. Therefore, any understanding of the world situation would need a transdisciplinary, global, future-oriented, and policy-relevant outlook which is difficult to find in present-day social sciences of whatever descent. The reform so desperately needed would be far-reaching, even fundamental, and comprise the global society together with all its regional, national, and local subunits. The problématique, to use the term proposed by the Club of Rome to emphasize the interrelatedness of all symptoms in the syndrome of global crisis, does not meet any adequate institutional regulatory capacity. It would be easier to demonstrate the inability of present mainstream scientific endeavours than to find realistic signs of hope. Against popular belief and the academic search for colonizing issues in disciplines claiming exclusive responsibility, sustainable development is not about environmental protection, it is about society in a holistic sense.

In a rapidly urbanizing world, there are many reasons to bring the two together: sustainable development, and the future of cities. It might well be that the future of mankind is decided by the capability of urban areas to change their paths of development from material, economic and population growth to an ecological one, i.e. low resource orientation, and an adequate form of social organization. Despite the great number of suggestions in this direction, despite the theoretical consensus on this point expressed during HABITAT $\overline{2}$, there is little or no noticeable change in urban reality. Urban population growth increases in the metropolises of all Third World countries, as do agglomeration processes in the North as, for example, in the "Blue Banana" of Western Europe stretching from southeast England down to Lombardy in Italy. With urban population growth, we observe increasing energy consumption and traffic; solid, liquid, and gas wastes; decreasing availability of sinks; more pollutant hazards; and degrading technical infrastructures. While tropical rain forest depletion, climate change, or health effects of environmental degradation receive much attention, and of course for good reasons, the enormous waste of natural and human resources caused in the urban areas of the world remains underestimated.

The reason for this stunning contradiction is not that we would not have enough information, or technical recipes, or creative imagination, or scientific and technological research. All proposals for intelligent and ecologically sensitive energy supply based on the use of renewable primary energies and small-scale distribution, decentralized production, least cost planning, etc., have been on the table for years, and the same holds true for strategies of decentralized urbanization, or transportation. But there is no city on earth supplied or designed according to our best ecological knowledge, not to mention residential, commercial, or industrial quarters. Most public awareness is misled and misleading insofar as it does not pay attention to problems of power structures and decision-making processes. It is, first of all, social structures where promising answers to the "global problématique" can be found. It seems, however, that Western social scientists have given up hope to shed light and contribute to change such structures, and instead have in resignation turned to the micro-aspects of society like values, life-styles, or individualization.

This is where the Global and the Local are most obviously interdependent: transnational corporations and the supporting national governments set the conditions for development on the local and regional scales. But the actors appear either to be anonymous like the incredible amount of global financial speculation, or like natural laws as the ups and downs at the stock exchange. We tend to forget that social structures are man-made and therefore changeable, and that democratic societies must find the means to control for exploitation and abuse, and secure the means for basic needs satisfaction of all human beings. This is what sustainable development is about. Therefore it is not confined to mitigating environmental pollution. Its economic and social aspects go inextricably together with its ecological content. If we are not willing or not able to face this complex though essentially simple interdependency, it will mean that socio-economic-ecological polarization between the haves and have-nots will not only increase but accelerate, and with it conflict and tension. The basic question behind sustainable development comes down to be: Who is consuming Which quality and quantity of natural resources for What purpose, for Whose benefit and at Whose cost? No serious discussion of the global problématique can avoid this central issue.

This opens a large array of problems and questions which no single discipline or profession can hope to answer although all disciplines, all professions, all regions of the world have important insight and experience to offer for a better understanding. Cultural diversity is as enlightening a source of knowledge as is history, or gender, or age, or class. In this understanding, there is no "developed" as distinct from an "underdeveloped" region of the world. The cultural dominance claimed by the countries of the North is totally contradictory to their part in global environmental destruction, and much wisdom lies in "underdevelopment" where it goes together with modest and self-reliant life-styles and social development. The North should not only listen carefully to the lessons taught by the South, but also consider its own pre-capitalist history. Even the pre-capitalist history of the North would be full of learning experiences, without romanticizing its dark sides.

Between 1991 and 1994, four International Summer Seminars on Sustainable Development and the Future of Cities were organized at the Bauhaus Dessau, Germany. Participants from different countries of all world regions, from all age groups between 19 and 79, from many disciplines, professions and career phases worked together in an environment which is unique in its creative tradition and atmosphere. The seminar series was a part of the cooperation programme between the Bauhaus and the Centre for European Studies, Trier University, which dated back to days before the velvet revolutions turned the former German Democratic

Republic upside down. The programme received financial support from UNESCO, from the German Commission for UNESCO which holds a patronage over the Centre for European Studies, from the German Federal Ministry for Education and Science, the Friedrich Ebert-Foundation, the Bauhaus, and a number of other sources. The seminars had no fixed programme in the sense of the usual bunch of lecture-type of events. Instead, participants were asked to think carefully about the hopes and expectations which motivated them to attend and present these ideas to the organizers and to the first plenary. Participation was controlled so as to result in a group where half the participants were women, and roughly one-third coming from each group of Western, Eastern, and Third World countries. Close to 160 people from more than seventy countries participated. The first plenary usually served as a problem-defining session. After this the sessions were usually divided into working groups for informal, intensive and in-depth interaction. Regular plenary meetings and small group protocols allowed intense interaction between all. Each of the invited resource persons was asked to present lectures in his or her speciality along with which delegates could enter into discussions. It was even possible to spontaneously invite local experts in order to test some of the ideas developed in one of the groups. Many brought contributions for evening sessions, in the form of slide shows, videos, or lectures. Majority of the topics for the seminars were not imposed by the organisers, but were developed out of the discussion process involving a non-hierarchical, argument-based style of cooperation. Therefore, all seminars were different: the first (1991) emphasized problems of public planning capacity; the second (1992) discussed problems of global economics and their impacts on urban and regional areas; the third (1993) covered practical strategies of implementing sustainable development policies; and the fourth (1994) was on specific cultural and historical aspects of urban sustainability.

Almost all the material collected for this volume has been presented and discussed at these seminars. The papers are partly reflections after the events. All the papers have been revised by the authors for inclusion in this volume. Only a small selection of the papers presented could be included, for obvious reasons. On the other hand, although the book illustrates a rich variety of different aspects of the problem, it is certainly not comprehensive, nor does it intend to be used as a cookbook by planners. The editors have strived for a delicate balance between binding the diverse texts together as an integral entity and at the same time not censuring the individual approaches, epistemological backgrounds and attitudes of contributors. The collection is evidence of the heterogeneity of the urban sustainability debate, while witnessing the basic homogeneity in the understanding of what urban sustainability may be. This reflects nicely the seminar situation: despite the extreme diversity in the seminar group, there was an awareness of a common goal and a spirit of solidarity in achieving it. The papers have been organized into Three Parts.

Part I : Concepts, Theories, Problems—concentrates on the more theoretical issues

Part II : Regional Perspectives—gives an idea of regional differences

Part III : Local Answers—provides the practical solutions.

Part I—Concepts, Theories, Problems, discusses some of the theoretical issues involved in the ongoing debate on sustainable development. *William E. Rees* provides a conceptual framework for assessing ecological realities, planning theory and practice. He assumes a global perspective on the ground that if the basic argument is correct, the success of sustainable development initiatives anywhere add to sustainable development everywhere. Rees notes that the innocuously skeletal definition of sustainable development gave something to everyone. The Brundtland commission advanced economic growth as the principal vehicle for sustainability in the apparent belief that eventually the poor will benefit and sufficient economic surpluses will be available for ecosystems maintenance. Such an argument is patently wrong because economic growth is part of the problem rather than part of its solution. Rees makes a distinction between mere growth and development. This simple distinction is essential for a rational debate on developing sustainability. His thesis is that the dominant economic paradigm is fatally flawed, its limited content and false assumptions are self-defeating in the quest for sustainable development. A true alternative is congealing around new values associated with modesty in natural resource consumption, spiritual development, harmony with nature and mutual reciprocity. Disallowed in technical analysis, such unmeasurables have been relatively neglected in conventional approaches. Rees argues that serious analysis and interpretation of sustainable development raises it above mere technological adjustment and efforts to extend neoclassical economic analysis. Developing sustainability requires profound changes in existing power relationships, a reordering of cultural values, massive institutional reform, and reconsideration of the social role of economic growth. Enormous effort must be placed on managing the global transition from a world dependent on growth to one secure in sufficiency. For sustainable development the need is more for appropriate philosophy than for appropriate technology.

In the next paper, some of these arguments are taken up from a Third World perspective. Urban environments in developing countries have been worsening as a result of rapid growth in population and undesirable patterns of economic growth. The Western models of development which have been adapted and adopted by the governments in the Third World have resulted in providing expensive services to some and not even minimum facilities to many. This has led to severe environmental degradation and inefficient use of resources. *Pandurang K. Muttagi* has analysed the situation in select cities in Latin America, Africa and Asia. He argues that the urgent task in the Third World cities is managing the environment which includes a wide range of activities such as: prevention and control of water, air and noise pollution; maintenance of ecological balance and conservation of non-renewable resources, and proper and careful use of renewable resources. Some of these activities require the use of scientific knowledge and technological inputs, others need adopting less sophisticated, more conventional indigenous ideas and practices, but all of them call for an objective appraisal of the situation.

Environmental problems arise whenever wastes cannot be absorbed and integrated in the natural environment in innocuous ways. Strategies for sustainable development therefore, must be vitally concerned with the organization of flow of materials and energy between society and nature. *Marina Fischer-Kowalski* and *Helmut Haberl* have analysed the problem from a cultural perspective. The culture of each society, according to them, is characterized as a specific balance of reproduction, production, and resources and cultural evolution is a continuing struggle to maintain it. Sustainability is a problem of maintaining a particular social metabolism under given environmental conditions. In the pre-industrial era, the sustainability problem was manifest as a chronic shortage of nutrition, but in industrial societies, it is squarely rooted in the size and quality of their excessive metabolism. It is generally accepted that industrial societies are well on their way to producing irreversible changes in the functioning of the natural systems, but changing this orientation remains an intellectual exercise in obvious contradiction to a lot of seemingly everyday experiences.

Risks and their management are controversial and often present contradictory findings. The field has become increasingly chaotic after the catastrophies in Chernobyl and Bhopal. *On-Kwok Lai* highlights the context in which the states engage themselves in the politics of environment and space and mediate various socio-political constellations of modernity and the emergence of a new production mode. In the second part of the paper, the author discusses four propositions which shed light on the contingent role and limits of the state in environment-spatial processes for sustainable development. These are concerned with the euphoria and uncertainty of state intervention, the legacy of the New Social Movements, the concern for quality of life and the development of the local and global organizations. He observes that the state will still be subject to various socio-economic forces within and increasingly those beyond the nation boundary, and thus it continues to be the mobile locale of strategic dilemma and contradictions concerning environment and space.

Nikolai Genov's paper presents the findings of the nation-wide study on risk perception carried out in Bulgaria, separately for the capital city of Sophia and for the rest of the country. The findings indicate that a sizeable section of the population felt that the problem of pollution is either non-existent or not serious. They perceived unemployment and crime as more serious problems. The author observes that the troubles facing the management of environmental risks in Bulgaria are not the exception but rather the rule in the emerging democracies in Eastern Europe. The factors determining the current situation and the future prospects of risk management are deeply rooted in previous developments and in the present-day critical situation of the Bulgarian society. He is sceptical about the capacity of the well-established institutions managing the multi-dimensional risk situation facing that society and adds that instead of becoming more influential in the course of democratic transformations, the environmental and non-governmental organizations have lost a substantial element of their appeal and fellowship. The paper has been placed in this part because its findings are easily applicable beyond the Bulgarian context.

A genuine task for the social sciences and, among them, for environmental sociology is to suggest a sustainable mode of production and living and indicate the subsystems that will ensure that the right alarms will ring. Legislation, rules and regulations, and bye-laws are the important means of regulating development. In his paper *Peter Marcuse* discusses Property Rights as a tool for desirable development. He observes that these rights can provide very flexible instruments to meet basic human needs, distributing power democratically, achieving a desired level of equality, stimulating accumulation of wealth and providing for sound city planning. Further that property rights, imaginatively defined and implemented, could provide an effective and flexible means of achieving a wide range of public policy goals.

Salah El Shaks focusses on long-range processes and their implications for the planning of mega-cities to create sustainable systems. He discusses growth patterns, polarization reversals and their implications for long-range planning, and makes several observations which are particularly relevant for developing countries. For example, he says that the spatial distribution of urban population and activities within the settlement subsystems of mega-city regions in LDCs becomes a crucial developmental and ecological issue. His observations on the efficient use of urban land and energy resources through an optimum distribution of population within a balanced system of settlements would go a long way towards preserving the natural capital. The risks we face are global, indivisible and multiply themselves at a geometrical rate and exponential scale. They are associated with people, nature and technologies.

Part II—Regional Perspectives, gives an insight into problems and perceptions related to Sustainable Development and the Future of Cities, each from a regional point of view.

With the growth of urban populations comes the more widespread acceptance of urban lifestyles. The growth of the built environment is, itself, an ecological problem, and generates a number of other related difficulties. *Charles Middleton* discusses some issues for the design profession to promote sustainability in the built environment. He points to the fact that the consumption of natural resources is disproportionately high in the Western capitalist societies as compared to the developing world. Change must begin here to have a sizeable global impact. In order to attain sustainable development as a basis for the future of cities in both more and less advantaged countries, the current energy-consuming development of the built environment must be challenged by those who participate in design. Referring to the problems of high resource consumption, the author suggests that the issues should be addressed primarily by economies of the capitalist persuasion rather than by others. It is extremely relevant at the time when media have chosen to boost the advantages of free market economy.

Responding to the challenges for sustainable development in a developing country is a difficult task. It is much more complicated in an environment where the economic and social disparities between the affluent and the underprivileged are glaring. Introducing appropriate legislative measures, rules and regulations, ensuring their implementation and empowering people to take appropriate steps to help achieve desirable goals. *AlexB. Brillantes* discusses the significant role played by the Local Government Code of 1991 in the Philippines in ensuring economic, social and political sustainability. The code provides the foundation of sustainable development and helps transform local authorities into development managers of their own municipalities and play a major role in all spheres of development—economy, governance, resource management and social services. It is significant to note that the code encourages and lays the ground for direct and active participation of NGOs and POs in local government structures and processes.

After decades of communist regime, societies of post-communist countries have lost the ability to self-organization. At the same time their demanding and dependency attitudes are prevailing. The recent political changes introduced in the former communist countries have great potential support not only to build new democratic structures but also to work out new stategies for socio-economic development. *Miroslaw Grochowski* discusses the basic issues, problems and dilemmas which have resulted from the introduction of democratic rule in these countries. Euphoria and optimism characteristic of the first phase of the anti-communist revolution have been replaced by disappointment resulting from the limited possibilities of solving the many problems inherited from the communist system, and newly posed by the need of adaptation. The author has identified several obstacles such as barriers of social apathy which do not allow people to be involved in the process of reforms; barriers of magic thinking which make people ready to believe in easy and harmless solutions; barriers of traditional thinking about the blessing power of industrial development; barriers of environmental awareness which make people believe that they have time to improve their environment and resources.

In an urban-cultural context, *Ljubinko Pusic* notes that the term sustainability implies a satisfaction of social needs on a higher level of aspiration than is the case in a vulgar interpretation of the common mainstream economic and ecological assumptions. Urban areas should develop on their own and at their own pace. The heritage bestowed upon them should be preserved. The concept of sustainable development must be based on strategies which respect the patterns of the urban constitution as of the urban morphology. Rediscovery and reaffirmation of the lost architectural and planning context founded on regional values, and finally patient waiting to perceive improvement in the material and spiritual qualities of the city are needed. Sustainable urban development should respect cultural pluralism instead of being used as a pretext to homogenize cities according to the criteria of junk civilization.

Part III—Local Answers, consists of articles dealing with local solutions in varying socio-economic situations. The concepts of urban planning and technology are inadequate in solving the basic urban crises. In order to develop sustainable urban areas, we need concepts, techniques and measures which allow us to combine environmental policies with social and economic policies. *Ulrike Weiland* and *Lorenz Hilty* describe the existing computer-supported methodologies—Environmental Impact Assessment, Life Cycle Assessment, Eco-logistics and Material Flux Analysis. These instruments require completion and integration. Even if integrated in a holistic and consistent framework, they are not sufficient to bring about the paradigm shift from conventional urban planning to sustainable urban management. The new ideas such as the concept of fractal urban form, the sequential inter-industry model, the dynamic economic-ecological models and the like need to be developed and utilized.

William E. Rees and *Marc Roseland* in their paper "Sustainable Communities: Planning for the 21st Century", observe that strong sustainability has serious implications for urban form, for the material basis of urban life, and for community social relationships that must be expressed as practical measures in planning Canadian communities. These measures must emphasize the efficient use of urban space, reducing consumption of material and energy resources, improving community livability, and organizing administrative and planning processes which can deal sensitively and comprehensively with the attendant socio-economic and ecological complexities. International bodies and natural governments may struggle to formulate policies to achieve this goal, but it is at the community level where most of these initiatives will have to be implemented. Many local governments have taken action singlehandedly. They recognize that fiscal, economic and ecological benefits will accrue to those who get their environmental house in order.

Ashgar Zarrabi puts the development of the region of Isfahan, Iran, into a regional and national perspective. After having analysed the situation of the city which attracts a large number of migrants from poorer areas, he feels that attempts must be made to decentralize urbanization, stabilize the regions of origin, and establish conditions which especially allow the better educated to stay and contribute to the development of these regions.

Going to Scandinavia, the definition of Sustainable Development was written into the Finnish Building Law, and this is the most important paragraph of the law. The content, briefly translated, is that an area is to be planned in a way that saves natural resources and supports sustainable development of the environment. However, an ecologically sustainable city is an unimaginable utopia. We come closer to sustainable development when we reduce material and energy flows and attempt to return residual products to nature. Achieving these requirements means that we are approaching a city which is greener, smaller scaled and demands less traffic. A precondition for the principles of sustainable development to be achieved is a substantial increase in the awareness of the inhabitants. Conforming to this thinking *Aarne Tarumaa* presents three case studies representing ecology-based planning, EIA-related master-planning and development-based communicative planning procedures in which inhabitants are actively involved from the outset. On the basis of the findings of the case studies, the author concludes that the understanding and application of local tradition to the present is one of the basic prerequisites for a good solution.

Irena Jedrzejezyk presents the results of an empirical research on the economic structure of old industrial regions in Central and Eastern Europe. The prime focus of the research was to create a scientific basis for working out a strategy of sustainable development for the Voivodship of Katowice. The author observes that the environmental degradation of Silesia is caused by its high urbanization and industrialization and by its outdated economic structures, antiquated technologies and negligence in building appliances for the protection of the environment. Diversification of the economy is the key step towards sustainable development. The risk of unemployment and the fear caused by it are the most difficult obstacles that have to be faced. The relevance of the findings of the study to understand the problems in other old industrial areas, but also in developing countries, is obvious.

Jadranka Veselic-Bruvo's paper focusses on folk architecture in Croatia. On its space and time framework, the folk architecture reflects and expresses entire conceptual and emotional capabilities of the human society. It is defined by two groups of factors: natural conditions, and social implications. The first group includes the geological texture of soil, terrain configuration, climate, vegetation and available building material. The second group encompasses historical events, migrations, levels of welfare and ethnic characteristics of the population, organization of the family and the social group. The forced urbanization and industrialization after the Second World War, which were supposed to take us into the happy future while everything traditional was considered retrograde and outdated, brought neglect of agriculture causing further dissolution of rural regions and their social structure, degradation of traditional life-styles and economy, thus causing damage to the rural landscape. The author feels that while physical conditions of the environment are endangered to a considerable extent, the struggle for survival should be accompanied by devotion to the community elevating the living space on a creatively higher level, fighting against automatism, technicism and capitulation to practice.

Bernd Hamm describes a project which he conducted with his Trier University students in urban sustainable development planning. By examining existing projects, they came to the conclusion that ecological planning must have the strong support of the citizens, and therefore citizen participation became an essential aspect of their endeavour. They decided to adopt an action research approach. Although the project was an interesting learning experience, and in fact quite successful in directing the development planning process and a number of decisions made, the work with students also has its severe limitations, given the regular conditions of curricula, time frames, and experience.

The issues and problems of sustainable development of cities are complicated and cover almost every aspect of human life—from politics and economic relations to health, education, legislation, culture and the environment. This volume cannot touch all these aspects. The theoretical interpretations of sustainable development and its implications for planning vary as widely as the ideologies of its various proponents. This debate may continue to reside in academia. It should, however, not impede practical action. The general guideline of such action is that urban development should be directed towards the minimum consumption of natural resources. Among the important consequences would be minimum energy use and the transition towards regenerative sources; the minimization of transportation by, for example, bringing the places of home and work closer together, by gradually reducing import-export relations and favour the local and regional clientele, and by introducing electronic communication; the reduction of needless consumption and the reduction of packing; and the greening of urban spaces including roofs and facades. On the macroscale, decentralized urbanization would be a major goal. It is important and necessary to focus on the ecological necessities that must be accommodated by any realistic approach irrespective of the mostly ideological debates on interpretation. The authors in this volume argue that if economic growth is not equitably distributed, or if growth takes place without concern for education, for nature or for environment, no system can be effective or stable. The present pattern of urban development both in the developed and developing countries is ecologically inefficient and socially inequitable and therefore not sustainable. Sustainable development includes two key elements, one is the meeting of needs and in particular the needs of those who have been left far behind in a century of extraordinary growth. The second element concerns the limits which the world society must now impose to protect the resource base of our environment both locally and globally. Therefore sustainable development imposes standards of consumption which must be met within the bounds of ecological possibility. Both elements are multi-dimensional and extremely complicated to handle. The first one is primarily the problem in developing countries, the second one is that of the developed world, though it is applicable to the sizeable section of the affluent groups inhabiting the developing world. The first measure on the path of a stable social structure is the securing of basic human needs: food, housing, health, security, and education. Without increased investment in these areas, long-term economic prosperity is inconceivable. Social development must therefore be given priority in development aid just as in the countries' finance policies. Despite the almost extreme heterogeneity in the composition of the seminar groups, there was basic consensus on such principles.

There are no short-cuts to the process which requires strong and effective national governments to construct a civil society that can then stretch its hands across the globe on terms of equity. Without this emphasis the global village will resemble the landscape of medieval times with the peasantry and poor strewn across the countryside and nobles holed up in their castles. This is, beyond metaphor, the case until today. It remains true that the affluent countries of our world do deplete natural resources far beyond just proportions, as it is true that they use their power in the international institutions and in transnational corporations to appropriate the benefits and export the disadvantages of the global metabolism. But it is also true that countries like India or China being on the paths of rapid industrialization have tremendous and growing potential for the ecological orientation of their economies and societies. A consequent ecological orientation will unavoidably be followed by a thorough redefinition of justice and welfare. It will, however, result in increasing unemployment in the formal sector and a considerable expansion of informal economies; and, as the entire systems of state funding and social security are based on the premise of paid employment, will result in a reconstruction of social institutions. This is the task post-industrial society has to face on a global scale. It seems close to impossible that such a thing can be achieved; but only few years ago it seemed also impossible that a world organized in two hostile military blocks could be overcome.

The system of industrial production that emerged with the industrial revolution and has continuously been undergoing refinement and updating in terms of ever more efficiency, ever larger production, more raw materials, requiring more specialized skills and labour. If the present trend in industrialization, pollution, resource depletion, and species extinction continued unchanged, gradually there will be a breakdown of society and the irreversible disruption of life-support systems. This will end in sharpening distributional struggles and eventually in global harakiri. It is the system of industrial production which has to take the onus of the present environmental decay. In this context, Schumacher observed that it would be most appropriate to seek the root cause of the present crisis not just in the industrial system of production, but deeper still into that view of life, that philosophy of progress and that approach to human happiness which have sustained it and provided it with a certain legitimacy. A change in moral values could bring about a change in perception of social needs and this would enable the people to set limits to their consumption. But this means changing the social structures in which the value systems are embedded.

Part I
Concepts, Theories, Problems

Understanding Sustainable Development

William E. Rees[1]

PURPOSE AND INTRODUCTION

This paper discusses major themes and perspectives in the ongoing debate over "sustainable development". My aim is to contribute a conceptual framework that will assist academic and professional planners to assess how emerging ideas in sustainable development should inform planning theory and practice in the decades ahead. This task is not as simple as it sounds. Interpretations of sustainable development and its implications for planning vary as widely as the ideologies of its various proponents. However, rather than dwell on ideological differences per se, I focus on certain ecological realities that must be accommodated by any realistic approach to sustainable development. I also assume a global perspective on the grounds that if the basic argument is correct, the success of sustainable development initiatives anywhere are dependent on sustainable development everywhere. With this in mind, the paper concludes with an assessment of current global directions.

Some of the most substantive challenges to conventional thinking come from recent efforts to specify the limiting ecological conditions for sustainable development. Historically, the development debate in liberal democracies has been dominated by social and economic considerations. From this perspective, there are no absolutes—what constitutes sustainable development is largely a matter of subjective opinion and expressed public preference. Within a broadly utilitarian framework, a pluralist society will ultimately arrive at a politically expedient interpretation of the concept through the usual power-brokering, negotiation, and compromise among

---

[1]Part of an earlier version of this paper also appeared in Rees (1991).

competing interests and values. The acceptance of ecological constants obviously places unaccustomed boundaries on this debate.

This is not to deny that many dimensions of development remain subject to sociopolitical negotiation and control. For example, society might achieve sustainable development in ways that reduce economic disparities between the rich and poor, or in ways that exacerbate existing relative poverty (Boothroyd 1991). However, the point here is that the basic ecological requirements for sustainability are not negotiable. Industrial society is now constrained by biophysical realities which, if heeded, provide objective criteria for sustainability. Satisfaction of these ecological criteria is a necessary if not sufficient condition for sustainable development, whatever its political and socioeconomic character.

DEFINING SUSTAINABLE DEVELOPMENT

The concept of sustainable development has deep roots in early 20th Century theory of renewable resource management. Later advanced as a more fully integrated approach to conservation and development in the World Conservation Strategy (IUCN 1980), sustainable development has only recently been popularized by Our Common Future, the 1987 report of the World Commission on Environment and Development (The Brundtland Commission).

The Brundtland Commission defined sustainable development as "development that meets the needs of the present without compromising the ability of future generations to meet their own needs" (WCED 1987:43). This innocuously skeletal definition gave something to everyone, and academia, governments, and non-goverment organizations have been striving ever since to flesh it out. As global ecological trends worsen, any concept that implies we can eat our development cake and have the environment too naturally inspires enthusiasm on all sides of the debate.[2]

General concurrence on the need for sustainable development obscures equally widespread disagreement over the practical meaning of the concept. Environmentalists of all stripes and groups on the political left emphasize the "sustainable" part. They see a need to put Earth first, limit material growth, return to community values, and devise ways to share the world's wealth more equitably. Economic planners, the political centre,

---

[2]Daly and Cobb (1989: 75–76) suggest that the Brundtland Commission's vague definition of sustainable development may have been purposeful and politically astute. It generated serious debate of a full spectrum of possible interpretations. Similarly, Brooks (1990:24) notes that Our Common Future is important "not so much for what it says, but for the reaction it has generated. It has had a galvanizing effect on international development at a crucial time."

and all those to the right lay stress on the "development" component. From this perspective, there are no limits, growth comes first, the present system works, and the global expansion of market economies will create all the wealth needed for world ecological and social security.

While proponents of sustainable development occupy the entire political spectrum, the debate is becoming polarized around two distinctive worldviews each with its own normative assumptions and distinctive vision of humankind's role in the scheme of things. Milbrath (1989) labels these poles the "dominant social paradigm" and the "new environmental paradigm". Taylor (1991) calls them the "expansionist worldview" and the "ecological worldview."

The Brundtland Commission was curiously ambiguous in elaborating on its definition of sustainable development. Our Common Future defines "needs" as the "essential needs of the world's poor, to which over-riding priority should be given." It also acknowledges the "limitations imposed by the state of technology and social organization on the environment's ability to meet [those needs]" (WCED 1987:43). To people concerned about ecology and social equity, such words seemed to be a plea for political recognition of global economic injustice and limits to material growth.

But there is another side to Our Common Future that guaranteed its message would be as enthusiastically received in corporate boardrooms everywhere. The report reassuringly asserts that "sustainable development is not a fixed state of harmony, but rather a process of change in which the exploitation of resources, the orientation of technological development, and institutional change are made consistent with future as well as present needs" (WCED 1987:9). Achieving sustainable development is said to depend on broader participation in decision-making; new forms of multilateral cooperation; the extension and sharing of new technologies; increased international investment; an expanded role for transnational corporations; the removal of "artificial barriers to commerce"; and expanded global trade.

In effect, the World Commission equated sustainable development with "more rapid economic growth in both industrial and developing countries" on grounds that "economic growth and diversification...will help developing countries mitigate the strains on the rural environment" (WCED 1987:89). Consistent with this interpretation, the commission observed that "a five- to tenfold increase in world industrial output can be anticipated by the time world population stabilizes some time in the next century" (WCED 1987:213).[3] In recognition of the additional stress this

---

[3]While this may seem like an extraordinary rate of expansion, it implies an average annual growth rate in the vicinity of only 3.5–4.5% over the next 50 years. Growth in this range has already produced a five-fold increase in world economic output since the Second World War.

implies for the environment, the commission cast sustainable development in terms of more material- and energy-efficient resource use, new ecologically benign technologies, and "a production system that respects the obligation to preserve the ecological base for development" (WCED 1987:65).

Government response to the Brundtland Commission in the industrial democracies is perhaps typified by the report of the Canadian "National Task Force on Environment and Economy" (CCREM 1987). Taking its cue from Brundtland, the task force defined sustainable development as "development which ensures that the utilization of resources and the environment today does not damage prospects for their use by future generations." Ignoring the obvious difficulty posed by the consumption of non-renewable resources in any generation, the report goes on: "At the core of the concept...is the requirement that current practices should not diminish the possibility of maintaining or improving living standards in the future." Perhaps most revealing is the assertion that: "Sustainable economic development does not require the preservation of the current stock of natural resources or any particular mix of human, physical and natural assets. Nor does it put artificial limits on economic growth provided such growth is both economically and environmentally sustainable" (CCREM 1987:3). Certainly no one can accuse this task force of confusing sustainable development with any "fixed state of harmony!"

Both the Brundtland Commission and the Canadian Task Force reflect the prevailing interpretation of sustainable development in the political mainstream and on the right in industrialized countries. Governments and industry increasingly acknowledge that present development practices do produce significant environmental and socioeconomic stress. However, without pausing to examine its systemic roots, both reports assert that the solution to the global ecological crisis resides within the same socioeconomic structures that seem to have created it in the first place.[4]

Even fans of Our Common Future who recognize its radical implications acknowledge that its authors "have turned out to be their own worst

---

[4]Taylor (1991) labels sustainable development a "menace inasmuch as it has been coopted...to perpetuate many of the worst aspects of the expansionist model under the masquerade of something new." Even popular commentators now condemn sustainable development as "dangerous words now being used... to mask the same old economic thinking that preaches unlimited consumption in the crusade to turn more land into glorified golf courses, deadly suburban ghettos, and leaking garbage holes (so-called landfill sites)" Nikiforuk (1990). Nelson (1990) sees industry's enthusiasm for sustainable development as a dangerous "corporate takeover" and the accompanying green rhetoric as little more than public relations "ecobabble". In this vein, one participant in "Globe '90" (a major conference and trade show for the environment industry held in Vancouver in March 1990) observed that sustainable development had apparently come down to "business-as-usual with a treatment plant".

enemies—they failed to draw out the implications of their own statements" (Brooks 1990:24). More virulent critics argue that its analysis is "superficial or lacking". Because it fails to identify and analyse the causes of global poverty and ecological decline it advances solutions "that are the direct opposite of those required". By not challenging the assumptions driving an increasingly market-driven global economy; by ignoring the connection between global ecological concerns and profligate lifestyles of the industrialized countries; by putting their faith in the "indiscriminant growth and trickle down approach to third world development", the Commissioners produced a thoroughly conventional statement. The Brundtland Report "constitutes an enthusiastic and unquestioning reaffirmation of the system, lifestyles, and values that are causing the problems under discussion" (quotations from Trainer 1990:72).

Most important, Our Common Future advances economic growth as the principal vehicle for sustainability in the apparent belief that eventually the poor will benefit and sufficient economic surpluses will be available for ecosystems maintenance. Tenuous assumptions aside, many analysts find this continuing reliance on growth to be the most troubling aspect of the mainstream prescription for sustainable development. The World Commission "reveals no acquaintance with any of the extensive literature now supporting [challenges] the growth conception of development" (Trainer 1990:79). Indeed, the Commission's work was little influenced by science of any kind. Its mandate ensured that the Commission "was most concerned with values..." (Timberlake 1989:117). As a result, for all its pervasive influence, Our Common Future is a political document, not a scientific one. "The claim that we can have economic growth without damaging the environment is a sheer statement of opinion" (Timberlake 1989:122).

Perhaps the fixation on growth per se should come as no surprise. Our "...largely uncritical worship of...economic growth is as central to [capitalism's] nature as the similar veneration of...divine kingship or doctrinal orthodoxy has been for other regimes" (Heilbroner 1989:102).[5] Indeed, some economists believe "not only in the possibility of continuous material growth, but in its axiomatic necessity" (Georgescu-Roegen 1977).

Nevertheless, given the "sustainability" theme, it is remarkable that neither the Brundtland Commission nor the Canadian Task Force distinguish between growth, which "should refer to quantitative expansion in the

---

[5]Heilbroner notes elsewhere that growth through the reinvestment of profit is the unique essence of the capitalist system. As the "the life blood of capitalism", profit not only provides the "wherewithal for expansion" but also represents "the intangible structure of power, hierarchy, privilege, and belief that arise from the systems nature and that give rise to its logic" (Heilbroner 1985:76–77).

scale...of the economic system", and development which "should refer to the qualitative change in a physically nongrowing economic system in dynamic equilibrium with the environment" (Daly and Cobb 1989:71). By these definitions, sustainable growth in a finite environment is a logical impossibility but sustainable development contains no self-contradiction. This simple distinction between mere growth and true development is essential to rational debate on developing sustainability, but has scarcely entered the discussion!

There is an historical basis for this reticence. Economic growth has long been the principal instrument of social policy in capitalist societies. "If we can have perpetual growth, those who are relatively well off won't have to share their wealth with others" (Miernyk 1982:4). Thus, we refuse to fight poverty by redistribution and sharing... leaving 'economic' growth as the only acceptable cure...." (Daly 1990:118). The promise of an ever-increasing economic pie holds out hope that even the poor will eventually get an adequate share. This expectation reduces popular pressure for policies aimed at more equitable distribution of national incomes.

While morally bankrupt, this "solution" to social inequity posed no physical threat to society as long as the economy was small relative to the scale of the ecosphere. This is no longer the case, but in advancing growth-as-solution once again, our mainstream authors make no attempt to weigh the anticipated future scale of the global economy against the finite productive capacity of the ecosphere.

In fairness, we should note that conventional economic analysis cannot even pose the proper question. Macro-economic theory has nothing to say about the appropriate scale of the economy (Daly 1989,1990). The idea of continuous growth is so firmly entrenched that the issue of scale has apparently not been considered relevant. By contrast, from the ecological perspective, it is very much an open question whether it is possible to expand industrial production by a factor of five to ten while simultaneously guaranteeing "the sustainability of ecosystems upon which the global economy depends" (WCED 1987:67). How the world's dominant economic paradigm has drifted so far from what seems to be self-evident reality is the focus of the following section.

THE MECHANICAL ECONOMY

A given culture's "story" about reality provides "a context in which life [can] function in a meaningful manner" (Berry 1988:123) and profoundly affects how its members act in the world. The internal contradictions of our prevailing economic story can be traced to the 19th Century founders of the neoclassical school. Impressed with the successes of Newtonian physics, they set about to create economics as a sister science "the mechanics of utility and self-interest" (Jevons 1879, cited in Georgescu-Roegen 1975).

The decision to develop a mechanical rather than biological metaphor for the economy was a critical one. While economics is (or should be) a branch of human ecology, the central assumptions of modern economic theory are uninformed by ecological principles. Three closely related assumptions of the mechanical model are sufficient to illustrate this historic divergence.

1) Industrial society perceives the human enterprise as dominant over and essentially independent of nature. Indeed, we act as if the economy is somehow separate from the rest of material reality. The parallel notion of environment-as-separate entity is therefore a social invention reflecting the Cartesian subject-object dualism at the heart of western scientific materialism.[6] The very word becomes its own criticism diffidently declaring itself to be peripheral, unimportant, not to be taken seriously (Rowe 1989). The economy may use "the environment" as a source of resources and sink for wastes (Herfindahl and Kneese 1974), but beyond that it is perceived as a mere static backdrop to human affairs.

2) Economists have adopted the circular flow of exchange value as the starting point for analysis rather than the one-way entropic throughput of energy and matter (Daly 1989:1). The major consequence is an entrenched view of economic process as "a self-sustaining circular flow between production and consumption...". By this perception, "everything... turns out to be just a pendulum movement.... If events alter the supply and demand propensities, the economic world returns to its previous position as soon as these events fade out." Most important, "complete reversibility is the general rule, just as in mechanics" (Georgescu-Roegen 1975:348). Indeed, by inventing a perpetual motion machine economics seems to have done mechanics one better!

3) We have come to believe that resources are more the product of human ingenuity than they are of nature. According to the neoclassical theory, rising market prices for scarce materials encourage conservation on the one hand and stimulate technological substitution on the other. It is part of the conventional wisdom of many economic planners that these factors have indeed been more than sufficient to overcome emerging resource scarcities (Victor 1990:14).

---

[6]Descartes viewed the external material world "as a machine and nothing but a machine. There was no purpose, life, or spirituality in matter" (Capra 1982:60). He even extended this mechanistic view to living organisms: '...I do not recognize any difference between the machines mades by craftsmen and the various bodies that nature alone composes' (Descartes, cited in Capra 1982:61).

While standard neoclassical texts conclude almost conservatively that "exhaustible resources do not pose a fundamental problem" (Dasgupta and Heal, 1979:205), the most ardent (and influential) disciples of the substitutability principle are moved to idealistic, almost surreal, extremes.[7] Gilder argues that we "must overcome the materialistic fantasy: the illusion that resources...are essentially things, which can run out, rather than products of the human will and imagination which in freedom are inexhaustible" (Gilder 1981:232, cited in Daly and Cobb 1989:109). Similarly, Simon (1982:207) remarks: "You see, in the end copper and oil come out of our minds. That's really where they are." So pervasive is this doctrine that Block (1990:304) uses it to argue for further population growth on grounds that people "create the wealth they need to maintain themselves and more, thanks to free markets and technological progress."

To summarize, economic theory necessarily contains a model of nature. The key assumptions of the contemporary model range from mechanical dualism on the one extreme to metaphysical idealism on the other. Together they describe an economic system which, being functionally independent of physical reality, has unlimited potential to expand. Add open access to resources (the so-called "common property" problem) and future discounting (particularly in the face of uncertainty) and we have a system in which there are often "no economic forces whatever acting in favour of sustainable development..." (Clark 1991).

THE ECONOMY IN THE REAL WORLD[8]

Given its material success in the industrial age, countries almost everywhere now find the neoclassical paradigm a more compelling guide to economic policy and behaviour than is the biophysical reality from which it is abstracted. As with all models, its internal logic "heighten[s] the tendency to prize theory over fact and to reinterpret fact to fit theory" (Daly and Cobb 1989:38).[9] This section re-examines the internal logic of the model in light of ecological theory. My thesis is that the dominant economic paradigm is fatally flawed. Its limited content and false assumptions are self-defeating in the quest for sustainable development.

From the relative objectivity of scientific ecology, there is little to distinguish humankind functionally from the millions of other species with

---

[7]This reflects the Kantian argument that the human mind is not passive in its experience. It actively creates its own reality. "In fact, anything we can speak of... is in some sense a product of the human mind" (Daly and Cobb 1989:108).

[8]Based on Rees 1990 a, b, c.

[9]Daly and Cobb (1989) refer to this general problem as the "fallacy of misplaced concreteness" and provide several additional examples.

which we share the planet. Like other organisms, we survive and grow by extracting energy and material resources from the ecosystems of which we are a part. Like other species we "consume" these resources before returning them in altered form to the ecosphere. Thus, far from existing in splendid isolation, the human economy is and always has been an inextricably integrated, completely contained, and wholly dependent sub-set of the ecosphere.

While politicians and businessmen call for "environment-economy integration" as the solution to our environmental crisis, it is actually the present form of integration that is the cause of the problem. It follows that since we cannot separate the economy from the ecosphere, we must restructure the relationship to conform to ecological reality rather than to more comfortable but simplistic assumptions. Only in this way can economics finally become good human ecology.

Contrary to conventional wisdom, the ecologically relevant flows through the material economy are not circular but unidirectional. This is because the ultimate regulator of the economy is not mechanics but thermodynamics. In particular, the Second Law (the entropy law) states that in every material transformation, available energy and matter are continuously and irreversibly degraded to the unavailable state (see Georgescu-Roegen 1975:1977). Economic activity requires both energy and matter and therefore necessarily contributes to a constant increase in global net entropy (disorder) through the continuous dissipation of waste heat and residuals (pollution) into the ecosphere.[10]

Without reference to this entropic throughput "it is virtually impossible to relate the economy to the environment," yet the concept is "virtually absent from economics today" (Daly 1989:1).

In effect, thermodynamic law dictates that all material economic "production" is actually consumption. Herein lies the essence of our environmental crisis. Since our economies are growing and the ecosystems within which they are embedded are not, the consumption of resources everywhere has begun to exceed sustainable rates of biological production. Seen in this light, much of today's wealth is illusion derived from the irreversible conversion of productive natural capital into perishable human-made capital.

We now have the basis for a thermodynamic definition of sustainable development as development that minimizes the increase in net global

---

[10]For example, a finished automobile represents only a fraction of the energy and material (typically 25 metric tons) that has been permanently dissipated as pollution in the manufacturing process. Similarly, modern energy-subsidied agriculture consumes up to 10 fossil calories for every calorie of food energy produced.

entropy. (In theory, we could actually work with the ecosphere to reduce the entropy of the ecosphere.) By contrast, our present emphasis on material growth maximizes resource use and consumption, thereby maximizing entropy.

Wishful thinking aside, humankind exists in a state of obligate dependency on many critical products and processes of nature. Resource depletion therefore remains a fundamental problem. While market mechanisms may be effective at setting prices and finding substitutes for valued nonrenewables such as copper or oil, they are an inadequate solution to the depletion of bioresources on several grounds:

1) Price- or scarcity-induced substitution may occur too late to permit the recovery of renewable and replenishable resources that have been over-exploited;

2) Substitution does nothing to repair the pollution damage caused by the dissipation of the byproducts of previously depleted resources;

3) Some renewable resources for which there are markets (e.g., agricultural products) are dependent on material or process resources (e.g., soils and soil-building processes) for which there are none; and,

4) Other material (e.g., the ozone layer) and process resources (e.g., photosynthesis, climate stabilization) have not been recognized as economic resources at all.

These last two factors are particularly important. Markets are silent on the state of many ecologically critical materials and processes despite their immeasurable positive economic value. The primary scarcity indicator offered by the neoclassical school—pricing—fails utterly when the assumptions under which it operates do not prevail (Victor 1990). Traditional analysis can therefore lead to morally and ecologically indefensible tradeoffs and substitutions. Consumption and pollution destroy ecologically essential resources with no signal from the marketplace that the very basis of survival is being irreversibly eroded. And there are no technological substitutes.

These weaknesses in the neoclassical model illustrate a basic theorem of systems analysis and cybernetics. "We cannot regulate our interaction with any aspect of reality that our model of reality does not include because we cannot by definition be conscious of it" (Beer 1981:9).[11] In short, if critical dimensions of the global ecological crisis lie outside the parameters of existing economic models, conventional analyses have little to contribute to sustainable development.

_____

[11]Alternatively, "...the regulation that the regulator can achieve is only as good as the model of reality that it contains" (Beer 1981:9).

THE ECOLOGICAL BASIS FOR REFORM ECONOMICS

The fivefold increase in world economic activity since the Second World War has produced an increasingly integrated world economy whose scale now approaches that of the ecosphere itself. Existing data suggest that the present rate of economic throughput already exceeds the rate of ecospheric production in important ways. Encroaching deserts (6 million ha/year); deforestation (11 million ha/yr of tropical forests alone); acid precipitation and forest dieback (31 million ha damaged in Europe alone); soil oxidation and erosion (26 billion tonnes/yr in excess of formation); toxic contamination of food supplies; draw-down and pollution of water tables; species extinction (1000s/yr); fisheries exhaustion; ozone depletion (5% loss over North America [and probably globally] in the decade to 1990); greenhouse gas buildup (25% increase in atmospheric CO_2 alone); potential climatic change (1.5–4.5°C mean global warming expected by 2040); and rising sea-levels (1.2–2.2 m by 2100) and like trends are the result of either excess consumption or the thermodynamic dissipation of toxic byproducts of economic activity into the ecosphere (Data from: Brown et al. [Annual]; Brown and Flavin 1988; Canada 1988; Schneider 1990; US Environmental Protection Agency [reported in Stevens 1991]). These trends carry the ultimate threat of irreversible ecological disruption and attendant geopolitical instability.[12] Prevailing patterns of development are simply not sustainable.

Fortunately, the ecosphere has the capacity to recover from abuse. Unlike economic systems, ecosystems are inherently self-sustaining, and contribute continuously to reducing global net entropy. The ecosphere therefore appears to defy the entropy law: "...[the system] is in many respects self-generating—its productivity and stability determined largely through its internal interactions" (Perry et al. 1989:230).

The organizational property which enables living systems to produce themselves is known as autopoiesis (Maturana and Varela 1988:43). Autopoiesis is a product of the complex, interdependent relationships (energy, material, and information flows) linking the system's major components. The structural integrity of these relationships is essential not only to the functioning of the system, but also for the production and maintenance of the participating components themselves. Human disruption of

---

[12]The 1991 Persian Gulf war is a recent example. This war was very much rooted in defence of the profligately unsustainable oil-based lifestyles of western democracies. Had we adopted strong conservation measures and promoted more investment in ecologically benign solar technologies in the 1980s in response to rising energy prices and early warnings of atmospheric change in 1970s, we would be facing an oil glut in the 1990s. This would have reduced not only the inter-regional dependencies that led to war but also the threat of global warming.

ecosystemic relationships on a global scale would severely compromise the possibility of achieving sustainable development.

Autopoeisis is possible only because the stuff of ecosystems is constantly being transformed and recycled, and because ecosystems, unlike economic systems, are able to access an external source of free energy, the sun. In thermodynamic terms, photosynthesis is the most important productive process on Earth and the ultimate source of all the biological capital (low entropy resources) upon which the human economy depends.[13]

Since the flow of solar radiation is constant, steady, and reliable, production in the ecosphere is potentially sustainable over any time scale relevant to humankind. Nature's productivity is limited, however, by the availability of finite nutrients, photosynthetic efficiency, and ultimately the rate of energy input (the "solar flux") itself. Ecosystems therefore do not grow indefinitely.[14] Unlike the economy which expands through dominant positive feedback they are held in a dynamic, far-from-equilibrium "steady-state" by negative feedback.

The ecological bottom line for sustainable development should by now be apparent: humankind must learn to live on the "interest generated by remaining stocks of living 'natural capital'. Any human activity dependent on the consumptive use of ecological resources cannot be sustained indefinitely if it not only consumes annual production, but also cuts into capital stocks (Rees 1990a,b).

Recognition that bioresources can be treated as unique forms of productive capital is the major contribution to date of the emerging hybrid discipline of "ecological economics". This economic metaphor even provides new light in which to view the persistently negative ecological trends noted above—the growing global economy may already have reached the point at which the marginal costs of natural capital depletion exceed the marginal benefits of jobs and commodity production. In these circumstances, further growth of the material economy is, in fact, "anti-economic growth" that ultimately "makes us poorer rather than richer" (Daly 1990:118). We explore the implications of these ideas for sustainable development in the following section.

---

[13]The human enterprise already appropriates about 40% of terrestrial photosynthetic activity (Vitousek et al. 1986). Note that in a finite ecosphere, significant expansion of human populations and the material economy can only increase this ratio at the expense of other species.

[14]While production may be more or less continuous, biomass accumulation is limited and ultimately balanced by the decomposition of organic material (previous production). In a closed system, such recycling is essential to provide the material basis (e.g., nutrients) for current production.

MAINTAINING NATURAL CAPITAL: A NECESSARY CONDITION FOR SUSTAINABILITY

Sustainable development, as a goal, rejects policies and practices that support current living standards by depleting the productive base, including natural resources, and that leave future generations with poorer prospects and greater risks than our own (Repetto 1986:15).

There can be little doubt that our present reactive responses to global ecological deterioration compromise our own potential and [shift] the burden of environmental risks to future generations" (Pearce et al. 1989:19). Any proactive prescription for sustainable development must acknowledge the primary role of bioresources in human survival and the inequity inherent in current practice. Maintenance of the functional integrity of the ecosphere is a necessary prerequisite to extending the time horizon for economic policy and to elevating both intra- and inter-generational equity to a place of prominence in developmental decision-making.

The developmental implications of this convergence of ecological and economic thinking are currently being explored through various interpretations of a "constant capital stock" criterion for sustainability (Daly 1990, Pezzey 1989, Costanza and Daly 1990, Pearce et al. 1989, 1990). In essence, adherence to this criterion would require that each generation leave the next generation an undiminished stock of productive assets. There are two possible interpretations of the constant capital stock idea (adapted from Pearce et al. 1989).[15]

a) Each generation should inherit an aggregate stock of manufactured and natural assets no less than the stock inherited by the previous generation. This corresponds to Daly's (1989) conditions for "weak sustainability".

b) Each generation should inherit a stock of natural assets alone no less than the stock of such assets inherited by the previous generation.[16] This is a version of "strong sustainability" as defined by Daly (1989).

The first interpretation reflects the neoclassical assumption that human-made and natural assets are substitutes and that biological assets (e.g., forests) can rationally be liquidated through "development" as long as subsequent investment in manufactured capital (e.g., machinery) provides an equivalent endowment to the next generation.[17] Pezzey (1989:22) seems

---

[15]Both interpretations assume that existing stocks are adequate. If populations are growing or material standards increasing, the stock of productive capital will have to be increased to satisfy the sustainability criterion.

[16]"Natural assets" encompasses not only material resources (e.g., petroleum, the ozone layer, forests, soils) but also process resources (e.g., waste assimilation, photosynthesis, soils formation). It also includes renewable as well as exhaustible resources. For ecological reasons, our primary interest is in maintaining physical stocks biological resources. (Note that the depletion of non-renewables could be compensated for through investment in renewable assets.)

to lean towards this version noting that applying the principle "inevitably boils down to deciding how essential to and substitutable in production are the different components of capital: machines, technical know-how, renewable and non-renewable resources."

The second interpretation better reflects the ecological principles advanced above. In particular, maintaining natural capital stocks recognizes the multifunctionality of biological resources everywhere, "including their role as life support systems" (Pearce et al. 1990:7) In this respect, strong sustainability" recognizes that manufactured and natural capital "are really not substitutes but complements in most production functions" (Daly 1989:22).

The reliability of the ecosphere's life support function is positively correlated with high levels of species diversity and structural complexity. Maintaining biological diversity is therefore a primary goal of natural capital conservation. Diverse natural systems and dependent economic systems display greater resilience (resistance to shock or stress) than species-impoverished managed systems such as agricultural monocultures. More important still, robust ecosystems, unthreatened by irreversible species loss, are essential for autopoiesis. Sustainable development is impossible in a thermodynamically far-from-equilibrium world unless the ecosystems upon which humans depend are capable of continuous self-organization and production.

Pearce et al. (1990) observe that conserving natural capital may seem particularly relevant to developing countries in which socioeconomic stability is immediately and directly threatened by deforestation, desertification, soil erosion, falling water tables, etc. In these circumstances there can be little doubt that existing stocks of natural capital are well below bioeconomic optima and must actually be enhanced for survival let alone sustainability.[18]

However, they also note that further reductions of natural capital may impose significant risks on society, even in countries where it might appear we can afford to reduce stocks. These risks reside in our imperfect knowledge of ecological functions, the fact that the loss of such functions may be irreversible, and our inability to substitute for those functions once lost. In short, because of the unique and essential services provided by ecological capital, we cannot risk its depletion.[19] "In the face of uncertainty

[17]"Equivalent endowment" would be defined in terms of monetary value, wealth generating potential, jobs, and similar economic criteria. (It is worth nothing that humankind has regrettably failed to achieve even the modest objectives of "weak sustainability" in much of the world.)
[18]In economic terms, the optimal stock is the theoretical point at which the marginal costs of further development exceed the marginal benefits.
[19]For example, the present unaccounted economic value of the world's remaining forests

and irreversibility, conserving what there is could be a sound risk-averse strategy" (Pearce et al. 1990:7).

We should note that "constant capital stock" could be interpreted to mean constant economic value which would allow for declining physical stocks with rising real prices over time. Alternately, it might mean constant price over time in situations where intensified exploration or technological substitution are able to compensate for increasing resource scarcity (Pearce et al. 1990:10). However, the foregoing analysis makes clear that the only ecologically meaningful interpretation for renewable resources is in terms of constant physical stock. The constant capital stock criterion therefore overturns the conventional wisdom that "sustainable economic development does not require the preservation of the current stock of natural resources or a particular mix of human, physical and natural assets" (CCREM 1987).

THE LIMITS OF RATIONAL ANALYSIS

The extension of benefit/cost and marginal analysis to ecosphere functions is a conceptually powerful step towards the recognition and protection of ecological values. However, the practical reality is that we are not likely, in the foreseeable future, to quantify adequately the "life support functions" of ecosystems, let alone ascribe a money value at the margin. Having established a seemingly rational framework for "environment-economy integration", there is way to apply it with accuracy or precision. Economic analysis is presently incapable of specifying the optimal stock and appropriate mix of natural assets.

Of course, the possibility remains that inaccurate use would suffice. For example, Amazonian deforestation claimed some 50,000 km^2 in 1989 but clearing fell to 20,000 km^2 in 1990, greatly reducing carbon releases to the atmosphere and the region's contribution to global warming. Pearce (1991) estimates the resultant economic savings (in the form of damage avoided from sea level rise alone) at $ 1300 per hectare for a total of $ 3.9 billion for the 3 million hectares not cleared. He also conservatively estimates the existence value of the Amazon forest (the amount adults in the developed countries might be willing to pay simply to conserve the forest) at $ 3.2 billion per annum. These figures each approximate 20% of the annual economic output of Amazonia. It is conceivable that combined with other ecosystems benefits and option values the estimated total non-market value of the remaining forest would be adequate to preserve much of it intact.[20] It

---

in terms of climate regulation, the stabilization of water regimes, and as carbon sinks may well exceed their market value as wood fibre.

would be in Brazil's interests to accept this sum "as compensation for foregone development benefits if it exceeds the value of those benefits" Pearce (1991:47).

In present circumstances, a much simpler approach might be more procedurally rational (see below). A "sound risk-averse strategy" would involve international agreement that, while technically unestimable, the life support (indirect use) values of critical stocks of natural capital are greater than any stock-depleting direct development values however large the latter might be. Given the enormous threat to global security associated with irreversible disruptions of the ecosphere, and the increasing probability of such events under prevailing development approaches, we are dealing with a category of "strong catastrophic risk". Such risks should, in the limit, not be undertaken at any price (Collard 1988:80).[21]

Decision-makers disturbed by the sweeping uncertainties of economic analysis for sustainable development will hardly be comforted by recent developments in ecology. Unlike the smoothly varying equilibrium models of neoclassical economics, real-world ecosystems, as self-organizing systems characteristically exhibit unexpected non-linear behaviour particularly when perturbed by exploitation (Holling 1986). Indeed, scientists now recognize that even simple deterministic systems with only a few variables can generate seemingly random behaviour. It is characteristic of such "deterministic chaos" that "any effect no matter how small, quickly reaches macroscopic proportions" (Crutchfield et al. 1986:49). Since initial measurements are always uncertain, long-term predictions of dynamical systems behaviour are intrinsically impossible (Crutchfield et al. 1986; May 1989; Davies 1990). Even near-perfect knowledge of the current state of a chaotically self-organizing system does not confer the ability to predict any future state.

These observations could hardly be more unsettling for current development and resource management models. The central assumptions of the "normal" predictive science upon which they are based simply do not obtain. Substantive rationality assumes perfect knowledge, and a substantively rational choice requires that the outcomes of alternative strategies be calculable. By contrast, adequate data—economic or ecologic—on nature's

---

[20]Critics are wary that the dollar valuation of nature's services implies acceptance of the prevailing paradigm and undermines non-economic arguments for conservation (see Ehrenfeld 1978). Pearce (1991:48) acknowledges the anthropocentric and utilitarian nature of this approach but denies that it undercuts other rationales. However, he does assert that "it may not be necessary to resort to moral arguments... if economic arguments alone are sufficient to justify [conservation]".

[21]If either of these approaches is adopted, we would still face the additional wicked problem of [finding] mechanisms for international transfers to compensate the developing world for foregoing legitimate development projects (Pearce 1991:49).

life support functions are not forthcoming, and even if they were, such data would not necessarily improve our capacity to enhance global ecological or geopolitical security. When it comes to managing the ecosphere for sustainability, it seems that the final product of the steady progress of science is a rational argument for decreased reliance on strictly scientific rationality.

It should be clear by now that planning for sustainable development will require procedurally rational approaches that enable "'reasonable men' [to] reach 'reasonable' conclusions in circumstance where they have no prospect of applying classical models..." (Simon 1978:14). The risks and uncertainties associated with global change require that economic and development planners "adapt not just the techniques they use, but possibly the whole way they think about their role and their profession" (Cartwright 1991:54).

TOWARD A TRULY NEW PARADIGM

Such thinking as this reinforces the views of those who believe that the mere extension of existing models cannot solve our problems. To them, industrial society is confronted with a deep cultural malaise whose resolution will require profound changes in traditional beliefs about our relationships to each other and about our place in the natural world. The failure of conventional analyses creates the psychological space necessary for serious contemplation of alternatives and for the emergence of a truly new development paradigm.

Fortunately, there is no shortage of "unscientific" (but otherwise rational) concepts relevant to sustainable development. Numerous authors have begun to articulate new worldviews and corresponding development principles that transcend the conventional emphasis on hard technology, material growth, and the marketplace as the wellspring of all social value. Their writings can be found in a literature ranging widely from appropriate technology through social ecology, ecofeminism, and community development, to bioregionalism and so-called "deep ecology". (See Gardner and Roseland [1989a,b] for an introduction to some of these.)

Where they deal with sustainable development directly, most of these authors address one or more of the following substantive principles or objectives: the maintenance of ecological integrity; the achievement of social equity (within and between generations); the fulfillment of human needs (material and non-material); keeping options open; and support for self-determination (Jacobs et al. 1987; Dorcey 1991). Gardner (1990) distills four additional process-oriented principles from the literature for planning purposes. Taken together, these principles lead to an emphasis on spiritual as well as political freedom, long-term ecological security ahead of short-term economic gain, cooperative social relationships, and community values.

Much current writing addresses only one or a few of the changes needed to preserve ecological integrity or enhance social equity. For example, focussing on the values required to achieve intragenerational equity, Boothroyd (1991) makes an eloquent plea for "compassionate" sustainable development. A common theme in the social ecology/ecology stream is rejection of egocentric individualism and with it the human domination of nature as the key to ecological security (Bookchin 1980). Indeed, ecofeminism treats the continuing domination of women and of nature as two reflections of the same behavioural pathology (Salleh 1984). The major related contribution from deep ecology is recognition that humans are organically inseparable from the non-human world and that "all organisms and entities in the ecosphere as parts of the integrated whole, are equal in intrinsic worth" (Devall and Sessions 1985:67; Naess 1986).

Because of its emphasis on the ecology of place, bioregionalism is worth a special note. This is a "teaching which helps people both to describe the bioregion where they live and then to live within its natural capacity to support life on a sustainable basis by ecological laws (Aberley 1985:145). Bioregional concepts offer much to sustainable development from the sociopolitical perspective as well. For example, bioregionalists treat appropriate scale as the single critical and decisive determinant of all human constructs... on grounds that: "The only way people will... behave in a responsible way is if they have been persuaded to see the problem concretely and to understand their own connections to it directly—and this can be done only on a limited [spatial] scale. It can be done where the forces of government and society are still recognizable, where relations with other people are still intimate, and where the effects of individual actions are visible..." (Sale 1985:53–54).

Recently, a few authors such as Milbrath (1989), Daly and Cobb (1989), and Brown et al. (1990) have attempted comprehensive syntheses of sustainable development. Significantly, the latter two volumes accept the maintenance of natural capital as a prerequisite to sustainability. This should suffice to illustrate that even if extensions of traditional analyses are inadequate in themselves, they may well be essential in the transition to, or as components of, more radical interpretations of sustainable development.

This brief introduction to the new "ecological worldview" cannot do it justice. The point here is to emphasize that while the mainstream sees sustainable development in terms of marginal adjustments to the status quo, a true alternative is congealing around new values associated with spiritual development, harmony with nature, and mutual reciprocity. Disallowed in technical analysis, such unmeasurables have been relatively neglected in conventional approaches.

CONCLUSIONS: THE (IM)POSSIBILITY OF SUSTAINABLE DEVELOPMENT

"...it would appear we are poised on the horns of a difficult dilemma—unable to live with economic growth for reasons of ecological limitation, but unable to live without growth for fear of the social and political spectre that might follow in its absence" (Sanders 1990:395). To the modern mind, high on the rhetoric of global expansionism, the alternative literature seems politically naive and economically simplistic. However, alternative concepts are often more firmly rooted in the soil of real human and ecosystems behaviour than is the dominant paradigm. This should be kept in mind as we contemplate the present prognosis for sustainable development. It is argued here that serious analysis and interpretation of sustainable development raises it above mere technological adjustment and efforts to extend neoclassical economic analysis. Developing sustainability requires profound changes in existing power relationships, a reordering of cultural values, massive institutional reform, and reconsideration of the social role of economic growth. The problem is that "sustainability is not regarded seriously by those who really count, namely those at the top of political structures and those who control the flows of national and international capital" (O'Riordan 1988:39).

Ironically, the failure of present development approaches to increase self-reliance and economic security in much of the world actually increases resistance to change at the popular level. Despite the growing threat of ecological instability, people's greater fear seems to be the socio-political chaos that might accompany deliberate economic stagnation or contraction.[22] In the absence of feasible alternatives, no country has voluntarily made the necessary institutional adjustments or abandoned the pursuit of growth as the preferred means to sustain "development".

Indeed, quite the opposite has happened. With the triumph of capitalism and the collapse of industrial socialism, "neoclassical economics and market liberalism are riding the crest of near-universal acclaim and celebration" (Sanders 1990:400). Accordingly, the blueprint for an increasingly global economy is being drafted in terms of expanded world trade governed by the harsh logic of the marketplace. The accompanying rhetoric

---

[22]Ironically, it is the rampant individualism, the destruction of community, and the erosion of the social contract characteristic of growth-bound neoconservatism that feeds this fear.

already resounds with the hollow ring of cliche. Nations everywhere are honing their competitive edges, the better to exploit whatever comparative advantage they might enjoy on the level playing field of the global free market. Meanwhile, social programmes wither and the environment is in danger of being forgotten altogether.

The idea, of course, is to stimulate growth with that maximum of economic efficiency possible only in a deregulated market. The chief instrument with the potential to achieve this latter condition is the General Agreement on Tariffs and Trade (GATT), now World Trade Organization (WTO) whose purpose is to liberalize trade by reducing import and export controls and by eliminating non-tariff trade barriers. "Environment" is not mentioned in the GATT. On the contrary, the terms of GATT largely reflect the profit-maximizing interests of transnational corporations in obtaining raw materials and resource commodities at the lowest possible prices and selling value-added products in the world's richest markets. In a free competitive environment this mitigates against any resource protection measures that would add to costs or reduce competition and virtually assures the continued liquidation of natural capital particularly in the developing world. With environment still considered a market externality, "trade agreements will often institutionalize principles that are at odds with, and at times antithetical to, the objectives that are being pursued through international environmental agreements" (Shrybman 1990:31; see also Bown 1990 and Morris 1990).

The world is clearly setting off with renewed vigour down an historically well-worn path confident that the economic future will resemble the past, only more so. However, if the thesis of this chapter is correct, the customary path leads nowhere near sustainable development. Long before we achieve the five- to tenfold expansion of industrial activity anticipated by the Brundtland Commission, humanity may find itself in a politically dangerous world of fouled waters, ravaged soils, and erratic climate where the life-giving sun has itself become a hazard to existence. One wonders if anything short of planetary destruction will convince the leaders of the industrialized world that our present social myth, however well-sustained by the evidence to date, is little more than what Beer (1981) would call a collection of "shared illusions"?

In a variation of the common property problem, there is little incentive for even a committed nation to go it alone—the initial internal costs would be substantial and the potential benefits overwhelmed by the inaction of others. On the positive side (and contrary to some opinion) the cooperation of all 180 sovereign states would not necessarily be needed at the outset. While sustainable development is often seen as a Third World issue, it is the 25% of the world's population in the industrialized North who, by consuming 80–86% of the world's nonrenewable resources and up to 50% of food supplies (WCED 1987), create most of the problem. If the industrial minority would lead, the developing majority would have to follow. Unfortunately, as the main beneficiaries both of material growth and the prevailing development model, the wealthy nations are often the least inclined to change their profligate ways.[23]

EPILOGUE: A CAUTIONARY NOTE FOR PLANNERS

Clearly, the socio-political barriers to sustainable development are formidable and the prognosis, at least in the mainstream, is discouraging. However, if we are to have an ecologically habitable, economically viable, and politically secure world in the 21st Century the barriers must be overcome. Of all development professionals, planners with their multidisciplinary training and integrated perspective are the best placed to act as midwives to the emerging new paradigm. Ultimately, and despite current emphasis on deregulation, the need for positive governance and proactive planning can only escalate in an increasingly populous world demanding ever more of an increasingly unstable ecosphere. In the meantime, enormous effort must be placed on managing the global transition from a world dependent on growth to one secure in sufficiency.

There is an important proviso. In all this work planners will acquire maximum leverage by shifting the focus of their efforts from changing the environment to changing human minds and redesigning social institutions. This chapter suggests that we do not have an ecological crisis, the ecosphere has a human crisis. Our "story" about our place in the scheme of things has somehow gone awry in the industrial age. For sustainable development, therefore, the need is more for appropriate philosophy than for appropriate technology. If we tend to ourselves, nature will take care of itself.

REFERENCES

Aberley, D. 1985. Bioregionalism: A territorial approach to governance and development of Northwest British Columbia. Unpublished M.A. Thesis. Vancouver: University of British Columbia, School of Community and Regional Planning.
Beer, S. 1981. I said, you are gods. *Teilhard Review* 15:3:1–33.
Berry, T. 1988. *The dream of the earth*. San Francisco: Sierra Club Books.
Block, W. 1990. Environmental problems, private property rights solutions. In: *Economics and the Environment: A Reconciliation*, W. Block (ed.), Vancouver: The Fraser Institute.
Bown, W. 1990. Trade deals a blow to the environment. *New Scientist* 128:1742:20–21.

---

[23]The United States, Canada, Great Britain, Japan and the Soviet Union are prominent among industrial countries resisting firm targets for CO_2 emissions reductions.

Bookchin, M. 1980. *Towards an Ecological Society.* Montreal: Black Rose Books.

Boothroyd, P. 1991. Distribution principles for compassionate sustainable development. In: *Perspectives on Water in Sustainable Development: Towards Agreement in the Fraser River Basin,* A. Dorcey (ed.), Vancouver: The University of British Columbia Westwater Research Centre.

Brooks, D. 1990. Beyond Catch Phrases: What Does Sustainable Development Really Mean? IDRC Reports, October 1990.

Brown, L. et al. (Annual) State of the World. Washington: Worldwatch Institute.

Brown, L., and C. Flavin. 1988. The Earth's vital signs. In: *State of the World 1988,* L. Brown et al. (eds.), Washington: Worldwatch Institute.

Brown, L. C. Flavin and S. Postel. 1990. Picturing a sustainable society. In: *State of the World 1990,* L. Brown et al. (eds.), Washington: Worldwatch Institute.

Canada. 1988. Conference Statement (The Changing Atmosphere: Implications for Global Security; Toronto, 27–30 June, 1988) Ottawa: Environment Canada.

Capra, F. 1982. *The Turning Point.* Toronto and New York: Bantam Books.

Cartwright, T. 1991. Planning and chaos theory. *APA Journal,* Winter 1991:44–56.

CCREM. 1987. *Report of the National Task Force on Environment and Economy.* Ottawa: Canadian Council of Resource and Environment Ministers.

Clark, C. 1973. The economics of overexploitation. *Science* 181:630–634.

Clark, C. 1991. Economic biases against sustainable development. In: *Ecological Economics: The Science and Management of Sustainability,* R. Costanza (ed.), New York: Columbia University Press.

Collard, D. 1988. Catastrophic Risk: or the Economics of Being Scared. In: *Economics. Growth and Sustainable Development,* D. Collard, D. Pearce, and D. Ulph (eds.). Macmillan Press.

Costanza, R. and H. Daly. 1990. Natural Capital and Sustainable Development. Paper prepared for the CEARC Workshop on Natural Capital. Vancouver, BC, 15–16 March 1990. Ottawa: Canadian Environmental Assessment Research Council.

Crutchfield, J., J. Farmer, Il. Packard and R. Shaw. 1986. Chaos. *Scientific American* 255:46–57.

Daly, H. 1989. *Sustainable Development: From Concept and Theory Towards Operational Principles.* (Hoover Institution Conference). Manuscript prepared for special issue of Population and Development Review.

Daly, H. 1990. Boundless Bull. *Gannett Center Journal,* Summer 1990:113–118.

Daly, H. and J. Cobb. 1989. *For the Common Good: Redirecting the Economy Towards Community, the Environment, and a Sustainable Future.* Boston: Beacon Press.

Dasgupta, P. and D. Heal. 1979. *Economic Theory and Exhaustible Resources.* London: Cambridge University Press.

Davies, P. 1990. Chaos frees the universe. *New Scientist* 128:1737:48–51.

Devall, B. and G. Sessions. 1985. *Deep Ecology: Living as if Nature Mattered.* Salt Lake City: Gibbs M. Smith, Inc. (Peregrine Smith Books).

Dorcey, A. 1991. (ed.) *Perspectives on Water in Sustainable Development: Towards Agreement in the Fraser River Basin.* Vancouver: The University of British Columbia Westwater Research Centre.

Ehrenfeld, D. 1978. The conservation dilemma. In: *The Arrogance of Humanism.* New York: Oxford University Press.

Gardner, J. and M. Roseland. 1989a. Thinking globally: the role of social equity in sustainable development. *Alternatives* 16:3:27–33.

Gardner, J. and M. Roseland. 1989b. Acting locally: community strategies for equitable sustainable development. *Alternatives* 16:3:36–47.

Gardner, J. 1990. The elephant and nine blind men: an initial review of environmental assessment and related processes in support of sustainable development. In: *Sustainable Development and Environmental Assessment: Perspectives on Planning for a Common Future,* P.

Jacobs and B. Sadler (eds.). Ottawa: Canadian Environmental Assessment Research Council.

Georgescu-Roegen, N. 1975. Energy and economic myths. *Southern Economic Journal* 41:347–381.

Georgescu-Roegen, N. 1977. The steady state and ecological salvation: a thermodynamic analysis. *BioScience* 27:4:266–270.

Gilder, G. 1981. *Wealth and Poverty*. New York: Basic Books.

Heilbroner, R. 1985. *The Nature and Logic of Capitalism*. New York: W. W. Norton.

Heilbroner, R. 1989. The triumph of capitalism. *The New Yorker*, 23 January, 1889.

Herfindahl, O. and A. Kneese. 1974. *Economic Theory of Natural Resources*. Columbus, Ohio: Charles E. Merill.

Holling, C. 1986. The resilience of terrestrial ecosystems: local surprise and global change. In: *Sustainable Development of the Biosphere*, W. Clark and R. Munn (eds.). International Institute for Applied Systems Analysis, Laxenburg, Austria; Cambridge, UK: Cambridge University Press.

IUCN. 1980. *World Conservation Strategy*. Geneva. International Union for the Conservation of Nature.

Jacobs, P., J. Gardner and D. Munro. 1987. Sustainable and equitable development: an emerging paradigm. In: *Conservation with Equity: Strategies for Sustainable Development*, P. Jacobs and D. Munro (eds.). Cambridge, UK: International Union for the Conservation of Nature.

Jevons, W. 1879. *The Theory of Political Economy*. 2nd edition. London: Macmillan.

Maturana, H. and F. Varela. 1988. *The Tree of Knowledge*. Boston: New Science Library.

May, R. 1989. The chaotic rhythms of life. *New Scientist*. 124: 37–41.

Miernyk, W. 1982. *The Illusions of Conventional Economics*. Morgantown: West Virginia University Press.

Milbrath, L. 1989. *Envisioning a Sustainable Society: Learning our Way Out*. Albany: State University of New York Press.

Morris, D. 1990. Free trade: the great destroyer. *The Ecologist* 20:5:190–195

Naess, A. 1986. The deep ecological movement: some philosophical aspects. *Philosophical Inquiry* 8:1/2:10–31.

Nelson, J. 1990. Deconstructing ecobabble: notes on an attempted corporate takeover. *This Magazine* 24:3:12–18.

Nikiforuk, A. 1990. Sustainable rhetoric. *Harrowsmith*, October 1990:14–16.

O'Riordan, T. 1988. The politics of sustainability. In: *Sustainable Environmental Management*, R. Turner (ed.). London: Belhaven Press and Boulder, CO: Westview Press.

Pearce, D. 1991. Deforesting the Amazon: towards economic solution. *Ecodecision* 1:1:40–49.

Pearce, D., A. Markandya and E. Barbier. 1989. *Blueprint for a Green Economy*. London: Earthscan Publications.

Pearce, D., E. Barbier and A. Markandya. 1990. *Sustainable Development: Economics and Environment in the Third World*. Hants, England: Edward Elgar Publishing.

Perry, D., M. Amaranthus, J. Borchers and R. Brainerd. 1989. Bootstrapping in ecosystems. *BioScience* 39:4:230–237.

Pezzey, J. 1989. Economic analysis of sustainable growth and sustainable development. Environment Department Working Paper No. 15. Washington: World Bank.

Rees, W. 1988. A role for sustainable development in achieving sustainable development. *Environ. Impact Assess. Rev.* 8:273–291.

Rees, W. 1989. *Defining Sustainable Development*. CHS Research Bulletin, May 1989. Vancouver: The University of British Columbia Centre for Human Settlements.

Rees, W. 1990a *Sustainable Development and the Biosphere: Concepts and Principles*. Teilhard Studies 23. American Teilhard Association.

Rees, W. 1990b. The ecology of sustainable development. *The Ecologist* 20:1:18–23.

Rees, W. 1990c. Why economics won't save the world. Paper presented at The Ecological Economics of Sustainability, a conference sponsored by the International Society for Ecological Economics. Washington, DC: The World Bank (21–23 May 1990).

Rees, W. 1990d. Atmospheric change: human ecology in disequilibrium. *International Journal of Environmental Studies* 36:103–124.

Rees, W. 1991. The ecological basis for sustainable development in the Fraser Basin. In: *Perspectives on Water in Sustainable Development: Towards Agreement in the Fraser River Basin*, A. Dorcey (ed.). Vancouver: The University of British Columbia Westwater Research Centre.

Repetto, R. 1986. *World Enough and Time*. New Haven, Conn.: Yale University Press.

Rowe, S. 1989. Implications of the Brundtland Commission Report for Canadian Forest Management. *The Forestry Chronicle*, February 1989: 5–7.

Sale, K. 1985. *Dwellers in the Land: The Bioregional Vision*. San Francisco: Sierra Club Books.

Sanders, J. 1990. Global ecology and world economy: collision course or sustainable future? *Bulletin of Peace Proposals* 21:4:395–401.

Schneider, S. 1990. The Science of Climate-Modelling and a Perspective on the Global Warming Debate. Pages 44–67 In: *Global Warming: The Greenpeace Report*, J. Leggett (ed.). New York: Oxford University Press.

Salleh, A. 1984. Deeper than deep ecology: the eco-feminist connection. *Environmental Ethics* 6:4:339–345.

Shrybman, S. 1990. International trade and the environment: an environmental assessment of The General Agreement on Tariffs and Trade. *The Ecologist* 20:30–34.

Simon, H. 1978. Rationality as process and as product of thought. *American Economic Review* 68:2:1–16.

Simon, J. 1982. Interview with William F. Buckley, Jr. *Population and Development Review*. March: 205–218.

Stevens, W. 1991. Ozone layer thinner, but forces are in place for slow improvement. *New York Times* (9 April, 1991:B2).

Taylor, D. 1991. *Sustaining Development or Developing Sustainability?: Two Competing World Views*. Alternatives (in press).

Timberlake, L. 1989. The role of scientific knowledge in drawing up the Brundtland Report. Pages 118–123 In: *International Resource Management: The Role of Science and Politics*, S. Andresen and W. Ostreng (eds.). London: Belhaven Press.

Trainer, T. 1990. A rejection of the Brundtland Report. IFDA Dossier May/June 1990:71–84 (International Foundation for Development Alternatives).

Victor, P.A. 1990. Indicators of sustainable development: some lessons from capital theory. A background paper prepared for a Workshop on Indicators of Sustainable Development. Ottawa: Canadian Environmental Advisory Council.

Vitousek, P., P. Ehrlich, A. Ehrlich, and P. Matson. 1986. Human Appropriation of the Products of Photosynthesis. *Bioscience* 36:368–374.

WCED (World Commission of Economic Development). 1987. *Our Common Future*. Oxford: Oxford University Press.

Sustainable Development—A Third World Perspective

P.K. Muttagi

ABSTRACT

For the last several years, planners, policy-makers, administrators, activists, social scientists and others have been studying the socio-economic problems of developed and developing countries. They have been using various approaches and techniques to tackle these problems, but with little success. In recent years, the phrase sustainable development has come into wide use among them to signify the goal of an environmentally stable economy, especially in the Third World. It is an encompassing principle of the earlier concepts of development and emphasises the need to meet the present requirements without, in any way, compromising the future generation's capacity to meet its needs.

The paper briefly analyses the current environmental crises and indicates some measures for sustainable development.

THE GLOBAL SETTING

Technological advances have led to economic prosperity, changes in demographic, social, cultural and political systems of the community and psychological make up of the people all over the world. The consequences of such dynamic situations vary from one country to another, and also from one group to another within a country. The economic development may not always lead to improvement in the quality of life of the people of a region. It may frequently lead to reinforcement of the existing disparities and foster a fragmented sense of self and even to social unrest. The techno-economic and socio-political changes in the contemporary society are varied and inextricably linked with each other and with ecological changes at the local and global levels.

The advances, it has been argued, have also resulted in the environmental degradation: Acid rain, the hole in the ozone layer, the greenhouse effect, car exhausts, nuclear waste, water, air and noise pollutions, the destruction of the tropical rain forest, pesticides, whaling, famine and other environmental problems. The detrimental effects of man's activities on the environment now extend even to the most remote and inaccessible parts of the globe where man himself seldom, if ever, ventures. The depths of the oceans and the ice of the polar regions are tainted by the wastes he so carelessly throws to the winds and the waters. But it is in his settlements, those parts of the global environment where the majority of men spend the greater parts of their lives, where their social and economic activities are most densely concentrated, and where the opportunities for individual and collective satisfaction and advancement are greatest, that the most dramatic changes take place and the most intensive conflicts occur. It is here that the quality of the environment is particularly critical to human beings' health, welfare and happiness (United Nations 1974). These problems have been frequently discussed in the media, they are increasing our awareness of the issues involved. But beyond the awareness and concern which many people increasingly feel, how do we now see our future environment? Is everything being tackled and solved, as some politicians would have us believe, or is everything getting worse? Are we hopeful of achieving some utopian state or are we pessimistic? Will we have pure rain, no pollution, lush forests, abundant wildlife and a comfortable quality of life with pleasant homes, security and the sustainable use of the available resources of the earth? Or will we disappear in a welter of environmental disaster and wars over territory, resources and living space (Trudgill 1990)? To answer some of these questions we must know the present state of affairs and what prevents us from solving the environmental problems.

DEMOGRAPHIC CHARACTERISTICS

Today's environmental trends are a consequence of the 20th century's exponential growth rates. In 90 years, world population has tripled, the global economy has grown twenty-fold and fossil fuel use tenfold. It took all of human history for the world economy to reach $600 billion in 1900, but it now grows by more than this sum every two years. The population curve is equally daunting. It took some 50,000 years for the human population to reach 2.5 billion in 1950, but only 37 years to double to 5 billion. We are now adding nearly one billion people a decade (Speth 1990). Aside from population growth and its consequences, rapid urbanization has become the dominant demographic trend of the late 20th century. Urban residents are increasingly concentrated in very large urban agglomerations. In 1950, there were only 10 metropolitan areas with populations of 5 million people or more. In 1990, there are 3 metropolitan areas with 5 million people or more, 15 with 10 million people or more, and 6 with 15 million people or more. It will remain a dominant trend well into the 21st century when population growth is expected to moderate (Camp 1990). Now standing at 5.7 billion, the population of the Earth will swell to over 8 billion by 2020. Coping with such a rapid growth is the key strategic issue.

Large cities in developing countries are growing much faster than cities in the industrialized world ever have. London, which was the first industrialized city to top 1 million, took 130 years to reach a population of 8 million. By contrast, Mexico City's population which stood at only a million people just 50 years ago, has crossed 20 million. Cities in the industrialized world have been growing at slow rate of 0.8 per cent per year and this rate is likely to decline in the coming decade. Cities in the developing regions have been growing at 3.6 per cent a year—a rate they will maintain through the 1990s and which represents a doubling time for urban populations of less than 20 years. Africa's urban population is growing at 5 per cent a year, representing a doubling time of only 14 years. By the end of this century the urban population of the developing world will be almost double the size of that in the industrialized world. Urban migrants, including squatters, tend to upgrade their housing over time, with or without the help of governments. But the continued rapid pace of urban population growth ensures a constantly expanding fringe of newly arrived squatters. Investments in urban infrastructure never have time to catch up. According to the World Commission on Environment and Development, between 1985 and 2000, developing countries will need to have increased by 65 per cent their capacity to build and manage urban infrastructures, including transportation and sanitation systems, utilities, schools and hospitals. Developing countries cannot cope with it.

Many cities in the industrialized world likewise face the need to refurbish crumbling urban infrastructures. Often they must do so at a time when their industrial base has weakened and their populations have aged, with a now smaller proportion in the tax-paying work force. Air pollution, traffic congestion, noise and urban violence are similar in large cities around the globe. But with their slower rates of population growth, greater financial resources and more educated populations, the cities of the developed world are much better prepared to resolve urban problems. In cities in many of the less-developed countries urban problems will worsen substantially through the coming decade and beyond, as population growth outruns investments in new urban infrastructures.

THE SOCIO-ECONOMIC SCENARIO

After several decades of efforts to achieve rapid economic and social progress, we have been witnessing a severe contradiction in the levels of investments, growth of production, international trade, consumption and distribution systems in different parts of the world. To shape future programmes and direction, we must understand the present programmes and policies and about the changes which are taking place in global development activities and relationships, in attitudes and perceptions and the change in the economic, social, cultural, political and technological spheres which have been affecting the environment. Western countries and some Asian countries have continued to achieve rapid growth and expanding industrial sector. In the OECD countries we observe that things are going rather well for about two-third of the population, but that the situation for the remaining one-third is deteriorating. In a sense, one can also speak here of involuntary delinking. For example, how can governments of the European countries continue to say that the economy is doing well, that Europe is entering the eighth consecutive year of economic expansion, without giving top priority to the 10–14 per cent unemployment that Europe has had during most of the 1980s (Compass 1990).

The human distress in rich societies needs to be understood. The social fabric in these countries is getting weaker with drug crimes, rape, suicide, murders, single-parent families, illegitimacy rates and divorce rates. In a sense the problems in these societies are a direct result of their economic affluence. These social problems are also found in the Third World in addition to poverty, illiteracy, unemployment and external debt. Many Latin American countries, despite appreciable progress and basic economic strength, are facing severe stagnation because of external debt. Most seriously affected are the countries of Sub-Saharan Africa which are struggling to implement economic recovery programmes which have been largely built on external trade prospects. High aid levels have not offset trade losses or alleviated crippling external debts. The continuing downward spiral of poverty and environmental degradation undermines productive capacity. Also, relatively low investment in food production in the past, rapidly expanding populations, and civil conflicts have greatly set back Africa's development (Williams 1990). The economic progress in the case of certain Asian countries is not only uneven, but even alarming. Despite appreciable progress in the recent past and the potentialities for growth in certain sectors, they are encountering severe stagnation and inequality. In South Asia, the top 5 per cent of the population controls 22 per cent of the national income, while the share of the bottom 20 per cent is less than 6 per cent.

The Third World is made up of poor nations, poor societies and poor people. These are the live societies that have social and political dynamic of their own. Because of the impact of social change, population growth, education, communications, and exposure to the media, there are powerful processes at work in these societies which are not tending towards stability, but are instead giving rise to expectations and aspirations which governments practically everywhere find difficult to respond to. These countries are less stable than they themselves were during the earlier period. One by one the Third World countries are becoming ungovernable. No matter what the complexion of the governments—right wing, left wing, military or democratic—they are all in situations of not being able to respond adequately to the expectations of their people aroused by media, communications, and education (Corea 1990).

ENVIRONMENTAL CRISIS IN THE THIRD WORLD

Environmental deterioration in the Third World can be attributed to industrialization, depletion of traditional sources of energy and raw materials, constant population growth, pollution of natural resources, the destruction for economic ends of various animal and plants species, water, air and noise pollutions, and the negative genetic consequences of industrial pollutants. The ecological crises in the agro-ecosystems arising out of the erosion of soil, water and genetic diversity are related to the increasing tendency to view the agricultural sector as the consumer of industrial products like fertilizers, pesticides and hybrid seeds. The agricultural policy which affects rural development directly is increasingly focussing on providing these inputs at the neglect of maintaining and strengthening the intrinsic ecological stability and productivity of agro-ecosystems. The crisis emerging from the technological changes is not restricted to agro-ecosystems only. What is done to the land also affects the waters since the marine ecosystem is the final repository of our lost soil, pollutants, urban wastes, as well as being damaged by activities like dredging, trawling, and reclamation.

Environmental crises are due to wrong orientation of science and technology, misuse of political and administrative powers; rampant corruption, nepotism, favouritism in most of the departments; misuse of funds; lack of interest in welfare activities; deterioration in public morality; lack of national character; implementation of the plan by untrained personnel; escapism from responsibilities; and division of society on the basis of caste, creed, class, religion etc. The developing countries are imitating the Western world and using their technologies without considering the ecological impact. Environmental crisis is the cause as well as the consequence of rural and tribal environmental degradation.

The environmental stress has often been seen as a result of the growing demand on scarce resources and the pollution generated by the rising living standards of the relatively affluent. But poverty itself pollutes the environment, creating environmental stress in a different way. Those who are poor and hungry will often destroy their immediate environment in order to survive. They cut down forests, their livestock overgraze on grasslands, they overuse marginal land, and in growing numbers they crowd into congested cities. The cumulative effect of these changes is far reaching and makes poverty a major global scourge. Increasing demand for various products and services due to population growth and the changing power equations between different social classes have sharpened the resource conflicts. The hazards overspill political boundaries to affect vast geographical regions, they also embrace the world ocean and ultimately develop into an international menace. Some of these global hazards are directly related to international politics. The spread of radio-active radiation in nuclear tests, arms race and military operations and pollution of the oceans have directly or indirectly some bearing on politics. The greatest danger to environmental standards however, arises from the lack of development itself. Lack of safe drinking water, housing, inadequate transportation, food, clothing and other basic needs are elements of poverty, and sources of danger and degradation to the human environment. They can be tackled only by all-round development in industry, agriculture and forestry, the infrastructure and other services. Both socio-economic and politico-administrative aspects are involved in environmental crises. Deterioration in an area is not always confined to that area, but spreads to different areas and regions. The nature and depth of environmental crises in developing countries raise serious doubts about the correctness of the growth-based strategy of economic development. Unless there is a drastic shift in the policies to development based on sustainability, safety and associated environmental considerations, the process of growth will neither be able to sustain itself nor can the large-scale under development of the poor and marginalized majority be avoided.

Development scientists have been pursuing different approaches starting with growth in terms of Gross National Product (GNP), slowly turning to growth with fair distribution of that growth and shifted to the basic needs approach with emphasis on improvement in the standard of living of the most disadvantaged, but with little success. It was soon realized that these approaches are inadequate, that economic growth is a mixed blessing and there are definite limits to the growth that can be achieved as certain resources from nature, needed for the growth are incapable of reproducing themselves if once exploited. Today, they are talking about sustainable development. Being popularized by the Report of the World Commission on Environment and Development (The Brundtland Commission WCED 1987) it has become a key concept to explain the economy-environment relationship. It implies that the basic needs for food, clothing, shelter and jobs must be met in such a way that they do not compromise the ability of future generations to meet their own needs (WECD 1987).

ECOLOGICAL APPROACH

Economists and planners generally assume that economic growth can take care of the environment through proper pricing of goods, greater efficiency of resource use, improved technology and better management techniques.

Many ecologists feel that this sort of assumption is based on the superficial understanding of the environment. If we continue like this, we may be fast approaching absolute limits to material economic growth. Trading off ecological damage for economic benefits and still hoping to achieve sustainable biosphere cannot be done. They consider certain ecological and thermodynamic principles that must be respected and add that the basic ecological requirements for sustainability are not negotiable. The following arguments advanced by William E. Rees summerise the ecological approach.

All material production is actually consumption since our economies are growing and the ecosystem within which they are embedded are not. The consumption of resources everywhere has begun to exceed sustainable rates of biological production. Consumption and pollution destroy ecologically essential resources with no signal from the market place that the very basis of survival is being irreversibly eroded, and there are no technological substitutes. Ecosystems are inherently self-sustaining and contribute continuously reducing global net entropy, but human disruption of ecosystemic relationships on global scale would severely compromise the possibility of achieving sustainable development. Humankind must learn to live on the interest generated by remaining stocks of living natural capital. Further, the acceptance of ecological constants, obviously places unaccustomed boundaries on the debates of arriving at a politically expedient interpretation of the concept through the usual compromise of interests. The basic ecological requirements for sustainability are not negotiable. However, satisfaction of ecological criteria is a necessary but not sufficient condition for sustainable development. Any proactive prescription for sustainable development must acknowledge the primary role of bio-resources in human survival and the inequity inherent in current practice, maintenance of the functional integrity of the ecosphere is a necessary prerequisite to extending the time horizon for economic policy and to elevating both intra and intergenerational equity to a place of prominence in developmental decision-making.*

---

*These are some of the arguments advanced by W.E. Rees in the seminar on Sustainable Development held at Bauhaus, Dessau, in September 1991.

AN APPRAISAL

In advancing his thesis, Rees has marshalled evidences from a large number of sources. The notes and references are exhaustive and impressive. These include the writings of medieval continental thinkers, present-day economists, ecologists, planners and others. It has referred to the views of the contemporary thinkers like Capra and presumably to Teilhard de Chardin. However, a researcher will get additional insight into the intricate issues by considering the views of thinkers like Schumacher (small is beautiful) M.K. Gandhi (Community self-reliance, mass production vs. production by masses, each according to his/her own needs trusteeship and so on). Referring to the distinction between growth and development. Rees observes that growth is quantitative change in a physically non-growing economic system in dynamic equilibrium with the environment. Sustainable growth in a finite environment is a logical impossibility but sustainable development contains self-contradiction. This distinction between growth and development is extremely important.

Interpretations of sustainable development and its implications for planning vary as widely as the ideologies of its various proponents. It is necessary to focus on ecological realities that must be accommodated by any realistic approach irrespective of interpretation. One can assume a global perspective on the ground that if the basic argument is correct, the success of sustainable development initiatives anywhere are dependent on sustainable development everywhere. Such an assumption helps to view the developmental issues from a wider perspective.

To develop sustainable urban communities it is necessary to take several actions. Rees' article on sustainable communities (plan Canada May 91) outlines in tables 1 through 6 several kinds of initiatives by government and public bodies. These include traffic planning and traffic management initiatives, energy conservation initiatives, waste reduction, improving community livability etc. to deal with socio-economic and ecological complexities. These measures include initiatives like bicycle transportation, street redesign, community land trusts, solar oven cookbook, packaging restrictions, gender equity, eco-counselling (Rees, 1991). These have been used in several urban settlements in different countries. It is necessary to examine their effectiveness in sustainability and explore the possibility of using them in other countries.

On the basis of the findings of his studies, Rees proposes 25 practical guides to global sustainable development. A study of these principles shows that some of them are statements of facts, some are beliefs, some can be implemented with certain adjustments within the system and some are extremely difficult to implement in the present socio-economic situation, but all of them need to be studied, discussed and evaluated before communicating them to planners, policy makers and other concerned.

Further, sustainable communities, it can be argued, will be cleaner, healthier and less expensive; they will have greater accessibility and cohesion; will be more self reliant in energy, food and economic security than the communities now are. Someone has to demonstrate leadership in developing the knowledge, alternatives and technologies which the world requires for sustainability.

Some thinkers believe that such a development demands cessation of growth and major reconstruction of the whole global economy along conservationist lines. However, there are others who believe that it is not possible to maintain the natural resources without any change. A strictly conservationist position is not practicable for it is impossible to use even a renewable natural resource and at the same time leave it unaltered with exactly the same quantities as before, nor can human needs be satisfied without some consumption of non-renewables. The real problem is on the one hand, there is demand for resource destruction which cannot be stopped, at the same time reliance on natural renewability is not practical. Under the circumstances there are no easy solutions.

Harold C. Brookfield feels that undoing unsustainability and building sustainability in its place will be an enormous task, against great opposition and made much worse by uncertainties, aggravated by human action, with which we have to live in the foreseeable future. It is further made worse by the widespread distrust of government, the interventionist role of which is critical to success. Sustainability does demand attention the regenerative capacities of the biosphere but there is much that human artifice and a wise technology can do to assist this necessary set of adaptations, while improving both the natural and human condition at the same time. These observations need to be investigated carefully in order to develop management strategies, technology and artifice that will ensure sustainable growth (Brookfield 1991).

It has been argued that sustainable development includes two key elements: one is the meeting of needs and in particular the needs of those who have been left far behind in a century of extraordinary growth, the second concerns the limits which the world society must now impose to protect the resource base of our environment both locally and globally. Therefore, sustainable development imposes standards of consumption which must be met within the bounds of ecological possibility.

Both the elements are multidimensional and extremely complicated to handle. The first one is primarily the problem in developing countries. The second one is that of the developed world, though it is applicable to sizeable section of the affluent groups inhabiting the Third World.

Developed countries have reached certain levels of growth. They have accumulated huge capital, skills, technology and other resources. Population is literate and not growing alarmingly. The number of the poor is significant, but hopefully manageable. These countries are culturally more homogeneous than some of the developing countries and have necessary infrastructure. By utilizing the existing resources efficiently and making marginal adjustments in their pattern of consumption and lifestyle, it is possible for them to provide the necessary comforts for the entire population. They can, and should, introduce measures of sustainable development. Some attempts have already been made in the developed world.

The socio-economic situation in developing countries is far more complex and merits discussion. An overwhelming majority of the population (80%) lives in rural areas. A majority of them is poor, illiterate and carry on the same traditional occupation without resorting to modern technology. The ecological crises in the agro-ecosystems arising out of the erosion of soil, water and genetic diversity are related to the increasing tendency to view the agricultural sector as the consumer of industrial products like fertilizers, pesticides and hybrid seeds. Environmental deterioration in urban areas can be attributed to industrialization, depletion of traditional sources of energy and raw materials, constant population growth, pollution of natural resources, destruction of various animal and plant species for economic ends, the artificial sound amplifiers and other noise-making systems including heavy traffic and the negative genetic consequences of industrial pollutants.

The environmental stress has often been seen as a result of the growing demand on scarce resources and pollution generated by the rising living standards of the relatively affluent. But poverty itself pollutes the environment, creating environmental stress in different ways. Those who are poor and hungry often destroy their immediate environment in order to survive: they cut down forests, their livestock will overgraze grasslands, they will overuse marginal land, and in growing numbers they leave rural areas and crowd into congested cities and join the households living in slums and shanty towns. By and large, each settlement is divided into unplanned sector and planned sector. The latter is always in danger of being surrounded by the unplanned sector. In these countries there are large numbers of people who have been deprived of basic necessities for survival; water, sanitation, housing, employment and medical facilities including vaccination and inoculation. Further, developing countries are totally diverse in the development that they have been able to achieve. Each country differs from the other in every conceivable dimension such as size of the population, homogeneity of culture, capacity to mobilize resources, infrastructure facilities, trained and skilled personnel and technological management.

While a country like India has become almost self-reliant in many fields, there are several others that are still to be even convinced of the possibility of their attaining self-reliance. Some of the countries have enacted social legislation to help the poor to seek justice, but the implementation machinery is poor. Both government and non-government organizations have been making efforts to bring the poor and other underprivileged groups together to form them into an organisation in order to empower them, but without much success. In some countries the NGO movement is strong and growing from within.

Developing countries have been striving to meet the socio-economic needs of their people with the help of the developed nations, particularly in the last 40 years. They have been receiving in large quantities both financial and technological aid for ameliorative as well as developmental purposes. This process has led to establishing a complex set of institutions; multi-lateral, bilateral, official and non-government—which has resulted in establishing peculiar relationship with the native institutions. Incidentally, it will be interesting to find out whether these institutions are part of the problems or part of the solutions. If they are part of the problems is it due to their concept of development. What needs to be noted is that not-withstanding all the development efforts that have been carried out in the recent past, and are still being carried out with a view to improving the situation, nothing substantial has been achieved in improving the quality of the life of the poor. The severe economic deterioration of the majority of the countries, coupled with increased evidence of widespread degradation of the environmental and natural resource bases on which the economies of these countries so largely depend has forced the re-examination of the development experience and the premises on which it is based. In short, despite massive help, poverty is increasing and environment is deteriorating. This is the most serious threat the world is facing.

Researchers have attempted to analyse the causes of ineffectiveness of the development programmes. They have found, for example, that the international agencies and official and non-governmental agencies from the developed world assume that technological and capital transfer could bring about desirable change. They invested their money, time and expertise to bring about desirable changes. Failure is attributed to the lack of participation from the beneficiaries and poorly managed delivery system to distribute the benefits of development to the poor. It should be noted that technology and financial aid may be part of development but they are only small parts. More significant are the people's determination to make things better for themselves; the accountability of those in power to those they propose to help develop, people's willingness to change their cultural patterns, their administrative patterns, their educational systems and sometimes their political systems. These are all parts of development. Development involves change in all aspects of any system which is developing.

There have been inequalities in income, employment opportunities, educational skills and health. These are along ethnic, religious, gender, caste or tribal dimension. But the important point is that on each dimension, there are some haves and many have-nots, a small group of elites and large numbers of masses. The haves get greater access to information and opportunities to make money, to acquire education and skills and lead good life at the cost of the deprived and the damned. The development has actually reinforced the existing economic disparities.

Development efforts should recognize that equity is a necessary condition and the authorities must ensure that the needy people are benefited. If the rich get richer and the poor become more in number and less in wealth, such development does not lead to desirable results. If development discriminates against women and children and if it ignores the minority groups and the minorities do not join the mainstream in developmental activities no development can sustain. The existing strategy has contributed to the economic growth of several project areas, but not to social justice and ecological balance.

There was no proper appreciation of the strengths and weaknesses of the institutions and individuals who are involved in development activities. Project management was entrusted to the people who utilized the opportunity to exploit the poor to make money and to enrich those who kept them in power. The greatest need of the hour in developing countries is inspired and committed leadership at the top, at both official and non-official levels, to plan and implement the programmes with vigour and devotion. Such leadership at the top and with a top down approach alone not bottom up, will succeed. The leaders can motivate the people down the line, change the indifferent administrative set-up, educational and political systems and deliver goods. Leaders in the Third World have done it in many places in the past and are still doing it. Some are running development projects efficiently and by setting good example, they have changed the people below them. They may not be well-qualified professionals but highly committed workers. The projects run by these leaders are productive, efficient and sustainable. They are based on the traditional approach to development. It is not the professional expertise but committed leadership which delivers goods. Modern development projects like integrated community development programmes and social forestry have been managed by qualified and experienced personnel, some are professionals. They have been implemented enthusiastically and with due publicity. We are not quite clear about their impact on improving the quality of life of the rural people and preserving the environment.

Poverty is not new to the developing countries. A good majority of the people have always remained poor. The rural and tribal groups have learned strategies of survival in their own ecological niche. Over the generations and by trial and error, they learned the techniques of coping with poverty and in their own way preserved the environment. It has been preserved through beliefs, customs and traditions. All of them did not contribute to the preservation of the environment. Even those customs and traditions which help to maintain an ecological balance are gradually disappearing on account of modernization. Public disregard for local and traditional knowledge has been destroying the wealth of information that has taken thousands of years to build up. Systematic efforts need to be made by the authorities to record such knowledge, identify those aspects which contribute to ecological balance and encourage the people to retain them.

Today, on account of scientific and technological progress, particularly mass media of communication, people in developing world are exposed to Western values, life styles and comforts enjoyed by the people in the developed world. In many countries, economic progress has led to the rise of new elite groups who imitate the Western life-style and imbibe their values and culture. In the context of the rising awareness for improvement in their economic status, the economically and socially deprived groups have been demanding a greater share in whatever is produced. Everyone would like to enjoy the comforts and luxuries. Both poverty and the feeling of deprivation need to be tackled. Motivating the poor is not enough. Their needs and requirements should be satisfied. Under the circumstances rapid economic growth appears to be the only solution. One cannot fuel development so conceptualized without an increase in the consumption of matter and energy resources, some of them non-renewable and with toxic waste products. On the other hand, mass aspirations for products of modernity and good life have been fired to such an extent, the cultural changes that imply high resource use have occurred so fast, that no mass-based politician can hope to even reach first base if he or she advocates a zero-growth, a purely environmentalist agenda.

The existing models of development have led to severe economic deterioration and environmental degradation. In view of this, policy makers and change agents will have to rethink the basis of development cooperation and technology transfer. To achieve rapid economic growth, perhaps major changes in institutional framework, administrative set-up and re-examination of developmental strategy for efficient use of existing resources are necessary. The present planning strategy has led to providing expensive services to some. It should at the same time aim at providing the minimum to the rest. The new developmental strategy has to be a combination of Western and native ideas. The new policy should focus on larger

productivity, greater self-reliance and a much better economic growth and efficient and equitable distribution of goods and services. Any measure which is
aimed at achieving sustainable development will receive a setback.

It is important and necessary to appreciate that sustainable development
involves several continuous on-going processes of change and adaption in
which the exploitation of resources, the direction of investment, the orientation
of technological development and institutional change are all in harmony with
each other and together aim to satisfy the needs and aspirations of all people,
keeping in view the requirements of the future generation. Sustainable
development is based on the processes that are efficient, equitable, environmentally sound and endogenous. Developing countries must achieve
economic growth with equity first and then strive for sustainable development. There is no shortcut.

ACKNOWLEDGEMENTS

The Author is grateful to Professor William E. Rees of the University of
British Columbia for giving his articles and ideas. He also thanks Professor
Bernd Hamm, ZES, Universitat Trier for his valuable guidance and en-
couragement to include the dimension of the development of the Third
World in this perspective.

REFERENCES

Brookfield H.C. 1991. "Environmental Sustainability with Development"—Extracts from a
    speech at the EADI General Conference, "Development", Journal of the Society for Inter-
    national Development, Rome, 1. p. 118
Camp, S.L. 1990. Life in the World's 100 Largest Cities, Metropolitan Areas, Population Crisis
    Committee, Washington,.
Compass. 1990. One World or Several: Towards a Strategy of Growth, Sustainability and
    Solidarity in an Interdependent World, Compass, "Development". Journal of the Society
    for International Development, Rome, March, p. 2
Corea, G. 1990, Global Stakes Require a New Consensus, "Development". Journal of the Society
    for International Development, Rome, 3/4, pp. 17–22.
Rees, W.E. and Roseland. 1991. Sustainable Communities: Planning for the 21st century, Plan
    Canada, May pp. 18–22.
Speth, J.G. 1990. Environmental Security for the 1990s, "Development". Journal of the Society
    for International Development, Rome, 3/4, p. 10.
Trudgill, S. 1990. Barriers to a Better Environment, What Stops Us Solving Environmental
    Problems? Belhavan Press, London, p. 1.
United Nations. 1974. Human Settlements: The Environmental Change. A compendium of
    United Nations Papers prepared for the Stockholm conference on the Human Environ-
    ment 1972, the MacMillan Press Ltd., London, p. 3.
WCED. 1987. Our common future: Oxford University Press, New Delhi.
Williams, M. 1990. Changing Development Realities and Trends: Impact on SID's Future
    Programme, "Development". Journal of the Society for International Development, Rome,
    March, p. 1.

Sustainability Problems and Historical Transitions— A Description in Terms of Changes in Metabolism and Colonization Strategies

Marina Fischer-Kowalski and Helmut Haberl

INTRODUCTION

The emergence of "sustainable development" as a key concept in the debate surrounding environmental issues has stimulated an interdisciplinary dialogue which has increasingly brought together scientists from most divergent fields as well as conflicting political and social groups. The wide variety of conceptions concerning sustainability that has emerged in the wake of this process calls for operationalization if it is to be relevant in terms of political and economic strategies.

Accordingly, societies may be conceptualized as subsystems of the biosphere. Such a conception, of course, does not fit within what Catton and Dunlap (1978) have identified as the paradigm of "human exceptionalism" predominating within the social sciences. Whereas the biosphere, that is the global eco-system, is closed materially, it is an open system with respect to energy. Societies are subsystems which are open with respect to both matter and energy (Daly 1994). Strategies for sustainable development, therefore, must be vitally concerned with the organization of flows of materials and energy between society and nature or, in other words, with social metabolism (Ayres and Simonis 1994a, Fischer-Kowalski and Haberl 1994). Essentially, metabolism is a biological concept which refers to the internal processes of a living organism. Organisms maintain a continuous flow of materials and energy with their environment to provide for their own functions, for growth and/or reproduction. In an analogous way, the social systems convert raw materials into manufactured products, services and, finally, into wastes—processes which economists describe as production and consumption (Ayres 1994; Ayres and Simonis 1994b).

Environmental problems arise, on the one hand, when societies consume minerals, fossil fuels, uranium, biomass, oxygen, etc. as "inputs". Historically, this process of "productive consumption" has time and again been strained by the scarcity of resources, and societies have traditionally attempted to resolve this constraint by migrating to more fertile regions, reducing procreation, changing nutritional habits or established modes of production, by means of trade, expelling other peoples, and by many other measures. With respect to "output", environmental problems arise whenever wastes cannot be absorbed and integrated in the natural environment in a useful or, at least, innocuous way. In order to maintain their metabolism, societies transform natural systems in a way that tends to maximize their usefulness for social purposes—natural ecosystems are replaced by agricultural ecosystems (meadows, fields) designed to produce as much usable biomass as possible, or are converted into built-up space, genetic codes of species are altered to increase their resistance against pests or pesticides, or to produce pharmaceuticals. We refer to this mode of intervention into natural systems as "colonization" (Fischer-Kowalski and Haberl, 1993) and define it as the conundrum of social activities which deliberately induce disequilibrium into natural systems and maintain them in that state.

Past societies may be classified according to the ways in which they have organized their metabolism and colonized their natural environment. To our knowledge the best guideline for such an analysis is the approach of materialist cultural anthropology outlined by Harris (1989, 1990). Societies—according to this paradigm—are exclusively expected to sustain mankind as a species and have evolved from rather small, egalitarian groups of hunters and gatherers to the highly specialized industrial societies. The culture of each society may be characterized as a specific balance of reproduction, production, and resources. All of these are faced with problems of sustainability, and cultural evolution may be viewed as the continuing struggle of societies trying to solve these. If, for example, populations reproduce too fast, traditional resources will not suffice to provide enough food; as a consequence, new resources must be found and/or new production techniques have to be developed—or else people will starve. Harris (1990), however, focusses on the explanation of cultural traits like food taboos sustained by ecological necessities. We will use his approach to describe the cultural evolution of sustainability problems in a more general manner.

Cultural evolution—interpreted in terms of sustainability problems— may serve to explain dramatic changes in the mode of production, the resources utilized, the forms of population control, and in the complex interrelations among these factors. This may be expected to cast some light on the question why some cultures broke down while others proved to be "superior". Our analysis provides a kind of framework to distinguish cultures according to their characteristic relationship with nature. Since sustainability problems may be viewed as problems of maintaining a particular social metabolism under given environmental circumstances, it is first necessary to point out the essential attributes of this metabolic process:

1) *Materials flow:* The social metabolism may be measured as mass throughput [kg·a^{-1}] for nutrition, shelter, clothing, buildings etc. From this point of view, societies are complex material systems, ingesting various resources and emitting diverse waste substances.

2) *Energy:* Like any other dynamic system of material stocks and flows, social systems are driven by a flow of free energy. Every society has at least the biological energy turnover of its members. Nowadays, in industrial societies the energy input per capita is at least 40 times the biological energy requirement of humans.

The metabolism of a human society at a certain time in a certain region may be characterized by its mass and energy input. Input per capita and year is largely determined by the mode of production, which can only be sustained if the necessary resources are available in sufficient quantity and quality. It is the size of the population, then, that determines the overall input of both energy and mass. On the other hand, the sustainable population density is determined by the mode of production and society's ability to exploit certain key resources.

SUSTAINABILITY PROBLEMS: FROM HUNTERS AND GATHERERS TO INDUSTRIAL SOCIETIES

The metabolism of a society is at least equal to the sum of the metabolisms of its members. The evolution of mankind has seen the expansion of social metabolism far beyond this minimum level, as societies began to colonize more and more natural systems for their own purposes and have intensified their intervention into natural processes ever since.

The history of this process may be broken down into three main stages (Sieferle 1993): (1) hunter-and-gathering societies, (2) agrarian societies, (3) industrial societies.

1) Hunter-and-Gathering Societies

People have lived as hunters and gatherers, moving about in groups of 20 to 50 people, for 99 per cent of the history of mankind. The metabolism of hunters and gatherers did not significantly exceed their biological metabolism. Migrants that they were, they probably had few heavy goods to carry, nutrition was provided by gathering fruits and other edible parts of plants, by hunting and fishing, with the ratio of vegetarian food to meat and fish largely dependent on the environment. Whereas the Inuits almost exclusively lived on meat and fish, !Kung bushmen met 70–80 per cent of their energy demand from vegetarian foods. Tools were made of stone, wood and bones. Fire was used for cooking, to provide warmth and protection against carnivores, and to drive game animals over cliffs or into ambushes. Means of sustenance could be procured with about three or four hours of work per day (Harris 1991; Ponting 1991, Wing and Brown 1979) and ample leisure was a free luxury. Hunters and gatherers did not colonize nature, that is, they did not deliberately modify natural systems in order to make them more productive or suitable to provide for their needs. There was one exception though it seems that fire was used to burn down forests in order to promote herbaceous plants, which are usable for prey animals to a greater extent than woody species (Butzer 1984; Harris 1991).

The major sustainability problem was probably food supply which was limited by the rather invariable carrying capacity of the ecosystems that they were part of: Whenever the number of people exceeded a certain critical level, they either had to migrate to places with sufficient food supply or starve. Although regulatory mechanisms kept population growth at very low levels (Harris 1991), the hunters and gatherers spread to all continents and climate zones within a span of approximately 50 millennia.

This mode of production could no longer be sustained once the population increased unchecked. The hunters and gatherers were instrumental in the extinction of many big animal species. Ponting (1991) mentions that 86 per cent of the big animal species in Australia became extinct in the past 40,000 years, most likely because of hunting activities of the aboriginals. In South America 80 per cent of the bigger animal species became extinct, in North America 73 per cent. The "invention of agriculture"—the neolithic revolution—seems to have occurred as a response to the growing scarcity of food. This change in the mode of production coincided with a major climatic turn at the end of the last glacial period. Temperature increases changed forests to grasslands and promoted the domestication of animals rather than hunting them. Harris (1990) argues that it was not the lack of technological abilities which retarded an earlier development of agriculture, since hunters and gatherers knew some agricultural techniques long before they were widely practised. They did not use them simply because agriculture is a much less convenient way of food production than the one they were used to.

2) Agrarian Societies

The major innovation of agricultural societies is that most of their metabolism is based on "colonization", on the deliberate transformation of natural ecosystems by means of the continuous application of human labour. Concomitantly, ecosystems are subjected to a state which is far from their natural balance but, at the same time, yield more produce that is available for the metabolism of society.[1]

The metabolism of agrarian societies is still based on biomass for nutrition. Compared to hunter and gathering societies, however, the necessary output per capita has multiplied since it contains food for humans as well as for domestic animals and puts wood as a natural resource to an ever-widening range of uses. To an ever-increasing extent, the biomass required for nutrition (grains, animal milk and meat) must be extracted from "colonized environments". Specific natural cycles need to be sustained by human labour, and social wastes (in particular, human and animal faeces) must be utilized in order to retain soil fertility. This, in turn, must be supported by "colonizing" local and regional water systems. Irrigation systems need to be established, the water supply of larger settlements must be organized,[2] wet areas need to be drained and cities protected from flooding. Forests—formerly an abundant resource—are mostly exploited in much the same way as the sea is harvested for fish, with society relying completely on the self-regenerating capacities of nature.

As a consequence of the sedentary way of life, mineral materials are used for construction—housing, public buildings, infrastructure (transport, defence)—and resources like metals and salt are introduced which account for a small but crucial fraction of the social metabolism (salt is a key prerequisite for the domestication of animals).

With reference to the interplay between reproduction, production and resources, we may summarize our findings as follows:

1) Initially, the "sustainability problem" became manifest as a chronic shortage of nutrition resulting from very slow but steady

---

[1]As soon as human labour ceases to be applied, these ecosystems become renaturalized. Domestic animals regain those traits which were successful in natural selection, gardens and fields return to forest and grassland. Some of this renaturalization has to be permitted periodically to maintain the regenerative qualities of the ecosystems—wild species must be crossed in with domesticated plants and animals, forests need time to recover in slash-and-burn agriculture in tropical zones, and follow periods have to be established in rainforest agriculture.

[2]One of the most fascinating examples is 17th century Edo (later Tokio) that supplied its almost one million inhabitants with fresh water and at the same time carefully collected their "nighe soil" (faecal matter and urine) to be purchased(!) by the peasants supplying the city with agricultural produce. In terms of the concepts used in our approach this serves as a very good example of outputs of societal (and in this case even biological) metabolism being used for the colonization of natural environments that in turn provide for inputs.

population growth and, at least regionally, was aggravated by a major climatic change.

2) A new mode of production evolved which "colonized" parts of the natural environment instead of merely exploiting it. Increased application of labour to these "colonies" multiplied returns yet, at the same time, did not deplete the resource base, since much of this labour served to upgrade the carrying capacity of natural systems (e.g. ploughing, fertilizing, flooding and irrigating, or feeding of animals). This intensification of labour and the concomitant increase in labour productivity both induced and permitted an excess population to profit from it, to organize it—and to avoid it. Thus, much larger societies with an elaborate social hierarchy and division of labour could evolve and exist in the same environments at a much higher population density.

3) This transformation also involved changes in the cultural regulation of reproduction, since a sedentary way of life and the new value of child labour stimulated population growth. Although practically all agrarian societies apply some kind of birth control and, therefore, have population growth rates much below the rates that are biologically possible, the population of the ancient empires, for example, grew at rates of approximately 0.5 per cent annually (compared to about 0.001 per cent in hunter and gathering cultures; Hassan 1981, cited in Harris 1991:96). Thus, human populations tend to outgrow their nutritional base.

4) One way to respond to this was to culturally regulate what should legitimately be considered a "resource". Duby (1984:70), for example, reports that during the 6th century strong taboos predominated in Europe against the cutting of trees—taboos which the Church had difficulties to overcome despite an abundance of undernourished people. Harris (1990) provides several examples referring to food regulation, such as the prohibition of eating pork (3rd book Moses) or the institutionalization of the "Holy Cow" in India.[3] As is well known, all forms of vegetarianism require less (by a factor of approximately 10 less) plant biomass than eating animal products or animal meat (which have to be fed on plants before); thus, religious prescriptions of vegetarianism can be found in many agrarian cultures. Other ways to respond are migration, colonization or the conquest of new territories,[4] or civil wars

---

[3]The prohibition of eating pork in the Middle East corresponded to pigs becoming direct nutritional competitors of humans as a consequence of deforestation in this region—before, pigs had been able to feed on themselves in the woods. Had there not been established a general religious taboo, the further breeding of pigs would have required sacrificing the grains and other increasingly scarce resources like shadow and water pools needed for the direct supply of humans (Harris 1990, p. 180).

[4]The importing of slaves as in Ancient Rome has a similar effect: It "externalizes" the biological costs of child-bearing and child-rearing to a different territory.

which decimate the population. Finally, nature herself may regulate numbers by means of positive checks, by famines and epidemics. Agrarian cultures have practiced a variety of means over the centuries, and for most of them malnutrition of the majority of the population was as common as childbirth, hard labour and cruelty.

Despite the fact that they lasted for a few millenia and gradually colonized most of parts of earth which could be easily settled in, agricultural societies developed a way of life that was "unsustainable" in the long run—they depleted many of the natural resources they depended upon, such as forests and arable soil, and eventually could provide no more than a fairly miserable, hard-working and badly nourished life for most of their members. Improvements in technology such as the use of iron ploughs and horses brought only temporary relief soon to be countered by population growth. The "natural limits to growth" were set by the amount of available land and its capacity for food production; the margin of soil productivity increases which were amenable to technological manipulation was not very substantial.

3) Industrial Societies

Parallel to this colonial expansion of agrarian cultures a new mode of production gradually emerged within Europe, for which this expansion and the accompanying improvements in the means of transportation (and increased possibilities of trading) were of key importance. The final breakthrough of this new mode of production, however, depended on the use of a qualitatively new resource, i.e. fossil fuels. First, and for a long time, this involved only coal, with oil and gas becoming ever more important. In view of the constant scarcity of the life-sustaining resources of the agricultural era, this may be looked upon as an environmentally beneficial innovation: There is no other living system that human societies might depend on that is vitally interested in fossil fuels or in the many other subterrestrial resources which—with the help of fossil fuels—may now be effectively utilized. Thus, the social metabolism can be greatly increased without depleting the base of human nutrition.

Unfortunately, however, this induces new problems which, in the long run, may certainly affect inputs, yet become manifest more immediately with respect to the output of social metabolism. The mobilization of huge amounts of materials stowed away for geological periods in subterrestrial sinks and their eventual deposition in the biosphere kicks off biochemical processes on a planetary scale and at a speed beyond the reach of gradual evolutionary adaptation. Local and regional consequences of this were felt quickly (e.g. fogs detrimental to human health and agricultural productivity in 19th century England, but global and long-term consequences will be felt for centuries to come. Thus, intermediate "bottlenecks" checking population growth and/or the scale of metabolism, e.g. the scarcity of energy based on current biomass, have been overcome (at least within industrial societies) only to be substituted by an environmental "bottleneck" induced by "output" or off-products resulting from industrial processes. (Of course, resource scarcity will once again raise "input bottlenecks" with the depletion of so-called "non-renewable resources".)

With respect to reproduction industrialism seems to have had beneficial effects in the end. The transition to the industrial mode of production in Europe, North America and Japan, and currently spreading to the rest of the world, entailed the breakdown of traditional cultural regulations of population growth. In the early phases of industrialization, theories like that of Malthus made it seem inevitable that most members of industrial societies would have to be kept just at subsistence levels, or else they would bear more children than the labour market could absorb and the soil could feed (Sieferle 1990, p. 90). Later stages saw a shift in the cost-benefit ratio of having children, that is, decreasing benefits and increasing costs, so that it became culturally established to have very few children or even none at all (Heinsohn et al. 1979). This cultural change became effective even before the invention of elegant technologies of birth control. Thus, in the centres of industrialism the population does not grow any more, except by immigration. This, of course, is not the case at the "peripheries",[5] where it is still a matter of hope whether a "demographic transition" will take place.

The "sustainability problem" of industrial societies, therefore, is squarely rooted in the size and quality of their excessive metabolism—which is what we are going to analyze next.

THE SIZE OF THE INDUSTRIAL METABOLISM

As already mentioned in Chapter 2, one can think of two reasonable ways of looking at the "size" of the metabolism of a society: (1) The metabolism can be operationalized as "materials flow" (raw materials enter society, are processed internally and "excreted" in form of emissions), and (2) as "energy flow". Of course, the same material can be part of both flows (e.g. oil), but some will only be relevant in the materials flow (e.g. water, gravel, sand).

Let us first look at the amount of materials processed by an industrial society. These materials are extracted from nature, used and transformed in

---

[5]In several African countries, for example, population growth rates at present amount to an annual 3.5 to 6 per cent.

one way or another within society, and are eventually returned into natural cycles as wastes or emissions. This is a more or less simple input-output calculation in material units (e.g. tons) which may be computed—on the basis of some methodological assumptions and conventions that are gradually being agreed upon internationally (Ayres and Simonis, 1994b)—from standard economic statistics. This results in a kind of material "national product", with tons rather than particular currencies serving as accounting units. Divided by the size of the population, this figure provides the per capita metabolism of the average member of a society.

This per capita metabolism may be compared to the metabolism which—using historical and anthropological data—can be estimated for hunter and gathering societies, as shown in figure 1. Austrians or Germans currently maintain a metabolism which is about 40 times larger in scale than the metabolism of people who inhabited the same region some 4000 years ago. They use about 10 times as much air, 20 times as much solid "raw materials" and 60 times as much water (see figure 1). Accordingly, their stress on the natural environment is several times greater than that of their predecessors.

If 70 per cent of the world population now living under more or less agrarian circumstances changed to an industrial mode of living, the

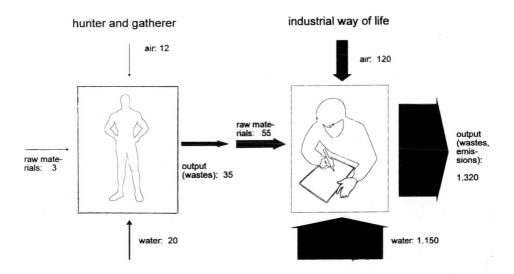

Fig. 1: Comparison of the social metabolism of hunters and gatherers compared with members of an industrialized society (in kg per capita and day)
© IFF-Social Ecology 1994

stresses upon the environment, judged by this crude measure, would multiply by a factor of approximately 10,[6] disregarding population growth.

The numbers given in figure 1 are valid for Austria, but comparable countries are very similar (see Schütz and Bringezu 1993 for Germany, Jänicke 1994 for a comparison of Austria, Germany and Japan). It appears that approximately 88 per cent of the socio-economic metabolism of industrial societies is water, 8 per cent air and 4 per cent "raw materials", which means solid materials (ores, gravels, sand, coal, biomass etc.) and liquid/gaseous energy carriers (oil, natural gas).

If we distinguish between "renewable" (mainly: biomass and water) and "non-renewable" (mainly: fossil fuels, minerals and metals) inputs, the major characteristic of industrial society of course consists in the enormous increase of the latter fraction: Among the raw materials (disregarding water and air) of contemporary industrial societies "non-renewable resources" make up for about two-thirds of input[7] in terms of mass. Tentative estimates for agricultural societies (based on Netting 1981; analyses for 6th century Byzanz and 15th century Venice are in preparation, Winiwarter 1994) show that metals and minerals amounted to certainly less than 10 per cent of their input. Nevertheless industrial development obviously also increases the amount of per-capita-input of "renewable resources", i.e. biomass, by more than 50 per cent.

Thus it seems there exists a per capita level of material input/output typical for highly developed industrial societies, far above the level for agricultural societies. Interestingly enough, as judged from the case of Austria, this enlarged metabolism still mainly consists in the extraction of raw materials from national territory. With respect to water and air, of course, this involves the local utilization of a good that is truly transnational by nature. But with respect to raw materials input of 157 million tons not more than 40 million tons (25 per cent) were imported from abroad[8]—with more than half of it being fossil energy resources.

---

[6]We do not yet have good estimates for the size of metabolism in agricultural societies, although we are currently working at the reconstruction of typical examples. Scales are difficult to establish since regional and temporal variance is substantial.

[7]The results of this calculation strongly depend upon the definition of "biomass":, i.e. whether its weight is calculated including natural water content or by dry substance. Here we used Austrian data natural water content. A pecularity of the German calculations (both from the Statistical Office and the Wuppertal Institute) is the exclusion of green fodder consumed by livestock, which reduces their proportion of biomass to 18 per cent of the total of raw materials (Kuhn et al. 1994).

[8]This calculation is not quite fair, though, since imported materials are only computed by the weight they have when they cross the national border. In their country of origin and by transportation they have accumulated an additional material "rucksack" not included here. Symmetrically, however, the "rucksack" of exports is included here.

Outputs originating from solid raw materials are more likely to be emitted as wastes to the transnational mediums like the atmosphere and the water system than to be "exported" as goods in the economic sense. 27 million tons[9] (i.e. 17 per cent of raw material input) are discharged into the atmosphere, mainly in the form of CO_2, and another 7 million tons (4 per cent) of residuals are discharged into the countries rivers (and part of it finally to the sea). Compared to this "export of emissions", commodity exports amounting to a total volume of about 16 million tons (10 per cent) are rather trivial (see figure 2).

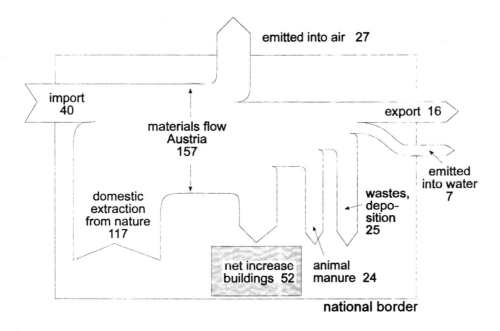

Fig. 2. Raw materials flow with reference to the national territory (in million tons per year) © IFF-Social Ecology, 1994, data: Steurer 1992

In figure 3 we present a comparison of the raw materials flow of Austria and Germany (ex-FRG only), which shows that the differences between the two countries are rather small. The total per capita raw materials flow in Japan is also very similar (Jänicke, 1994). But what is even more interesting to note in figure 3 is the similarity in growth rates. Whereas in Austria the raw materials flow has increased by a third within two decades, in Germany it took three decades.

---

[9]Counted as C, S, H ..., not as CO_2, H_2O, SO_2, ...(CO_2-emissions are approx. 60 million tons).

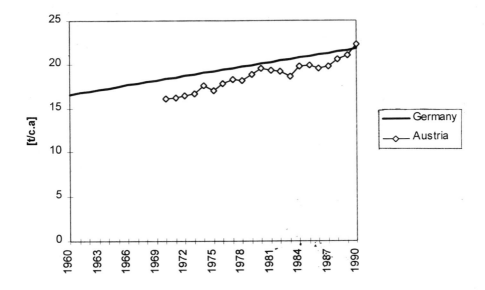

Fig. 3: Comparison of the per-capita raw materials flow in Germany and Austria, 1960–1990
© IFF-Social Ecology, data: Steurer 1994, Kuhn et al. 1994

Thus we may conclude that even in rich industrial countries economic growth still also means growth in the consumption of raw materials (and emissions). Whichever mechanisms may be at work to reduce material growth (such as increases in the material and energy efficiency, miniaturization of products or an increase in the relative importance of services) does not serve to stop material growth altogether.

But as may be judged from figure 4, we can observe a decrease in material intensity—Economic growth in terms of monetary values (i.e. Austrian Shillings at constant prices) during the last two decades has surpassed growth in terms of material tons. Material intensity (i.e. tons per shilling) has decreased by approximately one-third.

A second way is to look at the size of the metabolism of a society in terms of energy. Figure 5 shows a comparison of the energy input of hunter-and-gathering societies, an example from an agrarian society (Törbel 1875) and an industrial society (Austria 1990). Törbel, a small village in Switzerland, has been investigated in an in-depth study by Netting (1981), which allows extrapolations of the total energy and materials flows. The per-capita energy use of this agrarian village turns out to be about four times higher than our estimates for hunter-and-gathering societies. Industrial societies again use about 3.5 times more energy than agrarian

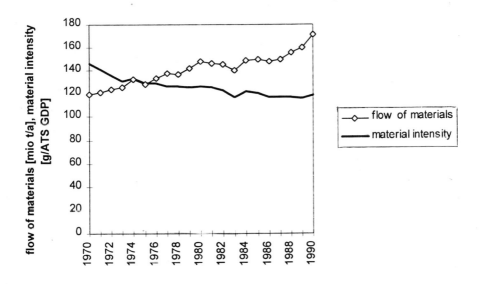

Fig. 4: Flow of raw materials related to GDP, Austria 1970–1990
© IFF-Social Ecology, 1994, data: from Steurer 1994

societies per capita. Interestingly enough, biomass use remained nearly stable (65 GJ/c.a in Törbel, 75 GJ/c.a in Austria 1990). This may be specific for Austria, since Austria's use of biomass is extraordinarily high compared to other industrialized countries. However, it is obvious that the enormous increase of per capita energy use was only possible by a shift to fossil fuels as new energy carriers.

As far as the total energy "income" from the sun is concerned, the energy inputs of social systems, even under industrial conditions, are very low. What is more relevant as a limit to natural "income" is the annual energetic net primary production of plants—sun energy incorporated into plant biomass within a given period of time. This energy is the nutritional base of all heterotrophic life on this planet. Humans live on this energy as well as all animals and all microorganisms that are not capable of photosynthesis. The amount of this net primary production (NPP) of plants depends on climate, soil quality and the availability of water, and on a planetary scale can only be marginally increased by human techniques.[10] The proportion

---

[10]It can more easily be reduced through overuse of land and consequent desertification, through toxic emissions etc. Most anthropogenic biotopes (such as corn fields or orchards) are less productive than the natural ones that would grow in the same place (such as natural forests).

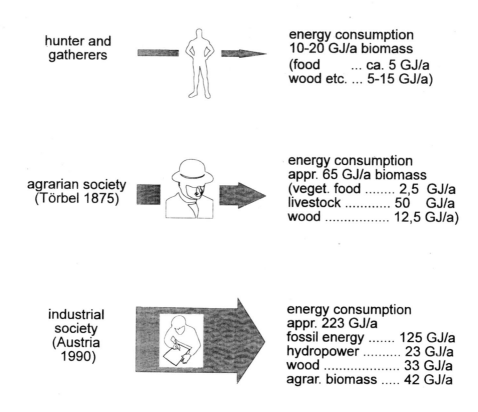

Fig. 5: Per capita energy flow of hunters and gatherers, an agrarian society and an industrial society
© IFF-Social Ecology, 1994, data: own calculations, Netting 1981

of this NPP that is appropriated by human societies[11] is, therefore, a good indicator of the "size" of social metabolism vis-a-vis its natural environment. As soon as societies appropriate more than 100 per cent of NPP, they

---

[11]Society may "appropriate" this energy in two different ways: a) By preventing its generation or reducing the quantity of energy being generated. Buildings or roads, for example, prevent the growth of plants in this area and thereby reduce the NPP that can be generated. In Austria almost 10 per cent of potential NPP is prevented by the built-up environment. Another way of preventing NPP is planting biotopes that are less productive than the natural biotopes that would evolve there in the absence of intervention—such as grasslands, gardens or fields (instead of woods). b) By harvesting the plants (or part of the plants) growing in an area. In Austria the harvest of wood accounts for almost 29 per cent of NPP-appropriation.

"consume more than what is growing" and very quickly deplete their own and only nutritional base. According to Vitousek et al. (1986), human societies appropriate about one-third of the world-wide terrestrial NPP — as a result of population growth alone—and this percentage may be expected to double within the next 35 years (Daly 1992). According to our calculations for Austria, this industrial society appropriates more than 50 per cent of the NPP on its territory.[12] Whichever way one prefers to look at it, the scale of the industrial metabolism is excessive compared to other modes of production and very large in relation to the natural environment that it feeds upon.

If one single species (together with its domesticated animals) needs half of the nutritional basis of all animal species taken together, it clearly competes with the rest to extinction.[13] A similar argument applies to the relation between the industrialized countries of the North and the mainly agrarian and industrializing countries of the South. By their excessive metabolism the industrialized countries just do not leave enough environmental "space" (be it in terms of raw materials or natural absorption capacity for emissions) for the South to develop along the same paths.

HOW CAN INDUSTRIAL SOCIETIES PERCEIVE THEIR OWN SUSTAINABILITY PROBLEMS AND RESPOND TO THEM?

From what we have seen so far, there is substantial reason to assume that industrial societies are well on their way to produce irreversible changes in the functioning of the natural systems that they vitally depend upon—they excessively emit substances which are either transferred from long-term planetary sinks or altogether alien to the biosphere, strain the natural energy household to the extent of severely reducing biodiversity, and may be expected to run into a threatening shortage of non-renewable resources. Although all of this may be true, and even many people may be convinced of this truth, this still remains an intellectual exercise in obvious contradiction to a lot of seemingly everyday experiences such as:

- raw materials are becoming cheaper and cheaper

---

[12]"Sustainability" originally implied not to exploit forests beyond thier reproduction rates—harvest rates are not supposed to exceed reproduction rates, which certainly does not mean to harvest a hundred per cent NPP on this territory, but 50 per cent at best. Still, this does not take into account the living conditions of all the other species for which forests provide. They were disregarded and successively extinguished by the application of this "sustainability rule". According to Weterings and Opschoor (1992), sustainable amounts of social NPP-appropriation should not exceed 20 per cent in each territory if a reasonable degree of biodiversity is to be maintained.

[13]For an in-depth case study of the scale at which the industrial metabolism of Austria is operating see Fischer-Kowalski and Haberl (1994) and Steurer (1994).

- agriculture is producing an excess of goods that cannot be sold on regular markets at regular prices
- people in industrial societies live longer, may be even healthier and more comfortably
- they do not depend on their territories but, on the contrary, gain a lot by far-reaching exchange and transport
- they can keep their labour force busy most of the time, although it may be hard to procure a sufficient amount of work
- they can resolve, or at least moderate, their internal social problems by stimulating economic growth and, finally,
- most parts of the world strive to imitate the industrial mode of production and living.

Why, then, should people believe in intellectual, scientific insights rather than in their reinforcing day-to-day experience?

The real problem, therefore, in taking a turn towards a more sustainable mode of production and living is to create conditions that provide the subsystems of society, in particular the economic subsystem, with experience[14] that will make the right alarms ring. To find out how this could be done is a genuine task for the social sciences and, among them, for environmental sociology.

We will proceed by checking some measures that are politically feasible as to whether they qualify in the light of this reasoning.

1) Social-Ecological Tax Reform

The international division of labour, notwithstanding increasing scarcity, consistently cheapens raw materials while, at the same time, it tends to raise the price of industrial labour. Industrial societies, therefore, exhibit a strong tendency to curb expenditures on labour instead of employing human capital to develop more elegant forms of utilizing natural resources. Rationalization aggravates the redundancy of human labour and eliminates an ever-increasing number of people from productive processes.

It is not only direct wages but also a relevant margin of "political costs" that increases gross labour costs by an additional ≈50 per cent (taxes, social insurance etc.). Social-ecological wage reform implies a gradual shift from taxing wages to taxing energy and raw materials in order to cheapen labour-intensive forms of production, e.g. services, whereas energy- and raw materials-intensive forms of production will become more expensive. Reform policies may be expected to promote the development of technologies which, by employing labour power, economize on natural resour-

---

[14]This type of reasoning, although put in different terms, very much resembles what Luhmann (1986) has called the problems of environmental communication.

ces. This, in turn, should increase the demand for labour and, therefore, is also socially advantageous.

A recent study by the German Institute for Economic Research (DIW 1994), financed by Greenpeace Germany, has tried to develop an econometric model of the economic effects of taxing energy and repaying the extra tax income to employers via a reduction of their share in social security payments for employees, and to households by means of what is called an "eco-bonus" (a fixed monthly sum per person)—the results were very reassuring for both a five- and a ten-year interval: There was no reduction of economic growth, a slight increase in employment and a degressive effect on household incomes. According to the model, the tax would induce a reduction of energy consumption by about 20 per cent. The results of this study are quite in line with OECD's evaluation of distributional effects of economic instruments in environmental policy (OECD 1994).

As far as we know, no comprehensive models have as yet been developed to evaluate the effects ensuing from taxing raw materials use, especially with reference to agriculture; currently, there does not even exist a consensus among environmental scientists, since many of them still consider the substitution of "non-renewable" by "renewable resources" a useful strategy, which—as far as biomass is concerned—we doubt very much in the light of the argument elaborated above. Taxing agricultural raw materials, however, might prove to be beneficial both with regard to the existing inequity in the international division of labour and with respect to the dilemmas associated with agricultural subsidies in industrial societies.

2) Paying Gains in Labour Productivity in Time Rather than in Money

Although only a minority of predominantly middle-aged males actually work "normal hours", this group of employees staffs highly influential positions when it comes to determine the standards of "normality" with respect to production and consumption. Hard workers that they are, they are invariably hard consumers as well, turning over substantial amounts of energy in both spheres. Breathless, potent, and generally short of time, excessive consumption of ready-made goods and services seems to be the only way to satisfy similarly excessive wants. If this dominant model of allocating time were gradually phased out, a good many substitutes promising satisfaction might become redundant and pass away, eventually, to leave room for services which are more effective to achieve the satisfaction of needs and wants.

Henceforth, productivity increases might be rewarded by time rather than with money. Since productivity gains are not distributed equally across the economy, the distribution of increased leisure across society will be subject to bargaining—especially since it is not clear yet, to what extent productivity gains are currently being achieved by "technization" (applying mainly to industry) and by means of "improvements in organization", respectively (which applies at least as much to services as well). This classic distinction advanced by Lutz (1969) might prove very useful when one analyses the potential means available to reduce material metabolism on the level of single working processes or firms. It is patent ecological non-sense, however, that the traditional lower class culture of "hard labour" established in the agricultural era—where it was quite neccessary given prevailing ecological conditions—has been generalized for all classes in industrial society.

3) Cultural Variety

Last, but not least, there must be room for social and cultural experience to try out new and different ways of life. Once again, we are considering several problems simultaneously: The gradual dissolution of traditional family structures and regional communities, migration movements, the omnipresence of markets, bureaucracies and the media, and the lack of affection and social recognition—that is, the deficiency in "positional goods" associated with that—are phenomena which frustrate an ever-increasing number of people in their endeavour to gain recognition within their social environment. Consequently, efforts are increasing to achieve this by means of spectacular expenditure on energy as well as on resources, or by means of intimidation and violence. It is impossible to create "communities" by means of policy measures—and even the mere attempt to pretend doing so is bound to face terrible consequences—but it is possible to grant them the space that they need to unfold, to try out ways of life that are better sustainable with respect to ecological concerns.

REFERENCES

Ayres, R.U. 1994. Industrial metabolism: theory and policy. In: *Industrial Metabolism. Restructuring for Sustainable Development*, R.U. Ayres and U.E. Simonis (eds.), pp. 3–20, Tokyo, New York, Paris: United Nations University Press.

Ayres, R.U. and U.E. Simonis (eds). 1994a. *Industrial Metabolism. Restructuring for Sustainable Development*. Tokyo, New York, Paris: United Nations University Press.

Ayres, R.U. and U.E. Simonis. 1994b. Introduction. Pages xi–xiv In: *Industrial Metabolism. Restructuring for Sustainable Development*, R.U. Ayres and U.E. Simonis (eds.), Tokyo, New York, Paris: United Nations University Press.

Butzer, K.W. 1984. *Archaeology as Human Ecology*. 2nd Edition. Cambridge: Cambridge University Press.

Catton, W.R. Jr. and D.E. Dunlap. 1978. Environmental sociology: a new paradigm. *The American Sociologist* 13: 41–49.

Daly, H.E. 1992. Vom Wirtschaften in einer leeren Welt zum Wirtschaften in einer vollen Welt. Wir haben einen historischen Wendepunkt in der Wirtschaftsentwicklung erreicht. Pages

15–27 In: *Nach dem Brundtlandbericht: Umweltverträgliche wirtschaftliche Entwicklung.* R. Goodland et al. (eds.), Bonn: Deutsche UNESCO-Kommission.

Daly, H.E. 1994. Die Gefahren des freien Handels. *Spektrum der Wissenschaft* 1/1994: 40–46.

DIW 1994. Deutsches Institut für Wirtschaftsforschung: Wirtschaftliche Auswirkungen einer ökologischen Steuerreform. Hamburg: Greenpeace.

Duby, G. 1984. Krieger und Bauern. Die Entwicklung der mittelalterlichen Wirtschaft und Gesellschaft bis um 1200. Frankfurt: Suhrkamp.

European Centre. 1993. *Welfare in a Civil Society.* Vienna: Report for the Conference of European Ministers Responsible for Social Affairs.

Fischer-Kowalski, M. and H. Haberl. 1994. Auf dem Weg zur Nachhaltigkeit: Vom Stoffwechsel der Gesellschaft. Pages 113–131 In: *Tagungsband zum Symposium "Mensch und Landschaft 2000, Nutzung, Bedrohung, Chancen."* (17–18.2.1994), Technische Universität Graz.

Fischer-Kowalski, M. and H. Haberl. 1993. Metabolism and colonization. Modes of production and the physical exchange between societies and nature. *Innovation in Social Science Research* Vol. 6 No. 4: 415–442.

Fischer-Kowalski, M. and H. Payer. 1993. Gesellschaftlicher stoffwechsel und wirtschaftliche entwicklung. *Kurswechsel* 4/1993: 7–15.

Haberl, H. 1994. Der Gesamtenergieinput des sozio-ökonomischen Systems in Österreich 1960–1991, Zur Erweiterung des Begriffes "Energieverbrauch", Technical Report, Vienna: Research Report of the IFF-Social Ecology No. 35.

Harris, M. 1989. *Kulturanthropologie. Ein Lehrbuch.* Frankfurt/Main: Campus.

Harris, M. 1990. *Kannibalen und Könige.* Die Wachstumsgrenzen der Hochkulturen. Darmstadt: Klett and Kotta.

Harris, M. 1991. *Cultural Anthropology.* 3rd Edition. New York: Harper and Collins.

Heinsohn, G., R. Knieper and O. Steiger. 1979. Menschenproduktion. Allgemeine Bevölkerungslehre der Neuzeit. Frankfurt: Suhrkamp.

Institut für sozial-ökologische Forschung (ed.). 1993. Sustainable Netherlands. Aktionsplan für eine nachhaltige Entwicklung der Niederlande. Frankfurt a. M.

Jänicke, M., H. Mönch and M. Binder. 1991. Ökologische Dimensionen industriellen Wandels. Berlin: Research Report of the Research Center for Environmental Policy, Free University Berlin.

Jänicke, M. 1994. Ökologisch tragfähige Entwicklung: Kriterien und Steuerungsansätze ökologischer Ressourcenpolitik. Trier: Schriftenreihe des Zentrums für Europäische Studien, Bd. 15, Universität Trier.

Katzmann, W., S. Kux, H.P. Nachtnebel and J. Reitinger. 1989. *Umweltbericht Wasser.* Wien: Österreichisches Bundesinstitut für Gesundheitswesen.

Kuhn, M., W. Radermacher and C. Stahmer. 1994. Umweltökonomische Trends 1960–1990. In: Wirtschaft und Statistik 8 (1994), S.658–677.

Luhmann, N. 1986. *Ökologische Kommunikation.* Opladen: Westdeutscher Verlag.

Lutz, B. 1969. Produktionsprozeß und Berufsqualifikation. In: *Spätkapitalismus oder Industriegesellschaft*, T. Adorno (ed.), Stuttgart: Euke.

Netting, R.M. 1981. *Balancing on an Alp.* Cambridge/New York/Melbourne: Cambridge University Press.

OECD. 1994. *The Distributive Effects of Economic Instruments for Environmental Policy*, OECD, Paris.

Ponting, C. 1991. *A green History of the World.* London: Penguin.

Schütz, H. and S. Bringezu. 1993. Major Material flows in Germany. *Fresenius Environmental Bulletin* 2 (8): 443–448.

Sieferle, R.P. 1990. *Bevölkerungswachstum und Naturzerstörung.* Frankfurt: Suhrkamp.

Sieferle, R.P. 1993. Die Grenzen der Umweltgeschichte. *Gaia* Vol. 2, No. 1: 8–21.

Steurer, A. 1992. Stoffstrombilanz Österreich 1988. Vienna: Research Report IFF-Social Ecology No. 26.

Steurer, A. 1994. Stoffstrombilanz Österreich 1970–1990—Inputseite. Vienna: Research Report IFF-Social Ecology No. 34.

Vitousek, P.M., P.R. Ehrlich, A.H. Ehrlich and P.A. Matson. 1986. Human Appropriation of the Products of Photosynthesis. *BioScience* 36 (6): 368–373.

Weterings, R.A.P.M. and J. B. Opschoor. 1992. The Ecocapacity as a Challenge to Technological Development. Rijswijk: RMNO-Report No. 74a.

Wing, E.S. and A.B. Brown. 1979. *Paleonutrition. Method and Theory in Prehistoric Foodways.* London: Academic Press.

Winiwarter, V.1994. Umweltgeschichte am Beispiel der Stadt: Forschungsstand und Probleme. Unpublished manuscript, Vienna.

The New Politics of Environmental Governance: Sustainable Development on the Way to the Next Millennium?

On-Kwok Lai[1]

PUTTING THE NEW GLOBAL CHALLENGE IN CONTEXT

Sustainable development, since the Rio Earth Summit on environment, has become the major (perhaps, the only) global issue requiring both global and local socio-political governance. To elaborate the discourse on sustainability in the next Millennium, we highlight the new contextual contours on which nation states are likely to situate the politics of environmental governance and mediate various conflicts. To generate more propositions for future study, our discussions will be maintained at a general yet indicative one. Under this premise, this paper outlines the related contextual specificity of the problem, under which the state project engages in sustainable development, and examines the synergetic effects of various socio-political constellations of the modernity,[2] then the new form of Gemeinschaft, and lastly, the emergence of a new production mode.

[1]Dr. On-Kwok Lai is in the Department of Political Science and Public Policy, the University of Waikato, Private Bag 3105, Hamilton, New Zealand. E-mail:oklai@waikato.ac.nz. This paper is prepared with supports from Zentrum für Sozialpolitik, Universität Bremen and Deutscher Akademischer Austauschdienst (DAAD).

[2]The peculiarity of the modernity should be noted that "most modern writers have recognized that the only secure thing about modernity is its insecurity... Modernity, therefore, not only entails a ruthless break with any or all preceding historical conditions, but is characterized by a never ending process of internal ruptures and fragmentation within itself." (Harvery 1989: 11–12).

1) The Governance of Nature: Tragedy of the Commons

Industrialization, in a historical sense, is interrelated with urbanization, which in turn shapes the course of social life, the transformation of communal life (*Gemeinschaft*—community) to a functionally organized modern society (*Geschellschaft*—society) and environmental problems. In this respect, we can discuss the synergetic relations between industrialization, production, consumption, and environment. In the following paragraphs, we focus on the specificities of industrialization and environment under modernization process, consumption and environment as well as social response towards environmental problems, which all contribute to the understanding of analytical matrix of nature, society and community, as well as the context of environmental governance.

Environment here refers to the natural environment which constitutes and shapes the biological, physical, and chemical sphere, or in over-used terms: the non-territorial specific ecological system (Meadows et al. 1992). In this respect, it should be pointed out that we are used to conceive nature as external to society, and pre-people's existence; and following this way of thinking, the concept of nature is also universal and external to people (*Homo sapiens*). This conception only explains the universal nature, however, not the nature in a people society. This dualistic view of nature versus society does not explain the synergy between environment and people, nature and society, as technological advancement has changed the contours of the configuration of nature and society (Martell 1994, Milton 1993).

An alternative conceptualization on the nature and environment is that environmental quality has been reproduced by human society, or at least being (badly) shaped by people. In actuality, this conceptualization is fundamental to the (also underlying) thesis of most pro-ecological advocacies for environmental protection and sustainable development. 'Environment' used in this context refers to the differentiated unity of nature and society, the differentiation refers to the concrete activities of people and the natural process that are (re)produced partly through people activities. In other words, the unity of nature is not undifferentiated, it is a differentiated unity, not an abstract identity; and for sustainable development, it is therefore necessary to examine the role played by people's productive activity in the differentiation process of nature. Given the role of people as social agency in the differentiation process of 'nature', i.e. the built-environment, it is possible to outline this process concretely, for example, in terms of the changes in environmental quality as prescribed by most scientific methodologies. More specific, because of recent scientific findings, say, the problem of the ozone layer depletion, all enable us to examine the extent of the influence of people agencies in shaping the 'nature'. To denote such dynamic conditions and the related happenings, one distinct feature of the analytical matrix should be noted, namely, the Tragedy of the Commons.

Since environment, space and community are the Commons for all people, each individual tries to get most out of the limited natural resources (collectively!), this in turn engenders a degradation process in and through which the unsustainability of the ecological system develops. This threatens the survival of people (Hardin 1968, Herring 1990). To deal with this problem, two approaches might be adopted, despite their respective limits. First, the Commons could be (sub-)divided through the change of entitlement of the rights to use them, or the endorsement of the respective property rights of individuals. We may call this process the [total] privatization of the Commons. This process, in theory, could make the concerned individuals accountable to the Commons s/he has; accordingly, the overall Commons could be protected as each individual tries to exploit as well as to protect the allocated Commons within the valid period of the (property) rights to use the resources.

There are , however, two problems related to this approach: (1) individuals might try to exploit the given, limited remaining Commons for short-term profits, rather than long-term natural conservation, if property rights are transferable and have a limited time span. The most obvious case is the single, economic corp plantation developed on the biological productive "wastelands" (Shiva 1986). Here, this process is facilitated by a number of confusions, in the administration of the privatization process that relates to the confusion between "wastelands" as "commons", or "wastelands" as ecologically degraded lands, and between plantations and natural forests. In other words, the market, not the needs of the ecosystem determines the fate of the Commons. (2) the "externality" of the Commons, say, the emission of pollutant from one plot (as property of someone) to another place (of other property owners), has lessened the extent of the divisibility of the *Commons* according to property rights principle through privatization programs.

Another extreme solution proposed is the strong Leviathan state intervention that controls all the access/use of the Commons, this might be called "Eco-Stalinism". The principal feature of this organization of the Commons is the collectivization of the Commons within a set of rules and controls under the 'eco-socialist' state, in order to promote the viability and sustainability of the *Commons*. However, this approach has some fundamental problems too. Under what conditions should the allocations take place? Should it be auctioned, lottery drawn or left to the good intentions (ecological soundness) of the users? In short, there are no incentives for rational individuals to do good for the Commons. The socio-political significance of the rationality of social actors is that their rationally calculation constitutes the constraints of the governance over environmental issues. With this prelude, we can introduce the variations of environmental-informed discourses on the socio-political nexus of economic development and sustainability.

2) The Pathology of Technology-Risk-Environment Syndrome

Modernization goes with the everchanging uncertainty, one of the obvious products of modernization is the risk (versus safety) generation within a wider context of the 'Technology-Risk-Environment' Syndrome.[3] Here we examine the pathological contours of the Syndrome.

People-made disasters, some name them as "accidents", have again and again, shocked and changed people's world-view (*Weltanschauung*), as people had not well prepared for the invisible killers, vis-a-vis the "success" and hegemony of (perhaps the last) technological revolution. Nuclear energy is only one of them. We are now, in this (post)modernity, experiencing another historicity: Risk Society as named by Ulrich Beck (1986, 1987a, 1987b) that the risks are global and invisible, and they multiply themselves at a geometrical rate and exponential scale... and these constitute. In our terms, all these are parts of the "Technology-Risk-Environment" Syndrome. The Syndrome is defined here as the synergetic effects of technological development, associated risks and others, as calculated, reacted and felt by the public at large. The risks associated with our technologies, are being generated and communicated, the ramifications extend to various sectors of our society (Sjöberg 1987). This is not just the result of the structural changes of society with the technological revolution, but is also derived from the new historical relations between (socio-eco-technological) variables: people, nature, and technology (Beck 1987a). This also mirrors the change of technology and its ramification on socios-patial ordering which have been discussed by Castells (1989: Ch.1) and Lai (1991: Ch.3).

The predominant coping strategy, in the last several decades, is risk-assessment. But the coping mode is as problematic as the definition of the risks. A risk analyst once rightly pointed out that "if the [risk] analysis shows that a particular category of accident can be expected, say, on average once in 1000 years, it does not follow that such an accident will not happen tomorrow. Neither does it mean that the analysis was wrong if it does happen." (Cross 1982: 61). In this respect, risk and its managements

---

[3]Syndrome here is used to denote the complexity of related issues and problems and means the syndrome in medical model. The syndrome here mediates risks between technology and environment, naturally, as argued in Douglas and Wildavky (1982), Douglas (1985) that the risk has cultural and anthropological significance.

are controversial. Not only do the experts notice contradictory findings,[4] but the field has become increasingly more chaotic after the catastrophes in Chernobyl and Bhopal. People are more uncertain about "How safe is safe?" For the technocrats and politicians: "What level of (probability of) risk is acceptable?". In spite of these problems, risk assessment is still being used as the dominant tool in providing the answer for most of the discussions on the siting and operation of the mega-industries which further generates the Not-In-MyBackyard (NIMBY), and Not-In-Anybody's-Backyard (NIABY) protests (Armour 1991, Heiman 1990, Petts 1986).

State intervention in these controversies is a default condition. What state or quasi-state institutions have dealt with is the (re)production of the "acceptable level of risks" that is politically defined and determined, and is subject to the cultural (mis-)understanding of the communities involved. More concrete, this involves the dominance of state organizations in assessment, mitigating and accepting risks level (Clarke 1989). In other words, the "acceptable level of risks" is determined by bureaucracy, implicitly those who have authority to define or access knowledge concerning the "risks". What becomes more ironic is that the highly sophisticated risk models developed do not play a significant part to informing the political debates on the acceptance of the risk level. Perhaps this is one of the many manifestations of the poverty of science. In short, the decoupling between risk-assessment and the (institutional bound) acceptance on risks reveals one contradiction of the Syndrome.[5]

Another manifestation of the Syndrome, mirrored in the polity, is the politicization of production; namely, protests (rather than movements) against nuclear and hazardous installations (Conrad 1987, Offe 1983). This phenomenon was not only seen in European countries, but (as capital and the transnational corporations do) globalized and penetrated differently into various sectors of our living world as well. For people mobilization on environmental issues, the emergence of an alternative-green thinking has been providing a new momentum for social change, juxtaposing the emergence of post-material values. For this, critical analyses of Alan Touraine (1981) and Hegedus (1989) highlight the emancipatory function of the political mobilization towards the environmental sustainability, which has been informing the endeavors of the social agencies to realize the ideals of the modernity project. But the risk and uncertainty issues have also led

---

[4]See Kunreuther and Ley (1982), Kunreuther and Linnerooth, et al. (1983), Morone and Woodhouse (1986), for discussion. For the management of risks in the public sphere, see Gow and Otway (1990).

[5]On the extent of the influence of mass media, newspaper in particular, in shaping the risk-communication, see Stallings (1990), Gow and Otway (1990).

some people to retreat to their private sphere that is enabled by the new technologies, particularly the information technology which enables people to engage in the consumption and production process at home without much direct contacts with the external world society at large. In this instance, the ways of political articulation and the ways of living, lifestyles, are changing which are more fluid and flexible in form and content (Castells 1988, Saunders 1988).

Overall speaking, the quest for scientific understanding is still the dominant modus operandi in our modernity. Here, the question is: could "science",[6] at this historical conjuncture, provide us the protection against risks in our society? Often, though not always, it is through quantifying the risks and the related variables (e.g. faults-events analysis); however, that could not generate discussion beyond the expert's reasoning (that mostly is a close system of *a priori* assumptions). As rightly noted by the International Study Group on Risk Analysis: the whole analytical exercise (of risk analysis) might be considered to be objective. Yet, it must be realized that because of the large body of assumptions, estimates, judgments and opinions involved and thus much of the input information is often subjective.

In other words, despite the fact that the procedural aspects of estimation and modelling are usually perfectly done, the risk assessment is still biased (Douglas and Wildavsky 1982: 67–82). To conclude, the management of risks is very problematic and detrimental at this historical conjuncture that shapes the contours of the interface between technology and environment.[7] From a macroscopic account, the crisis-ridden system and the conditions of production in particular, namely the environment-cum-ecology contradictions of the capitalist system as highlighted by James O'Connor (1987, 1988) are causes of the contemporary crisis. The crisis is manifested as the limits of "science": the problematic of modernization process, on the one hand, and the New Politics that is related to the New Social Movements (NSMs), within and beyond the parameter of the polity, on the other (Cohen 1983, Dalton 1988, Hegedus 1989, Inglehart 1990: 371–392, Offe 1983, 1985a).

The catastrophes, also more important are the protest movements, which push both industry and state to exercise more control and planning through regulation of production, consumption and exchange (Castells

---

[6]Science used here denotes a sense of its hegemony over the community (Gemeinschaft), or in Habermasian terms: the colonization of the life-world.

[7]The related questions and problems of risk assessment, as discussed, are more problematic than what they intended to solve. It is suggested that their validity should be forgotten, rather, caution should be used with reference to their findings, however.

1977, Harvey 1979, Offe 1983, 1984).[8] Paradoxically, the decoupling between risk-assessment and its 'acceptability' which suggests that the state
(and other institutions) has no (political) mechanism whatsoever to prevent
the mega-scale technology-related disasters, nor steering the unprecedented ecological-risk problem.[9] In fact, the state is "Still Muddling (in the
embedded politics of production but) Not Yet Through", a phrase used by
Lindblom (1959, 1979). At this juncture, how state responds to these changes in the synergetic environmental-spatial process deserves some discussion. Before doing that, I outline the changing form of the community
(Gemeinschaft).

3) The New Gemeinschaft Form and Societal Dynamics

We are moving into a new historical era! The contextual specificity is the
new form of community (Gemeinschaft) in this historical conjuncture, or
the shift of the conditions of modernity. For this transformation, David
Harvey (1989: 111) highlights that the turn to postmodernism does not
reflect any fundamental change of social condition." That is, the change
only reflects a shift in the way in which capitalism is working. Similarly arguments referring to the emergence of the informational mode of development is also stressed by Castells (1989: Ch.1), in spite of Alex Callinicos'
(1990) claim that there is no such transformation towards the postmoder-
nist one.

It is more than obvious that two distinct albeit inter-related processes
are taking place: (1) the spontaneous development of the protest movements, and (2) some people return to their private sphere. Seemingly, the
first one has a longer life span and dynamism in the public sphere. Obviously, one major sea-change in the societal sphere is the explosion of the
New Social Movements (NSMs). The NSMs' quest for the "new" form of
Gemeinschaft that could fit into the mutual-development of people and nature, at both local and global scales (Melucci 1989, Scott 1990). Protests to
defence for one's interests or survival, Not-In-MyBackyard (NIMBY), on
the one hand, and against technology, Not-In-Anybody's Backyard
(NIABY), are just too difficult for government to mediate and tackle not

---

[8]Another controversial aspect of these phenomena, ironically, is the reproduction of risk
in genetic engineering, hazardous and defence industries that is supported by state and quasi-
state organizations, see Conrad (1987), Castells (1989), Clarke (1989).

[9]Regarding this assertion, see Beck (1986,1987a) and Luhmann (1986). An alternative explanation might be that communication failure and organizational dysfunction are two of the
causes of Chernobyl, Bhopal and other disasters, and the tragedies that followed. For empirical discussions, see International Conference of Free Trade Union and International Federation
of Chemical, Energy and General Workers Unions (ICFTU 1988), Bogard (1989), Medvedev
(1990).

just because of their specific claims, but more are their universial claims for local/global just and sustainable development which are belatedly taken into governmental and public development agenda (cf. Petts 1986, Armour 1991, Heiman 1990).

This upsurge of socio-political mobilization on environmental issues is being responded to perhaps wrongly by the political establishment. In the last two decades, the fetishistic development of Environmental Impacts Assessment (EIA) and the related modelings has been beyond the comprehension of the concerned citizens. Here, there is a mismatch and/or misplacement between citizens' quest for environmental quality and the state's environmental management. Here, the struggles for opposing the setting of hazardous industries and the controversies around EIA is not just a reflection of people's perception of risks or technology, but is also based upon the people's distrust on the creditability, reliability and regulation of the state and its agents (Armour 1991: 68).

More specifically in the name of natural sustainability, these movements are around three spheres of capitalism, namely cultural, political and collective consumption; particularly, the cultural and societal dimensions of the "new" meaning of these movements that shape the actual and discursive struggles between people and the market, between communities and the state (Castells 1983, 1985, Cohen 1983). The socio-political discourse also reflects the New Politics that has taken place beyond the state structure (Inglehart 1990: 378–85, Offe 1985a/b). In this way the controversies over risk are only part of the de-(r)evolutionary process of the modernity. More precisely they are the political struggles in the midst of the existential crisis of people, animals and nature, following the liberation (project) from the spiritual, social and sexual constraints that happened in the 1960s and 1970s, on the one hand, and the technological advancement, on the other (Batty 1989, 1990a/b, Castells 1985, 1989). Thus, the debates are on the shifting of the modernity and value-orientation towards, and for the search for, local and global sustainability of people and the nature.

What will be decisive, for our future, are the 'self-creative' societal forces which are likely to advance the boundary of and the creation of new public spaces beyond the technologically structured and defined society, and revitalize the old democratic forms (Cohen 1983, Hegedus 1989). It may be called the renewal project in 'another' modernity. Accordingly, people can foster a new capacity to invent and realize their future, and to politicize green issues and engage in every political discourse, because every political decision has green relevance (Naess 1989: 130-162). More than that, it is the politicization of technology (with and without risks) which critically re-examines technology against criteria of the environmental impacts and inter-generational effects. It is a revitalization of the ideals of the modernity project; not just to defend, but also to extend the public sphere, vis-a-vis state and economy. In Cohen's words: "Indeed, they [ecological movements] can be seen as attempts to draw on the beleaguered cultural tradition of modernity to new forms of cooperation and meaning outside the province of economic and political steering mechanisms" (Cohen 1983: 109).

This observation is shared by Melucci (1989) in a differential emphasis that NSMs are fragile and heterogeneous social construction and create 'new' meanings and identities for the collective actors. In other words, the movements foster a new post-humanist consciousness as a response to the challenges for One World to rescue it from the wild growth of both capitalism and communism in reality, as well as from environmental degradation.[10] However, it should be pointed out that the movements are fragile and subject to socio-political cyclical development (Frank and Marta 1987). Because of this peculiarity, the impact of social movements is transient and not long-lasting, and the rise and fall of the movements are therefore contextual and historical.

Nevertheless, the (ideological) claims of the NSMs are universal values (such as harmony between nature and people), with alternative forms of life styles and beliefs (e.g. commune, self-help, and gender issues) which mostly do not correspond to any social policies nor institutions, and thus are revolutionary and emancipatory in some sense, temporarily yet significantly. In and through these movements the new (albeit fragile) definitions of environment-space are being re-constituted (Castells 1983a: section III, Melucci 1989, Milbrath 1989, Naess 1989, Inglehart 1990). Under this circumstance, the challenge for the people is: What should be (re)produced and consumed collectively and individually, or in what ways will that ensure a sustainable development?

In spite of the challenges of the protest movements to society, the individuals respond differently towards the impacts as the available advanced technology could enable individuals to avoid some crises, for instance, some of them retreat to the private sphere to temporarily enjoy their limited autonomy. This process goes along with the increasingly fluid social encounters and the de-differentiation (Entdifferenzierung) social process.

4) Postfordism and Informational City in a Global System

Techno-economic change developed in the last decade has re-defined the socio-economic landscape of politicking and governance. Juxtaposing the

---

[10]See Hegedus (1989) for elaboration on the transnational movements that have an underlying meaning for the project of There is Only One World. Also, cf. World Commission on Economic Development (WCED 1987).

"emancipatory" forces of the New Social Movements in the socio-polity and the social process of "returning to private sphere", there is a global flexible production system or the Postfordist mode of regulation as it is often referred to (Boyer 1990, Lipietz 1986, Scott 1988), coupled with the increasingly "fluid" social encounters as noted by scholars like Berman (1982), Howe (1959) and Harvey (1989) that for instance, life experience is increasingly shapeless. From a macroscopic view, all appear or seemingly so as a 'disorganized' phase of (post) capitalism (Lash and Urry 1987, Offe 1985a) More important are their synergetic impacts on spatial and cultural development, upon which our discourses on the change and transition of the modernity rest. Some of the consequences are: spatial unevenness, polarization of life experience (including underclass), and the gentrification process. Are these possible forms of Heterotopias of the contemporary postmodern city?

All these 'post-' concepts should be taken with care as Harvey (1989: 119) points out, there is a transition or change, that is, the state of the production system should lie somewhere in between the extremes of Fordism and flexible accumulation (Postfordism). In other words, the sea-change should be viewed as a change in the form of the community (Gemeinschaft) and the production system, and thus the very nature of capitalism is here but withering away (Callinicos 1990, Castells 1989).

The global flexible production system still has impacts on the locality, i.e. in the United States, among others. It is the restructuring of household economic activities that shifts to the informal sector, which has strong implications for (but not limited to local) politics, for example, the development of the "quality of life" neighbourhood movement in Sunbelt cities, which is in fact anti- (or managed) growth oriented (Smith 1988: 217–222).[11] This finding shares the peculiarity found in the New Social Movements across the Atlantic, particularly in the post-model Deutschland (German Model) era, the quest for sustainable development and the restructuring of socio-spatial orders (Essser and Hirsch 1989, Frankland 1989, Poguntke 1989, Rüdig 1988).

On the other hand, this fragmented, polycentric and much more complex (de)urbanization process (governed by industrial capital) assisted the city (as the center of the polity) in escaping from agglomeration of working class militancy, with the following results: the shifting of (class) politics in production sector to collective consumption struggles (Castells 1977, 1983, Dunleavy 1980), and to the politics of production (Conrad 1987, Gerlach 1986, Offe 1983, 1985b). Do these contribute to or suggest the transition to

---

[11]For a review on the globalization impacts on the locality, see Smith and Feagin (eds. 1987), Soja (1989, Ch.8,9) and Cooke (1990).

another phase of, or the coming of another modernity (Barbermas 1985, Soja 1989), or to a disorganizing phase of capitalism?

For the logic of environmental-spatial development, the increasingly global flexible production process might also mean that national policies (via planning) try to attract such employment/capital-related industries to specific urban areas which result in the changing of national standards or other environmental policies (Button and Peace 1989: 153) For instance, the postmodern-architectural projects, which are often out of scale with the history of specific places, leading to the submersion of locality by superstar architecture that (bluntly) alters the planning law; this, at least, is the case with Helmut Jahn's architectural product in Philadelphia (Zukin 1988: 40, 43 note 3).

In this respect, the struggles for landuse, as one of the environmental-spatial resources, and other development control conflicts between the large corporation which supports the postmodern architecture and the public will be intensified on the one end of the planning-politics trajectory, juxtaposing the calls for alternative policies for sustainable growth on the other. What is significant here are the contradictions between capitalist production relations and production forces, between the production force and the conditions of production (i.e. environment), that are still mediated by the planning mechanism that is subordinated under state and economic power. The instrumentality of urban planning in the capitalist state's hegemony project, on the one hand (Harvey 1989: 222–223, Jessop 1983), and the 'immovable paradox' against the social movements, on the other, should not be forgotten.[12]

For the process of the development of the informational city, the search for higher productivity in the production sector for profit maximization and the appropriation of capital is coupled with the substantial change in the pattern of state intervention, mostly mirroring a shift from political legitimation and social redistribution (i.e. welfare provisions) to political domination and capital accumulation (supply-side macro economic management), juxtaposing the internationalization of all economic processes. Two particular characteristics of this development should be mentioned: (1) the new technology enables the increasing rate of profit and serves as a powerful instrument in sustaining the capital accumulation and domination functions of state intervention; (2) for the organization of

---

[12]Concerning the paradox, Harvey (1989:238) notes that "not only does the community of money, coupled with rationalized space and time, define them in an oppositional sense, but the [social] movements have to confront the question of value and its expression of space and time appropriate to their own reproduction. In doing so, they necessarily open themselves to the dissolving power of money as well as to the shifting definitions of space and time arrived at through the dynamics of capital circulation. Capital, in short, continues to dominate ..."

production there is a growing concentration of knowledge-generation and decision-making processes in high-level organizations, and a related flexible production process with decentralized networks. More specific, it is being argued that technology is the nexus established between labor and other variables in the production process, and technological knowledge and its mobilization and accessibility have become the key source of productivity upon which a new mode of development is based. More important, it is the flows and networking of high-tech knowledge that are likely to shape the socio-political power constellation (Castells 1989).

In addition, the very nature of the new form of labour requirements for the new informational mode engenders a new set of uncertain or fragile concerns, e.g. the "lifestyle" or "quality of life" of the new professionals or middle class, which shapes the politicking process in which the state engages, on the one hand, and the back to private sphere process that strives for better "quality of life", on the other. Thus the informational mode of development should be highlighted: the space of and logic of flows, and the possible articulation of the (beyond class-based) New Social Movements (Castells 1988). More specific, it is the expanding development of services that has grown out of a variety of social mobilizations, mostly through protest movements and the related political concessions, on the one hand, and the organization of services that is shifting more towards the network of information and decision, on the other. Thus, the flows, rather than organizations become the units of work, decision, and output accounting. For the environmental-spatial process, what is crucial is the relationship between the process of the concentration of high level (e.g. decision-making) activities in the city-centre and the decentralization process of back offices and retail services to smaller areas (Castells 1989: 168–169).

One of the results is the rise of the new Dual City.[13] The informational-based formal economy is juxtaposed by a down-graded labour-based informal economy resulting in a spatial structure, a city that combines segregation, diversity, and hierarchy, with the emergence of a suburban warfare state from an urban welfare-state with a shift of state intervention from the provision of collective consumption (e.g. housing and welfare services) to the promotion of new technologies that are, historically, military-oriented. This shift is actually related to the selective orientation of state programmes which allocates resources to different localities following the technology hierarchy which has significant repercussions on environment and space. This techno-spatial selectivity of the related sectoral policy, say, the defence industry, is important in shaping the environmental-spatial process and the manifestation of problems.

---

[13] A critique on the notion of Dual City, see Marcuse (1989).

After this synthetic snapshot of our discussions, a set of theoretical propositions for the understanding of the role of the state in context, the politics of environment and space, to cope with the problem is outlined.

ENVISIONING ENVIRONMENTAL GOVERNANCE IN THE NEXT MILLENNIUM

Having discussed the particularity of the state form and the contextual changes in various arenas, this thesis ends with five propositional summary remarks. Accordingly, they are concerned with the coming of a new environmental risk paradigm, euphoria and uncertainty of state governance, the legacy and transformation of New Social Movements, the concern for "quality of life", and the development of the state and people's organization at both the local and global level. These propositions can shed light on the contingent role (and limits) of the state in environmental/spatial governcane.

1) The Coming of a New Environment-cum-Risk Paradigm

Environmental concerns have been particularly articulated, chronologically yet ironically by those involving in the natural sciences advancement, in particular, as most of them likely tend to agree that, globally, there is a limit to growth following the thesis of the *Club of Rome*, and also locally, the rate and extent of environmental degradation are unacceptable in terms of any scientific, economic and societal standards (Meadows et al. 1972, 1992). The environmental awareness on the limit of economic growth is in fact a sort of extension of the neo-Malthusian conception on natural resources versus population(-cum-economic) growth, development versus urbanization. The very notion of this awareness is the potential, projected or actual scarcity underpins global market operation. This conceptualization of the limits-to-growth thesis was also reinforced by the global Oil Crisis 1973, and was contextualized in the crisis and ungovernability of the state in urban question. The synergetic effects of the global concern for nature are beyond the anthropo-centric vision of the *Club of Rome*.

The coming of a New Ecological [Environmental] Paradigm marked a watershed between the materialism and post-materialism in the Western soceity (Catton & Dunlap 1978, 1980; Inglehart 1997, Milbrath 1989). In Western sociological terms, the new paradigm is also a reflection of what sea-change has been happening since the Oil Crisis: from the industrial to a post-industrial society (Bell 1973), from a class to an non-class based society (Gershuny 1978, Gorz 1978, Gouldner 1980), and from traditional one of the politics *in* production sector (say class politics between capital and labour) to the New Politics *of* production sector (say, whether some products against environment be produced), resulting in the strong political challenge of New Social Movements (Conrad 1987, Dalton and Kuechler 1990).

The global socio-political change with respect to environmental issues is quite obvious in the 1970s. This is particularly evident in the concern for environmental degradation, crisis and catastrophes which focuses on the systematic production of by-products (e.g. CFC against the ozone layer), hazardous exposure (in Bhopal and Chernobyl), and industrial-cum-domestic waste. The technological advancement has changed the ecological system. One of the configurations of modernization in fact is its detrimental effect and ramification in creating a Risk Society (Beck 1986), namely, the ever multiplication of risks on a global scale and the penetration of techno-environmental risks in everyday social life, and the more problematic and fundamental domain, the ungovernability of the state and market mechanism on global risks (Daedalus 1990).

The new configuration of risks, in contrast to the natural disasters in pre-modern time, is the involvement of people (social agency)-cum-new (say, in energy, material, bio-chemical and information related) technologies. Previously, i.e., in pre-modern time, natural disasters and the related human casualties could be interpreted (and also reinforced by religious belief) as a result of the spiritual agency, say, God or Goddess. Yet, the "normal accidents" in modern era are rarely explainable in spiritual or devilish terms. The concept of risks depends a lot upon the cultural context in which the risks embedded (Douglas and Wildavsky 1982) and in the modern world, the state agency's definition on risk acceptability (Clarke 1989). In short, risks and disasters generated by people are an inevitable part of modernization.

The historical idea of Risk was a probability of the losses and gains. But the present concept of risk is associated at least with the potential of dangers (threats to survival) to several generations of people, animal and the ecological system. More important, the risks embedded in our (post)modern world are as real as they were in pre-modern time but their nature is contradictory to the project of modernity and rational control (say, in terms of cost-benefit analysis) over uncertainties and the prevention of risks in all sectors of living. In fact, our present (no matter you how you name it: post-material, post-modern) society faces more dangers than ever before, and the worst scenario of the complete depletion of the ozone layer could mean that civilization and the ecosystem are destroyed permanently! In other words, the very powerful scientific and moral threat of risk is the apocryphal notion of the end of all.

Risks, in most modern-day cases, are associated with modern technology that structurally shapes and is shaped by societal linkages. The greater problem is that risk is characterized by the so-called "interactive com-

plexity" and "tight coupling" synergy which has a strong potential for system failure and technology disaster (Perrow 1984: 75–92). In short, techno-
accidents are being normalized and embedded in our modern, industrial
society. These "normal accidents" (a term coined by Charles Perrow, 1984)
or technology disasters can only be explained and managed within a set of
rational and scientific modelings. Yet the related assumptions in managing
environmental disasters, on the one hand, and the technological risks, on
the other, are within a paradigm full of *a priori* assumptions and reasoning.

Deep anxiety and perplexity with technology are becoming the facts of
life, but they are not being responded to appropriately by the political institutions and scientific community. The latter group mostly expresses
them symbolically in mathematical terms, far from addressing the actual
"normal accidents" developed and the anxiety and uncertainty of the
general public over high-tech industries. At this historical conjuncture, it is
appropriate to describe our present form of civilization (i.e. modernity) as a
Technology-cum-Risk Society. The contours of the New Environment-cum-
Risk Paradigm are in fact characterized by the *Technology-Risk-Environment
(TRE) Syndrome*: the invisibility, penetration power and global nature of
risks, plus the geometrical multiplication of techno-risks at an exponential
scale.

Equally problematic is that our knowledge of environmental crisis,
risks in particular, is very much influenced by the competitive mass media,
which usually dramatizes (if not exaggerates) the extent of disaster, which
in turn reinforces the uncertainty and anxiety over industrial accidents
(Renn and Burn et al. 1992). Therefore, the management of the hazardous
exposure, the related controversies and their social acceptance are quite
controversial (Gow and Otway, 1990). Apart from its dependency on technological system, society is rediscovering how dependent it is on natural
systems and how vulnerable the people are to global risks in everyday life.
This rediscovery has significant implication for both socio-political
mobilization of environmental issues and the state's environmental governance. Perhaps, the most critical issue in this historical phase of modernity
is not only the state's promotion of a society in terms of fair, just and equitable distribution of wealth, but also the redistributive justice of risks with
particular reference to the distribution of (the rate, intensity and extent of)
eco-technological risks each individual could/should have and would accept, as well as the distribution of risks loading on each constituent (say,
animal, plant, even rock) in our Earth.

To recapitulate, the quest for environmentality has far-reaching implications, but the most important is the concern for the distribution and
reallocation of environmental quality and the associated risks to our
society. In the ecological system, it implies poisonous substances in food

chain; in the production sector it is the risk to occupational hazards; the rise of radioactive exposure. At the regional scale, for example, it is the locality exposed to excess ultra-violet-rays as a result of the depletion of the ozone layer and for each human being, the hazards of exposure to a polluted environment.

Societal responses are quite diverse, ranging from environmental protests to the one with more sophistication of environmental technological know-how development. At the supra-national domain, a new wave of global environmentalism has been supported by a supra-national state agency, such as the United Nations, the European Community (McCromick 1989). The ecological protests and lobbying for a greener environment or at least for preserving the original environmental conditions have been strategic in crafting out the new socio-political landscape which is receptive to sustainable growth. For this, the instrumental role of the community-based advocacies of the Not-In-My-Back Yard (NIMBY; Mowrey and Redmond 1993), Not-In-Anybody's Back Yard (NIABY; Heiman 1990) and Best-Appropriate Back Yard (BABY; cf. Wang 1993) should be emphasized.

In other arenas, for market response to the global challenge of environmental crisis, the issue of greening or cleaner production and consumption is quite obviously taken up by producers and consumers. Obviously, there are different motives and logic underlying the greening of consumption and production: whether it is only a fashion in favour of a cleaner or environment friendly consumption pattern? Or, is green consumption merely serving the individual's mission to *Save the World* under the motto of *Think Globally and Act Locally*? Perhaps, factors like the individual's search for a healthy and better quality of life and for collective identity of being environmental friendly, plus business corporate interests to promote more (green) consumption, accounted for the recent expansion of the green sector in our global market (Lai 1995). Obviously, this set of questions, for academic as well as praxis sake, should be explored if the project of environmentalism and sustainability is to be put on the socio-political agenda.

Finally, the emergence of new politics and new production-consumption relationships is qualitatively different from those in the production plant (between capitalist and proletariat), labour movements and the hedonism of mass consumerism. Perhaps, more worrying is the trend that the newly constituted green socio-political alignment via functional differentiation along production and consumption might be withering away in the turbulence of the multiplication of eco-isms: eco-consumerism, eco-socialism, eco-capitalism, eco-anarchism....(Pepper 1993).

2) The Trajectory of State Governance: From Euphoria to Uncertainty

With the hegemonic appeal for certainty, reliability and stability, state intervention with scientific rational approach for socio-economic development was praised for its success, and it was accompanied by the euphoric feelings of the people regarding the future prospect. However, as the state intervened into more new arenas than it had previously, the politicization of the related issues occurred synchronously which engendered more conflict between the state, market and civil society, and that also revealed the limitations and uncertainties of the state project.

At this particular juncture, the role of the state in organizing the society is being challenged not just by the traditional political activists from the (new) Left and (new) rights, but also by the new protest movements which have revealed the underlying predicaments of state intervention. Furthermore, the tragedies of welfare state intervention, say, the limited available choice for citizens under the state's provision of collective consumption, which partly induced people to return to their private sphere for self-determination. In other words, for citizens the sense of euphoria over state intervention is withering away and is being replaced by a mix of uncertainties, queries, and challenges in increasingly fluid social encounters which expose the fragile relationship between state and civil society. Two major implications of what the future role of the state will be in the environmental governance. First, it is the increasingly fragile state-civil society relationship which reinforces the decoupling of these two subsystems in a possible collaborative effort to prevent environmental degradation. Second, though it is not operating as a functional subsystem of the capitalist mode of production whose primary task is to create, maintain and restore the conditions for capital accumulation as it normally does, the state will tend to act according to its own logic that is not particularly oriented or sensitive towards the issues on environment and space. In other words, the state, for its survival in the world state (and economic) system, will try to formulate a nation-building strategy which might not fully appreciate the environmental quality. For this, and far from the policy and political convergence for sustainable development, the state (and its policy mechanism) still is the site of strategic dilemma and contradictions.

3) The Transformation of New Social Movements

The future role of the state in the environmental governance is also influenced by the degree and the way in which the NSMs are being absorbed and consolidated in social and state sectors, or in what form the legacy of the Movements exerts its influence. The significance of the NSMs rested upon an issue that has not been politically articulated in the public sphere. For the NSMs mobilizing efforts, there is a need for an issue that is attractive and urgent; this is also the case for the state which looks for issues upon which its legitimacy could be anchored. Environmental issue is only one of the many over the policy/political spectrum on governance. Sometimes but not very often, the environmental issue by virtue of its unpredictable nature related to the calculation of (unknown) future events could only be used as the anchorage where the state continues to claim its legitimacy to govern. If this happened, the NSMs will be incorporated into the institutional politics, and subsequently die down as there would be no more issues for them to exploit or articulate. Or if there are other compelling social issues, the quest for environmental policy rarely attracts socio-political attentions, for instance, the recent socio-economic development in a unified Germany seemingly suggests that environmental issue is no longer strategic for the state (hegemonic) project.

It is not surprising that both the New Social Movements and the state have tried to take up the ecological issue, but only in some historical instances. For example, the formation of the federal ministry for the environment in West Germany and the related environmental programme in the early 1970s even earlier than the full-fledged development of the ecological movement illustrates the point that green issues are not monopolized by the movements. In fact, both the state and the movements compete for the workable issues.

Worth noting is that on the way to search for workable green issues, the fluid nature of the movements might be an unconscious instrument to be used by the neo-conservative for the promotion of a privatization programme, that ends up in the return to the uncontrollable market mechanism, that is, the exploitation of people, environment and space.[14]

On the other hand, both the internal organization of the movement and the external political opportunity of it have influence on the long-term environmental movement. In Germany, for example, the problematic organizing of the Green Party's "anti-party party" which has generated more internal struggles within the party than between the party and the state. On the other hand, the Five-Percent-Hurdle in German election law, the related reimbursement of election expenses of those parties which could reach this hurdle, and the free broadcasting time enjoyed by a party during election in particular have restored some form of unity within the pluralist (sometimes conflicting) Green party. In spite of these, the ideological cleavage between the conventional parties and the Greens was comparatively greater which enabled the conflicts between the "Fundis" and "Realos" (vis-a-vis other political camps) to be reconciled within the party. However, as time passes,

---

[14]See Kreuder and Loewy (eds. 1987) for discussions on the return of (neo)Conservatism on socio-politics in West Germany in the 1980s.

the difference between Die Grünen and other political parties is not as sharp as the internal conflicts within the former party.

Historically, the Greens also took advantage of the fact that the governing leftist party (SPD) was unable to retain the loyalty of those committed to new civic action and environmental issues (Wilson 1990: 79). However, the 1990 Bundestag Election revealed the reversing trend, that is, the SPD took a large proportion of the support which previously belonged to the Greens as it put forward an environment-related political platform. In short, it should be remembered that some peculiarities and the identity of the Greens have been eroded under the "new" rules of the game (as compared to the movements per se) and the proliferation of green ideas: "they have been compromised, questioned, or silently dropped from the practice of Green parliamentary politics" (Offe 1990: 244).

4) The Differential Search for New Quality of Life

It is ironic that technological development has led to the concerns about "quality of life" that act against the interest of further technological development. Corresponding with this development, it is the change of value orientation and lifestyles which shapes the contours on which the state mediates in the conflicting claims for economic development and environmental conservation. The concerns for global (as well as individual) survival in general and environmental (living) quality in particular, after recognizing that there are limits to growth, have highlighted the importance of local actions and their coordination for sustainable growth (McCormick 1989, Meadows et al. 1972, WCED 1987).

The new concern for "quality of life" has two dimensions: (1) one's satisfaction as derived from consumption, and (2) the global question of sustainable development. The co-existence of these (sometimes contradictory) dimensions has made the consumption pattern more symbolic than substantial; that is, people concern themselves more with the form and way of consumption and how to utilize the remaining natural resources for their pleasure, rather than putting emphasis on traditional lifestyle (reducing consumption) for substantial environmental protection. Thus it could be argued that the new concerns are more superficial and differentiated than was once believed.

The likely phenomenon that people return to the private sphere for their pleasure might be, rightly or wrongly, due to the rational calculation of people in the dilemma (crisis) situation—the threat of the global environmental degradation. To maximize the individual gains, the person might choose to act at the expense of the environment (Goodin 1976). The phenomenon: recent increase of mass consumption on high-tech consumers goods, such as CD-players and satellite antennae, and the homework with computer for profits, might support the thesis that people retreat from public domain (politicking is subsumed in this dimension) and the concern for global issues, politically.

On the other hand, the activists believe in alternative courses and the related preventive measures for environmental conservation and sustainable development. They articulate their claim through their "negation" of the dominant trend of the large-scale infrastructure, for example, dams, airports, and highways, or mass production-consumption praxis. In actuality, they are searching for a "post-capitalist", "post-socialist" lifestyle, you might call it an ecosocialist way of living.

Interestingly, it may be justifiable that the state also tried to adopt the green way of governance that adhered to the new waves of the societal concerns. However, its course is still dependent on the overall functioning of the production sector. For instance, despite the claim for the building of a "green" airport in München (Wähner 1990), the impacts of the airport on the environment have been irreversible and permanent. The state can no longer reverse the damage. Thus the questions on technology, environment, and quality of life, which reflect dilemma of the state governance between economic and environmental, are yet to be resolved.

After decades of the "up and down" of protest movements and the "stop-and-go" of the state projects on environment, it is fair to say that the monetary and socio-environmental costs have been paid for development projects; however, the prescribed and expected benefits are yet to be realized. Nevertheless, both NSMs and the state project on governance have, perhaps by coincidence, provided an environmentally tunnel visioning for the next Millennium's agenda setting, especially for future sustainable development.

5) Environmental Governance: a Matrix of Local/Global State and Organization?

Under the hegemonic influence of the privatization, de-regulation, devolution and decentralization of the state authority, the state is becoming more differentiated in terms of its structure and functions which are inter-related with market forces. In particular, the new form of state organization (QUANGOs: Quasi-State Non-Governmental Organizations) and the related policies for deregulation and public management are pursuing their course of action with reference to market operation, that is, profit maximization, efficiency and economic accountability. This development, coupled with the increasing bureaucratization of politics, is likely lead to a market/business oriented political steering that lessens the importance of citizens' politics, the functioning of local and global environmental Non-Governmental Organizations (NGOs). A global trend is the withering away of the local state with a corresponding expansion of the scope of the quasi-state structure. But the control of the new state structure on the environment quality is however very limited, juxtaposing the increasing fluid societal interaction pattern and the logic of flows in the informational society. This condition will pose certain difficulties for environmental governance. In short, the state and people organizations can rarely echo with each other for a sustainable developmental course of action.

The development of a supra-national organization—say, the European Union, which is assuming more and more nation state's jurisdiction is an important variable that will influence the role of the nation state in managing the environmental quality. To what extent will this "unification" process shape the sustainability of the future environment is still unknown. Nevertheless, the change will not be anything of incrementalism because the new (supra-) state structure is more influential than the New Politics which had once altered some political contours of our contemporary society. To conclude, the politics of environmental governance in the next decade is likely under the strong influence of global and regional agencies who have a more environmentally informed perspective for governance and the local societal forces for local and global environmentalism, in spite of the fact that environmentalism is more proliferating, differentiated and in some instances, superficial. For the sustainable development of the next millennium and beyond, there is a strong need for the convergence of policy, coordination of the local and global endeavours, as well as the formation of political will to govern our remaining Earth.

REFERENCES

Armour, A.M. 1991. The sitiyng of locally unwanted land use: towards a cooperative approach. *Progress in Planning* 35: part 1.

Bahro, R. 1986. *Building the Green Movement.* Philadelphia: New Society Publ.

Batty, M. 1989. Editorial. *Environment & Planning B: Planning and Design* 16: 119–126.

Batty, M. 1990a. Invisible Cities. *Environment & Planning B: Planning and Design* 17: 127–130.

Batty, M. 1990b. Intelligent Cities. *Environment & Planning B: Planning and Design* 17: 247–256.

Beck, U. 1986. *Risikogesellschaft: auf dem weg in eine andere moderne.* Frankfurt/M: Suhrkamp Verlag

Beck, U. 1987a. The anthropological shock: Chernobyl and the contours of the risk Society. *Berkeley Journal of Sociology* 32: 153–165.

Beck, U. 1987b. Beyond status and class: will there be an individualized class Society. In: *Modern German Sociology.* V. Meja, D. Misgeld and N. Stehr (eds.). New York: Columbia University Press.

Bell, D. 1973. *The Coming of Post-Industrial Society.* New York: Basic Books.

Berman, M. 1982. *All That is Solid Melts into Air.* New York: Simon and Schuster.

Bogard, W. 1989. *The Bhopal Tragedy.* Boulder: Westview Press

Boyer, R. 1990. *The Regulation School: A Critical Introduction.* New York: Columbia University Press

Button, K J. and D.W. Peace.1989. Improving the urban environment: how to adjust national and local government policy for sustainable urban growth. *Progress in Planning* 32: 135–184.

Callinicos, A. 1990. *Against Postfordism: A Marxist Critique.* Cambridge: Polity Press.

Castells, M. 1977. *The Urban Question: A Marxist Approach.* London: Edward Arnold.

Castells, M. 1983. *The City and the Grassroots.* London: Edward Arnold.

Castells, M. 1985. High technology, economic restructuring, and the urban-regional process in the United States. In: *High Technology, Space, and Society*, M. Castells (ed.), London: Sage.

Castells, M. 1988. Social movements and informational city. Conference Paper, "Cultural Changes in the Period of Transformation in the Capitalist World System: Some Considerations", Hitotsubashi University (Japan), 19–20 September 1988, reprinted in *Hitotsubashi Journal of Social Studies*, 1990, 21(1): 197–206.

Castells, M. 1989. *The Informational City.* Oxford: Blackwell.

Catton, W. and R. Dunlap. 1978. Environmental sociology: a new paradigm. *The American Sociologist* 13(Feb.): 41–49.

Catton, W. and R. Dunlap. 1980. A new ecological paradigm for post-exuberant sociology, *American Behavioral Scientist* 24(1): 15–47.

Clarke, L. 1989. *Acceptable Risk? Making Decisions in a Toxic Environment.* Berkeley, CA: University of California Press.

Cohen, J. 1983. Rethinking Social Movements. *Berkeley Journal of Sociology* 1983: 28: 97–113.

Conrad, J. 1987. Technological Protest in West Germany: Sign of a Politicization of Production? IIUG Discussion Paper 87–8. Berlin: Wissenschaftzentrum, WZB.

Cooke, P. 1990. *Back to the Future.* London: Unwin Hyman.

Cross, A. 1982. Fault Trees and Event Trees. In: *High Risk Safety Technology*, A.E. Green (ed.) Chicester: John Wiley & Son.

Dalton, R.J. 1988. *Citizen Politics in Western Democracies.* New Jersey: Chatham House.

Dalton, J. and M. Kuechler (eds.). 1990. *Challenging the Political Order.* Cambridge: Polity Press.

Deadalus. 1990. Topical Issue on "Risk", *Deadalus* 119(4/Fall): 1–254.

Douglas, M. 1985. *Risk Acceptability according to the Social Sciences.* N.Y.: Russell Sage Foundation.

Douglas, M. and A. Wildavsky. 1982. *Risk and Culture.* Berkeley, CA: University of California Press.

Dunleavy, P. 1980. *Urban Political Analysis.* London: Macmillan.

Ely, J. and Heinz, V. 1989.The greening of rational choice Marxism, or bio-wine from sour grapes?—Interview with H. Wiesenthal", *Capitalism, Nature, Socialism*, 3:141–161.

Esser, J. and Hirsch, J. 1989. The crisis of Fordism and the dimensions of a 'Postfordist' regional and urban structure. *International Journal of Urban & Regional Research* 13(3): 417–437.

Frank, A.G. and F. Marta. 1987. Nine theses on social movements. *Economic and Political Weekly*, August 29, 1987: 1503–1510.

Frankland, G. 1989. The Green Party in West Germany. In: *New Politics in Western Europe*, F. Müller-Rommel (ed). London: Westview Press.

Gerlach, L.P. 1986. Protest Movements and the Construction of Risk Discussion Paper IIUG dp 86–10. Berlin: WZB.

Gershuny, J.I. 1978. *After Industrial Society.* London: Macmillan.

Goodin, R. 1976. *The Politics of Rational Man.* New York: John Wiley & Sons.

Gorz, A. 1978. *Abscheid vom proletariat.* Frankfurt/M: Euorpaeische verlagsanstalt.

Gouldner, A.W. *1980.The Two Marxisms.* New York: Seabury Press.

Gow, H.B.F and Otway, H. (eds.) 1990. *European Conference on Communicating with the Public about Major Accident Hazards.* London: Elsevier Science Publ.

Habermas, J. 1985. *Die Neue Unübersichtlichkeit.* Frankfurt/M: Suhrkamp Verlag.

Hardin, G. 1968. Tradegy of the Commons, *Science*, 162 (13 Dec.): 1243–1248.

Harvey, D. 1979. On planning the ideology of planning. In: *Planning Theory in the 1980s.* R.W. Burchell and G. Sterlieb (eds.). Rutgers University: Centre for Urban Policy Research.

Harvey, D. 1989. *The Condition of Postmodernity*. Oxford: Blackwell.
Hegedus, Z. 1989. Social movements and social change in self-creative society: new civil initiatives in the international arena. *International Sociology*, 4 (1):19–36.
Heiman, M. 1990. From 'Not in my backyard!' to 'Not in anybody's backyard'. *APA Journal* Summer: 359–362.
Herring, R.J. 1990. Restructuring the Commons: collective action and ecology, *Items*, 44(4 Dec.): 64–68.
Howe, I. 1959. Mass society and post-modern fiction. *Partisan Review* 26: 420–436.
Inglehart, R. 1977. *The Silent Revolution*. Princeton. NJ.: Princeton University Press.
Inglehart, R. 1990. *Culture shift in Advanced Industrial Society*. Princeton, NJ: Princeton University Press.
International Conference of Free Trade Unions [ICFTU] and Federation of Chemical, Energy and General Workers Unions [ICEF] (1988) The Trade Union Report on Bhopal. Geneva: ICFTU & ICEF.
Jessop, B. 1983. Capital Accumulation, State Forms, and Hegemonic Projects. *Kapitalistate* 10/11: 89–111.
Kreuder, T. and H. Loewy. 1987. *Konservatismus in der Strukturkrise*. Frankfurt/M: Suhrkamp.
Kunreuther, H.C and E.V. Ley (eds.) 1982. *The Risk Analysis Controversy: An Institutional Perspective*. Berlin: Springer Verlag.
Kunreuther, H.C. and J. Linnerooth, et al. 1983. *Risk Analysis and Decision Processes: The Siting of Liquefied Energy Gas Facilities in Four Countries*. Luxembourg: IIASA
Lai, O.K. 1991. The Role of the State in the Environmental-Spatial Process, Dr.rer.pol. Dissertation, Fachbereich 9 Universität Bremen.
Lai, O.K. 1995. Green Consumption. Towards a New Modernity? Occasional Paper No.5, Dept. of Applied Social Studies, Hong Kong Polytechnic University.
Lash, S. and J. Urry 1987. *The End of Organized Capitalism*. Cambridge: Polity Press.
Lindblom, C.E. 1959. The science of muddling through. *Public Administration Review* 19 (Autumn): 79–88
Lindblom, C.E. 1979. Still muddling, not yet through. *Public Administration Review* 39 (6): 517–526.
Lipietz, A. 1986. New Tendencies in the International Division of Labor: Regime of Accumulation and Mode of Regulation. In: *Production, Work, Territory*, A.J. Scott and M. Storper (eds.). Boston: Allen & Unwin.
Luhmann, N. 1986. *Ökologische Kommunikation*. Opladen: Westdeutscher Verlag.
Marcuse, P. 1989. 'Dual City': a muddy metaphor for a quartered city. *International Journal of Urban & Regional Research* 13(4): 697–708.
Martell, L. 1994. *Ecology and Society*. Cambridge: Polity Press.
McCormick, J. 1989. *The Global Environmental Movements*. London: Belhaven Press.
Meadows, D.H. et al. 1972. *The Limits to Growth: A Report for the Club of Rome's Project on the Predicament of Mankind*. New York: Universe Books.
Meadows, D.H. et al. (1992). *Beyond the Limits*. New York: Universe Books.
Medvedev, Z.A. 1990. *Legacy of Chernobyl*. Oxford: Blackwell.
Melucci, A. 1989. *Nomads of the Present*. London: Hutchinson-Radius.
Milbrath, L.W. 1989. *Envisioning a Sustainable Society*. Albany, NY: New York State University Press.
Milton, K. (ed.) 1993. *Environmental—The View from Anthropology*. London: Routledge.
Morone, J.G. and E.J. Woodhouse. 1986. *Averting Catastrophe: Strategies for Regulating Risky Technologies*. Berkeley, CA: University California Press.
Mowrey, M. and T. Redmond. 1993. *Not in Our Back Yard*. New York: William Morrow Co.
Naess, A. 1989. *Ecology, Community and Lifestyles: Outline of an Ecosophy*. Cambridge: Cambridge University Press.

O'Connor, J. 1987. *The Meaning of Crisis.* Oxford: Blackwell.

O'Connor, J. 1988. Capitalism, nature, socialism: a theoretical introduction. *Capitalism, Nature, Socialism* 1(1):38–55.

Offe, C. 1983. Competitive party democracy and the Keynesian welfare state: factors of stability and disorganization. *Policy Sciences,* 15: 225–246.

Offe, C. 1984. *Contradiction of the Welfare State.* Cambridge, Mass.: MIT Press.

Offe, C. 1985a. *Disorganized Capitalism.* Cambridge: Polity Press.

Offe, C. 1985b. New social movements: challenging the boundaries of institutional politics. *Social Research* Winter 52(4): 817–868.

Offe, C. 1990. Reflections on the institutional self-transformation of movement politics: a tentative statue model. In: *Challenging the Political Order,* R.J. Dalton and M. Kuechler (eds.), Cambridge: Polity Press.

Opielka, M. 1985. *Die Ökosozial Frage.* Frankfurt/M:FisherTaschenbuch.

Pepper, D. 1993. *Eco-Socialism.* London: Routledge.

Perrow, C. 1984. *The Normal Accidents.* New York: Basic Books.

Petts, J. 1986. Planning and Hazardous Installation Control. *Progress in Planning,* 29: 1–75.

Poguntke T. 1989. New politics and party system. In: *New Politics in Western Europe,* Müller-Rommel (ed.), London: Westview Press.

Renn, O., W.J. Burn and J.X. Kasperson et al. 1992. The social amplification of risk: theoretical foundations and empirical applications. *Journal of Social Issues* 48(4): 137–160.

Rüdig, W. 1988. Peace and ecology movements in western Europe. *Western European Politics* 11 (1): 26–39.

Saunders, P. 1988. The sociology of consumption: a research agenda. In: *The Sociology of Consumption,* P. Otnes (ed.). New Jersey: Humanities Press Inc.

Scott, A. 1990. *The Ideology of the New Social Movements.* London: Unwin Hyman.

Scott, A.J. 1988. *New Industrial Space.* London: Pion

Shiva, V. 1986. Coming tragedy of the Commons. *Economic and Political Weekly,* XXI (15; 12. April): 613–614.

Sjöberg, L. (ed.) 1987. *Risk and Society.*London: Allen & Wnwin.

Smith, M.P. 1988. *City, State and Market.* Oxford:Blackwell.

Smith, M.P. and J.R. Feagin (eds.) 1987. *The Capitalist City.* Oxford: Blackwell.

Soja, E.W. 1989. *Postmodern Geographies.* London: Verso.

Stallings, R.A. 1990. Media discourse and the social construction of risk. *Social Problems* 37 (1 Feb.): 80–95.

Touraine, A. 1981. *The Voice and the Eye.* Cambridge: Cambridge University Press.

Wähner, H. 1990. Großflughafen auf der grünen Wiese. *Treffpunkt: Flughafen-Magazin* 1/1990: 14–15.

Wang, J.C.S. 1993, Amenity Map and Environmental Territory: A Case Study for Urban Community Based Environmental Management and Education in Taiwan. Conference Paper 2nd Int'l Workshop on Community Based Urban Environmental Management in Asia, 6–11. Sept. 1993, Hong Kong.

Wilson, F.L. 1990. Neo-corporatism and the rise of new social movements. In: *Challenging the Political Order,* R.J. Dalton and M. Kuechler (eds.), Cambridge: Polity Press.

WCED (World Commission on Economic Development). 1987. *Our Common Future.* Oxford: Oxford University Press.

Zukin, S. 1988. The postmodern debate over urban form. *Theory, Culture & Society,* 5(2–3): 431–446.

DO NOT WRITE

ABOVE THIS LINE

PLEASE DO NOT WRITE ABOVE THIS LINE ←

QTY.	CLASS	DESCRIPTION	PRICE	AMOUNT
		B 2.06		
		SUB TOTAL		
		TAX		
		TIP		
		MISC		
		TOTAL	30	52

DATE 3 7 06

AUTHORIZATION

REFERENCE NO.

ID-FOLIO / CHECK NO. / LIC. NO. STATE | REG./DEPT | SERVER | CLERK

VISA   MasterCard   5938012

EXPIRATION

☐ DATE

CHECKED

3037046·0990
FREAKPOINT BOOKS
ROCKY RIVER OH

Cash

SIGN HERE

X

The Issuer of the card identified on this item is authorized to pay the amount shown as TOTAL upon proper presentation. I promise to pay such TOTAL (together with any other charges due thereon) subject to and in accordance with the agreement governing the use of such card.

Challenges to Sustainability: Risk Perceptions by 'Lay People' and Experts

Nikolai Genov

THE PROBLEM SITUATION

Bulgaria is at a critical stage of its transition to a market economy and democratic political institutions. The tide of mass enthusiasm caused by the desired but largely unexpected radical changes is over. Sobering realities of mass unemployment, skyrocketing consumer prices and looming crime rates face politicians, business circles and the common people (Genov 1997).

Once envisaging the complexity and brutality of economic and political problems the Bulgarian society has to cope with what one might be prone to suppress, is the very discourse on environmental issues. Indeed, the country has regions marked by environmental calamities. But there are also areas with varieties of biodiversity which are unique in Europe. Therefore, when confronted with the risks of a far-reaching economic decline, political instability and cultural disintegration should Bulgarians be better advised to forget the very topic of environmental sustainability at least for a while?

This argument and its practical effects have already been experienced during the period of rapid industrialization. No wonder that the resulting open conflicts on environmental issues in the late eighties signalled the end of the authoritarian regime. At the beginning of the nineties they became hot political topics all over the country mobilizing influential movements on a number of sensitive spots. The practical outcome of the activity of environmentalist movements was minimal. Nevertheless, they managed to raise public awareness about risks stemming from the systematic abuse of nature. This facilitated some legal changes. But the country is still on its way to the development of a national strategy for sustainable development. Moreover, the economic collapse and the continuing uncertainty as to the prospects of political and social development mark the instability of environmental policies as well. What will be the impact of the ongoing large-scale privatization on the environment? How will' the unavoidable restructuring of the national economy affect the implementation of the environmental protection laws? Will the de-collectivization of agriculture facilitate or hinder agricultural production which is friendly to the environment? Will there be movement of hazardous technologies and toxic wastes from the most developed countries toward Eastern Europe in general and Bulgaria in particular?

The questions are more rapid than the answers. In fact, there are no ready answers. Conditions are changing quickly. Knowledge and practical skills for managing complex situations are insufficient. The democratic political institutions still lack the stability and the operational efficiency needed to cope with the situation. The non-governmental organizations do not have the stable social background of a well-established middle class. Last but not least, research, development and practical measures in the field of environmental protection cannot have proper funding because of the critical state of the national economy (Genov 1993; Annual Report 1995). Against the background of the above complex problem situation it seems promising to approach a specific aspect of issues connected with the undermined sustainability of the national social and economic development. The overload of such issues in the capital city of Sofia could be a special point. As a result of the rapid industrialization by means of unsophisticated technologies there is a variety of production lines, transport infrastructures and communal activities causing environmental tensions and conflicts in the capital. The approach might even focus on one special dimension of the environmental imbalances in the capital—air pollution. This would be for good reason since with the high concentration of dust, sulphur dioxide, nitrogen dioxide, lead aerosols and phenols, air pollution in Sofia is undoubtedly serious. In fact, the subjective perception of risks caused by air pollution is much more intensive in Sofia as compared to the public opinion nation-wide (Table 1)[1].

With the analysis given in Table 1 of the high-risk perception it is tempting to seek the experts' opinion. Are they concerned as well? Moreover, it is intriguing to compare the individual public strategies for handling the environmental problems with the institutional strategies for

---

[1]The nation-wide study on risk perception and the local study in Sofia were carried out simultaneously as home interviews with 1402 individual cases nation-wide and N = 1194 in Sofia. Both samples were representative of the voting population in the country and in the capital city respectively. The samples were prepared using the lists of residential registration.

Table 1. Assessments of Air Pollution in the Place of Residence[1]

	Countrywide	*Sofia*
The problem does not exist	41.9	7.5
The problem is not serious	28.1	31.2
The problem is serious	18.3	34.6
The problem is very serious	9.3	24.7
I don't know	2.1	1.6
NA	0.3	0.4
TOTAL	100.0	100.0

coping with the same issues as these strategies are incorporated in the activities of experts.[2]

THEORETICAL IDEAS AND HYPOTHESES

The guiding assumption of the study is that the types of the risk perception and risk management are the most fundamental characteristics of a given historical situation. The more critical the situation, the more relevant are the parameters for understanding and influencing the situation. The concept applied further lays stress on the balance between conditions (structures) and agencies (actors). Since modern conditions of life are basically man-made, interest is directed towards structures and actions causing harmful effects on human beings and social institutions. The broader conceptual framework is organized around the idea of sustainability which is differentiated along its economic, political and cultural dimensions (see also Keating 1993). The specific questions are based on the assumption, however, that the economic and political determinants of risk perception and reaction to risks are themselves moulded by the cultural definition of the risk situation. Thus the following questions arise:

• What are the cultural factors modelling the perception of environmental risks by major social groups?
• To what extent are there similarities and differences in the assessment of enviromental risks on the part of "lay people" (voters) and experts? It is widely assumed that the assessments of the first group are basically moulded by the mass media transmitting the popular culture. The assessments of experts are supposed to be guided by professional standards implying a higher level of precision and objectivity than the assessment of the "lay people". Do both assumptions correspond to reality?

---

[2]The information source for the analysis were 59 standardized interviews carried out with 59 experts in the field of air pollution in Sofia.

- What are the typical personal strategies of "lay people" for coping with environmental risks?
- What are the typical institutional strategies of experts for coping with environmental risks?
- What is the level of correspondence between both types of strategies in theoretical discourse and in practical action?
- What are the prospects for integration of both types of culture and practical involvement in problem-solving activities as regards environmental risks? Answers will be searched for in the context of the theory of interaction of actors producing and reproducing social relations. More precisely, the interest is focussed on the crosspoints of individual action and institutional structures. In modern urban societies the crosspoints are most essential in two territories: residence (dwelling place) and work (work place) (Hamm and Neumann 1996) (235). So the problem under scrutiny will be analyzed using George H. Meads' concept of the spontaneous and creative individual "I" and the institutional "me" imposed on the individual. The interactions are performed by a variety of actors (A) bringing about changes in fundamental relations (see Fig. 1):

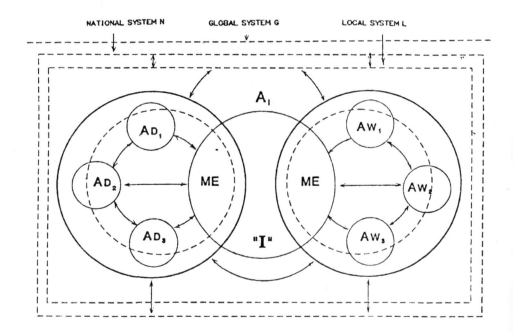

Fig. 1: The social context of environmental issues

- Persons Ad1, informal groups Ad2 and formal organizations Ad3 in the area of residence moulding the "me" of an individual who is a typical representative of a relevant statistical group;
- Persons Aw1, informal groups Aw2 and formal organizations Aw3 moulding the "me" of an individual at the workplace;
- Actors and institutional arrangements at the communal level L, the national level N, and the global level G influencing interactions connected with the environment in the place of residence and at the workplace.

Following this conceptual framework, the analysis is dedicated to the proof of five hypotheses:

1) There is an inherent contradiction in the widely spread mistrust towards social institutions and the rather limited individual initiative and responsibility towards the common good of the environment.

2) This is mainly due to the national tradition of retreat to private life in critical situations which threaten the common good.

3) The retreat to private life under critical conditions produces a homogenization of risk perceptions.

4) There is no congruence between personal experience of environmental risks, environmental anxieties and strategies for action towards alleviating environmental risks.

5) Experts and 'lay people' share basically the same assessments of the environmental situation due to commonly shared cultural models.

PUBLIC OPINION ON ENVIRONMENTAL RISKS

In developed countries public assessments of environmental risks are basically projected by the mass media. The intensity of media coverage of environmental issues declined in Bulgaria after the peak of their political usage in 1990–1991. But only 22.9 per cent of the interviewed 1,194 voters in Sofia maintained that their source of information about the state of the environment was their personal experience. The major part of 41.4 per cent pointed to the television as their major source of information. In addition, 7.2 per cent give a preference to the radio and 23.8 to newspapers and journals. Thus it is a fact that exactly like in the most advanced countries, in Bulgaria also, the public opinion on environmental issues is a 'second hand' vision of reality. What is this vision?

1) Environmental Issues in a Complex Situation of Risks

Given the overall critical situation of Bulgarian society one might assume that the sensitivity to environmental risks has been driven out of public concern. The assumption is only partly true. The picture is more complicated indicating a number of nuances in the current context of risk factors and their subjective experience. To start with, one may focus on the constellation of risk assessments. The operationalization of the issue is implemented in a composite question as to the threats which various factors pose to the country at present. The answers reveal a remarkable intensity of the perception of environmental risks in the given context (Table 2).

Table 2: Major Risks (five points scale, only position 5 "very serious problem", in per cent)

	Bulgaria	*Sofia*
Unemployment	64.4	41.5
Inability to tell good from bad	27.5	28.2
Political confrontation	44.7	45.6
Ethnic relations	25.3	30.6
State of the economy	73.5	76.5
State of the environment	44.2	60.6
Division between rich and poor	42.7	36.0
Crime	78.0	81.7
National security	27.1	32.3

As seen in this way the perception of environmental risks might be surprising since its intensity is higher in Sofia than the perception of the intensity of political confrontation as a risk factor—this in a society which is torn by political tensions. In Sofia only the state of economy and the level of crime are perceived as more serious risk factors. However, the shift of priorities determined by the present-day precarious situation of the national society becomes immediately evident in the range of answers to the question as to the relative urgency of one or another risk. It turns out that the relative weight of the environmental concerns is strikingly lower in this constellation (Table 3).

There is no doubt that the urgency of the economic situation and the closely-related unemployment are hardly comparable to the relative weight of other risks. So one cannot expect that decision-makers or the public at large would focus their attention on the management of environmental issues first of all. On the contrary, under the present-day conditions it is much more probable that in every particular situation at the communal or national level other priorities will take the lead at the expense of the financial or organizational support to solving environmental problems. The masterpiece of a realistic approach to the situation is to keep in mind this circumstance and not to give up the concern about environmental problems at the same time. There is no doubt that environmental problems together with other currently neglected risks like ethnic relations and national security are existentially important for the nation in the long run.

Table 3: The Most Serious Current Problem

	Bulgaria	*Sofia*
Unemployment	26.2	7.1
Inability to tell good from bad	2.7	4.6
Political confrontation	6.5	8.6
Ethnic relations	0.8	1.1
State of the economy	34.0	45.8
State of the environment	1.3	2.1
Division between rich and poor	5.8	4.4
Crime	18.3	19.8
National security	1.6	3.0
Anything else	2.2	2.7
NA	0.6	0.8
TOTAL	100.0	100.0

2) The Place of Residence as a Focus of Environmental Concerns

The impartial observer may describe, analyze and evaluate a given situation of risk without getting involved in emotional tensions. However, it is normal for human beings to get emotionally affected by existential risks of the type the environmental issues are. In fact, being asked about their personal anxieties concerning environmental risks in the place of residence the Bulgarian voters are quite definite (Table 4).

Table 4: Fear that Environmental Pollution in the Place of Residence could be Dangerous to Personal Health

		Bulgaria	*Sofia*
Does not fear at all	1	38.7	16.3
	2	17.5	17.3
	3	17.2	25.7
	4	11.9	17.7
Fears it very much	5	14.1	22.6
NA		0.6	0.4
TOTAL		100.0	100.0

Surprisingly there is a rather weak statistical correlation between gender characteristics and the level of anxiety caused by environmental issues in the place of residence (Cramer's coefficient $V = 0.086$). The age cohorts are also insignificantly differentiated along this line ($V = 0.054$). Even the educational level hardly plays any differentiating role ($V = 0.074$). So we can expect a clear case of opinion based on personal experience despite the vast information coming from the mass media about the environmental situation of the country in general. What is personal experience about the environmental imbalance in the place of residence in Sofia? (Table 5).

Table 5: How Serious are various Problems Around the Dwelling Place?

	Strong noise	*Air pollution*	*Pollution of drinking water*	*Pollution due to household wastes*
The problem doesn't exist	17.7	7.5	10.0	5.4
The problem is not serious	41.7	31.2	26.8	21.2
The problem is serious	25.1	34.6	37.2	37.1
The problem is very serious	14.4	24.7	19.8	34.5
Do not know	0.7	1.6	5.7	0.6
NA	0.4	0.4	0.5	1.2
TOTAL	100.0	100.0	100.0	100.0

The extent of similarity between data from objective measurements on environmental risks in Sofia and the data from the public opinion poll is striking. According to measurements carried out by the Ministry of Environment, 37 per cent of the population in Sofia live in areas where the noise exceeds the admissible level. Table 5, shows that 39.4 per cent of the voters in Sofia describe the level of noise in their place of residence as a "serious" or "very serious" problem. This fact supports the point that in their assessment of specific risks in their immediate environment, people rely basically on their personal experience.

The statistical correlation between the level of emotional tension and specific factors of environmental risks is another evidence of the close connection between the empirical reality and the assessment of specific risks. Cramer's coefficient of correlation between the level of fear caused by environmental imbalance in the place of residence and the perceived intensity of risks has the following levels:

- level of noise $V = 0.219$
- air pollution $V = 0.320$
- pollution of drinking water $V = 0.197$
- pollution due to household wastes $V = 0.202$

The picture is clear enough—persons who are exposed to a higher degree of specific environmental risks in the place of residence fear the harmful impact of the risks on their health more intensively. The situation however is not that simple. When asked about the level of information concerning dangers coming from the environment in the place of residence, a surprisingly high percentage of the interviewed voters stated that they did not know of the environmental situation at all (27.3 per cent) or almost not at all (15.9 per cent). Thus the most accurate picture of what the environmental situation really was always projected by experts. To rely on subjective perceptions and assessments by the public at large is not advisable for decision-makers dealing with management of environmental risks. Nevertheless, remaining at the level of the subjective reflections there is no doubt that a strong correlation exists between the assessment of the personal knowledge about environmental risks and the level of fears (Table 6).

Table 6: Correlation between the Level of Information about Environmental Risks and the Level of Anxiety

Anxiety							High	Total
Information		1	2	3	4	5		
Low	1	27.0	13.5	22.4	15.0	22.1		100.0
	2	10.6	29.66	29.1	17.5	13.2		100.0
	3	9.5	17.9	41.6	14.9	16.1		100.0
	4	11.7	16.4	20.5	32.7	18.7		100.0
High	5	17.0	12.8	14.5	13.8	42.1		100.0

$\chi_e^2 = 178.87$ $v = 0.194$

What kind of human activities cause the environmental problems in Sofia and to what extent? One may assume that in the area of the city, agriculture would play only a minor role in causing environmental imbalances. On the other hand, industry and transportation would usually be the primary polluters. While the level of specialized knowledge the lay people is not expected to be high, they do have a basically correct estimation concerning the causes and reasons of the major environmental risks in the area of residence. Table 7 proves this fact which has to be taken into account in every decision and practical action as to the management of environmental risks in the area of residence.

3) Environmental Issues at the Work Place

Like in residential areas, personal experience at the work place causes substantial emotional tensions among the 680 interviewed employed persons. The intensity of fears is distributed as shown in Table 8.

At first glance, basic sociodemographic characteristics play a minimal role in modifying these fears as was the case with environmentally determined fears in the place of residence. For instance, age has a negligible statistical correlation with the fears (V = 0.078). However, this is not exactly the case with gender. Although relatively weak, the value of the coefficient

Table 7: The Extent to Which Environmental Problems in Residential Areas in Sofia are Caused by Types of Activity

		Services	Households	Agriculture	Transportation	Industry
Cause(s) no problems	1	32.9	17.4	69.8	14.1	35.3
	2	21.8	18.0	7.6	12.0	10.2
	3	19.0	26.0	5.7	18.3	11.1
	4	11.2	20.9	2.4	21.8	14.0
Cause(s) very serious problems	5	8.6	13.7	2.9	30.2	23.3
Do not know		5.7	3.3	9.6	3.1	5.2
NA		0.8	0.7	1.8	0.5	0.9
TOTAL		100.0	100.0	100.0	100.0	100.0

Table 8: Environmental Fears at the Work Place

		Bulgaria	Sofia
No fears at all	1	48.4	32.5
	2	14.9	17.5
	3	16.1	22.2
	4	9.5	11.5
Very intensive fears	5	13.1	16.3
TOTAL		100.0	100.0

$V = 0.135$ indicates that there are gender-specific environmental anxieties. Contrary to common belief, men fear the dangerous impacts of the work environment more than women. The explanation of this difference is not focussed on biological factors but on occupational characteristics. Men predominate among those employed in heavy industry, mining and transportation where the hazards are greater. Almost 36 per cent of the employed in heavy industry greatly fear the harmful environmental impacts at their work place while this holds true for only 15.3 per cent working in light industry. The policies of managing environmental risks have to follow this difference precisely. What are the specific environmental risk factors at the work place as experienced by the interviewed persons in the capital city? (Table 9).

There is no doubt that the emotional tensions caused by the environmental imbalance at the work place are provoked mainly by direct personal experience. The strong statistical correlation of emotional tensions with the assessment of various risk factors provides the relevant evidence. Cramer's correlational coefficient of the 'fear' variable has the following levels in the given context:

Table 9: How serious are specific problems at the work place?

	Strong noise	Air pollution	Vibration	Radiation
The problem does not exist	33.1	19.6	50.0	64.0
It is not a serious problem	31.5	29.5	22.0	17.2
The problem is serious	21.4	29.1	14.8	9.1
The problem is very serious	13.6	21.5	10.4	6.8
Do not know	0.3	0.4	2.8	2.8

- with the variable 'strong noise' V = 0.252
- with the variable 'air pollution' V = 0.302
- with the variable 'vibration' V = 0.249
- with the variable 'radiation' V = 0.223

The fact that 15.9 per cent of the interviewed employed persons state that they are exposed to radiation which is a 'serious' or 'very serious' problem, casts some doubts about the connection between the objective environmental situation and the perception of environmental risks. The doubts might be strengthened by the fact that 23.1 per cent of the interviewed persons frankly say that they are not at all informed about the environmental risks at their work place. Whatever the doubts in this respect might be, we shall see that the experts' assessments of risks support the information obtained from the general public. Moreover, it is a well-established fact that employed people are rather sensitive to environmental risks connected with their occupations and that the perception of risks causes strong emotional and social tensions. What are the causes and reasons of environmental risks at the work place according to the results of the public opinion poll? (Table 10).

Table 10: Causes and Reasons of Environmental Risks at the Work Place

		Unsophisticated technology	Bad work-organization	Irresponsible behaviour
There is no such cause (reason)	1	40.6	40.7	35.1
	2	9.1	11.9	9.3
	3	14.1	17.6	14.7
	4	11.2	11.0	14.5
To a very high extent	5	18.2	14.6	21.3
Do not know		6.5	4.2	5.1
TOTAL		100.0	100.0	100.0

Despite the widespread opinion that the environmental issues at the work place are caused mainly by the technological underdevelopment of the production lines there is clear evidence that according to the people concerned there are substantial and even more important human and social reasons for the environmental imbalances in this area of human activity. Thus environmental problems turn out to be directly what they really are as seen from the point of view of their substance, first of all social problems. Another point strengthening this interpretation is provided by the data showing that 23.5 per cent of the workers fear the harmful impacts of the work environment on their health while this holds true for 11.9 per cent of the engineers. Therefore, the inequalities connected with environmental risks are definitely related to social inequalities. Consequently, these inequalities should be the subject of social policies as well and not of technological considerations alone.

LAY PEOPLE AND EXPERTS: MANAGEMENT OF ENVIRONMENTAL RISKS

Applying a famous distinction between two types of culture—the humanistic and the technocratic—we can develop another typology for the purpose of the current study. There is hardly any doubt that there is a distinction between the educational background of assessments of environmental risks made by the 'average' voter in Sofia and the assessment made by professionals who are supposed to know the situation better because of their specific knowledge and occupational skills. So we shall draw the distinction between the "laymen culture" diagnosed by the public opinion polls and the "experts' culture" diagnosed by means of specialized interviews and by means of analysis of documents. The 59 experts were selected from research and decision-making institutions at the national level, at the communal level in Sofia, from the managerial staff of industrial firms in Sofia, and from the Bulgarian Academy of Sciences. The key point is the comparison of convergence and divergence of assessments made by the public and by experts.

The ecological maps of Sofia based on objective measurements reveal a rather uneven distribution of environmental risks all over the city. So with a view to the specific personal experience there is a substantial percentage of voters in the city for whom air pollution at their place of residence is either not a problem at all, or, not a serious problem. The experts were expected to generalize by making a judgement about the extent of air pollution in Sofia as a territorial entity. That is why the picture is quite different. Only one of the 59 experts says that air pollution in Sofia is not a serious problem. Of the others, 52.6 per cent of them find the problem is serious, and 45.7 per cent say the problem is very serious. For comparison, 34.6 per cent of the 'lay people' assess the situation with the air pollution as serious and 24.7 per cent as very serious. The difference is due mainly to the difference in specific and general assessments. Both groups, however, show a remarkable similarity of their assessment of the attention paid by major social institutions to environmental issues. The outcome of both the representative survey and the specialized interviews with experts document a high degree of mistrust in the capacity of decision-makers to cope with existential dangers to public health (Table 11).

Table 11: Attention Paid by the Government and the Mayor's Offices to the Management of Environmental Risks (general public: risks in general; experts: air pollution)

	The government Public experts		Mayor's offices Public experts	
Less attention than necessary	92.3	83.1	94.1	93.2
As much attention as necessary	6.1	6.7	4.5	1.7
More attention than necessary	0.9	–	0.8	–
Do not know	–	8.5	–	5.1
NA	0.7	1.7	0.6	–
TOTAL	100.0	100.0	100.0	100.0

The syndrome presented in Table 11 is rather dangerous for social equilibrium. On the one side, there is the high intensity of risk perception on the part of the public at large and on the part of experts. On the other side, there is an obvious lack of trust in the crucial centres of decision-making which are normally expected to manage the environment for the common good. While the public might possibly be misled by its limited direct experience or by the propaganda of mass media, this cannot be the case with experts. They are assumed to base their opinion on well-founded knowledge.

What are the personal and the institutional strategies for managing environmental risks?

1) Personal Strategies for Coping with Environmental Risks

Confronted with a critical environmental situation and with the inability of major social institutions to manage it, Bulgarian voters might be expected to develop a wide range of personal strategies in order to live up to the challenge. One can assume that the lack of institutional initiative and responsibility is connected to the individualistic patterns of active participation in voluntary associations and movements. The environmental concerns seem to be the proper background for developing this type of social mobilization because they provide for the basis of identification and solidarity in modern societies.

The data reveal the personal attitudes towards managing environmental risks and behavioural strategies which do not necessarily support the

above assumption. The shift from a high intensity of environmental concerns as taken for themselves towards negligence of the environmental issues when regarded in relative terms was already indicated. There is a
similar shift from the cognitive and emotional states towards the real behaviour oriented towards the management of environmental risks. When
asked about the intensity of personal behavioural involvement in this type
of activity the interviewed persons give answers which only partly correspond to the high intensity of their cognitive and emotional environmental concerns (Table 12).

Table 12: Personal Attempts to Diminish the Environmental Problems in the Area of Residence

		Bulgaria	*Sofia*
Never attempted so far	1	50.7	43.1
	2	15.2	17.2
	3	14.6	19.6
	4	8.7	8.3
Attempted very often	5	10.3	11.0
NA		0.5	0.8
TOTAL		100.0	100.0

Compared to the large number of persons who declare that they have
never undertaken practical action towards environmental protection, the
proportion of the active and very active persons seems to be much smaller.
If calculated in absolute terms, however, one-third of the able-bodied Bulgarians involved in environmental protection (positions 3–5) means about
two million of the country's population. But what do people really mean by
answering the question about their behavioural activity positively? Refin-
ing the question further by introducing an one year time frame the picture
becomes clearer.

Table 13: Participation in Environmental Protection Activities During the Last 12 Months

	Bulgaria	*Sofia*
In organizations and movements for environmental protection	4.7	5.7
In cleaning and greening of streets and parks	44.2	49.8
In collecting money for environmental protection	5.3	7.9
In actions for closing production lines harmful to the environment	3.9	3.9

There is no noticeable difference between the levels of environmental
activities country-wide and in Sofia despite the much higher intensity of
risk perception in the city. In both contexts the environmental activity is

more an exception than a rule, the cleaning and greening of streets and parks notwithstanding. Having in mind the declared concerns about the state of the environment both in the area of residence and at the work place there is an obvious gap between these concerns and the intensity of the declared behavioural activity. There are various explanations for this. No doubt, in a situation in which 35 per cent of the interviewed persons in Sofia say that their most important personal problem is the shortage of funds, the concern about environment has to be given less attention. Given the economic conditions, 39 per cent of the employed persons in the capital city would prefer to get additional payment for being employed in harmful working conditions than to move to a safer but lower paid job. Thus in terms of both ultimate and instrumental values the management of environmental risks does not mean too much in shaping personal behavioural strategies.

The problem with the limited motivation for pro-active personal strategies in environmental management has another dimension as well. As many as 39.8 per cent of the interviewed persons in Sofia are convinced that improvement of the environmental situation in the area of their residence does not depend on their personal efforts at all. This percentage is even higher country-wide. So it is not surprising that instead of mobilizing personal efforts along the line of growing individualization of social life more than 80 per cent of the voters country-wide and in Sofia keep to the traditional institutionalist attitudes of focussing on the governments and mayor's offices for solving the environmental problems.

This is one of the most relevant paradoxes of the current transitional period. Despite the deepest disenchantment with the capacity of major institutions to solve social problems in general and environmental problems in particular, exactly the same institutions are expected to play a crucial role in solving the same problems. This, however, is not an exception. Medical care is also expected to be provided by the state free of charge by 52.9 per cent of the country-wide sample. Only 3.3 per cent go to the other extreme by insisting that medical care should be paid for entirely by the concerned individual. The move towards a more intensive involvement of personal initiative and responsibility is obvious in Sofia. There 35.9 per cent of the people would like to rely entirely on the state for medical care while 7.3 per cent would like to rely on individual responsibility alone.

There are two main lines for explaining the current disenchantment with institutions combined the strong reliance on them. The first explanation is based on the very function of these institutions in society—they have a more or less universal pattern of managing the common good which cannot be basically landed by individuals. The reliance on institutions for medical care or for environmental protection is currently strengthened because of the critical situation of large groups of the population which need public help. On the other side, like most Eastern European societies, Bulgarian society still has a strong paternalistic tradition. The smaller reliance of the inhabitants of the capital city on public help for medical care indicates, however, that the trend towards individualization is easy to recognize.

2) Experts in the Process of Management

When approached with the specially designed questionnaire the 59 experts in the field of the management of air pollution enumerated a number of institutional programmes for coping with the problem in Sofia:
- Systematic monitoring of the level of air pollution;
- Registration of emissions of greenhouse gases, SO_2, NO_x, etc.;
- Elaboration of methods of expertise of the level of air pollution;
- Elaboration on the geographic net of control points;
- Installation of dust respirators in metallurgical plants;
- Replacement of outdated vehicles;
- Construction of subways;
- Diminishing air pollution in the area of the 'Kremikovtsi' metallurgical works;
- Diminishing air pollution in the area of the 'Gara Iskar' non-ferreous metallurgical plant;
- Introduction of catalysts for vehicles;
- Introduction of new fuels for vehicles used in plants;
- Diminishing the NO_x and SO_x from the thermal power plants;
- Processing faecal waters;
- Shift of the bus public transportation to gas fuel;
- Development and maintenance of green areas;
- Move air polluting production lines out of Sofia;
- Limitations of traffic transitting through the city centre;
- Strengthening non-governmental organizations;
- Keeping purification installations in good order;
- Development of the system of central heating;
- Restrictions on the level of sulphur in fuels;
- Development of electrically-powered transportation in the capital;
- Enlighting the population about the dangers of air pollution and the ways to diminish them;
- Programmes for the maintenance of the public transportation vehicles;
- Move the airport outside of the capital;
- Regular cleaning of streets and parks;
- Construction of park lots at entrance to the city.

This broad range of programmes enumerated by the experts covers all aspects of the Complex Programme for Protection and Reproduction of the

Environment in Sofia and in the Conurbation System of Sofia until the Year 2000 which has been prepared during the eighties and updated several times thereafter. However, it is interesting to notice that with a few exceptions, these experts who had been selected with two recommendations by other experts, did not know about the programme. Moreover, some people who were regarded as experts and called themselves experts on air pollution, hesitated to mention any specific programme for the improvement of the air situation in Sofia. Out of the 59 experts 14 did not know anything about any such specific programmes.

The problem here is not merely the selection of experts. The selection is only part of the problem. There are at least three additional and relevant aspects of the issue:

1) There are both general and specific programmes or policies for managing air pollution in Sofia. Some of them are being implemented despite the severe economic crisis and the political uncertainty. But the design and the implementation of policies still remains the activity and control of a few technocrats and affiliated experts. The public at large and even the broader community of experts remain unaware.

2) Persons specially appointed to ensure the effective management of environmental risks at the national and local levels, or to directly take decisions in the field, could frankly tell the interviewers that they were not informed about current programmes for managing the air pollution in Sofia. It is hard to assume that they gave the answer because of considerations of confidentiality. Most probably, they really did not know about the programmes in question. The findings prove the fact that the recent personal and structural changes in decision-making bodies do not necessarily improve the level of competence there.

3) The practical irrelevance of the Bulgarian science has been confirmed in the study on experts. The academic scientists selected were dealing with the air pollution in general and even with the air pollution in Sofia in particular. But they openly showed their lack of any knowledge about and interest in the programmes for managing the air pollution in the capital city. This is a clear message that there is something wrong with the research strategy and with the patterns of financing Bulgarian science, allowing scientists to carry out research encapsulated from the practical needs and public concerns.

Despite these negative observations the interviews with experts really involved in managing environmental risks and the analysis of documents shows that the situation is not as grave as it might look at first glance. Timetables for the control on vehicles, for supply of fuels with lower percentage of sulphur, for better organization of the traffic, for accelerated construction of the metro, etc., were prepared at the beginning of the nineties although they were hardly followed. Basically, the numerous programmes for alleviating the negative effects of the production lines at the Kremikovtsi metallurgical works on the air pollution in the area of Sofia were more effective. Nevertheless, both the public at large and the experts are rather sceptical as to the effects of the current policies focussing on environmental protection (Table 14).

Table 14: Expectations for Change of the Environmental Situation in the Residential Areas in Three Years

	Public opinion		Experts
	Bulgaria	*Sofia*	*Air pollution in Sofia*
It will get worse	17.0	26.1	27.1
It will remain the same	45.5	44.2	49.2
It will improve	15.5	17.2	15.2
Do not know	21.6	11.7	5.1
NA	0.4	0.8	3.4
TOTAL	100.0	100.0	100.0

The interviewed experts live in Sofia. The very fact that their answers so closely resemble the answers obtained from the broad public questions the assumption about the substantially different culture of experts. Most probably, in this case we should lay the stress on the influence of general cultural models moulding the culture of both the lay people and experts.

DISCUSSION

The troubles facing the management of environmental risks in Bulgaria are not an exception but the rule in the emerging democracies in Eastern Europe. The factors determining the current situation and the future prospects of risk management are deeply rooted in previous developments and in the present-day critical situation of Bulgarian society. That is why they will remain relevant for social sciences and for policy making in the years to come. What are these factors according to the above analysis?

1) The technological level of Bulgarian society lags far behind the standards of modern production in economic and ecological terms. Bulgaria was, is and will probably remain in the technological periphery of the world at least in the foreseeable future. It is easy now to lay the blame for the current technological situation on the previous ruling elites. No doubt, false strategic decisions for technological innovations using technologies which require large quantities of non-renewable resources and which extensively pollute the environment have been taken up and implemented.

Having in mind the then existing international situation and the inherent deficiencies of overcentralized planning, it was hardly possible to go in a different direction of technological development. Now it is virtually impossible to switch on to environmentally friendly technologies in the short run. No doubt, some of the worst industrial polluters have already been closed because of environmental and more likely economic reasons. It is expected that other production facilities polluting the environment will be dismantled in the course of privatization since they will go bankrupt. In fact, this will be the fate of a number of key producers after the breakdown of the Eastern European markets. A smooth technological transition of this type seems to be out of reach at present. On the contrary, the generally unfavourable international economic situation makes the technological restructuring of the Bulgarian economy a rather slow and painful process. The policies for environmental risk management have to be attuned to these prospects. The facts of strategic disorientation, even on the part of experts, which were discovered in the course of the reported study, are indicative of the disarray of the current situation.

2) The recent experience confirms a long-lasting tradition of low administrative efficiency both at the national and community levels. In fact, the disappointment with institutions is so intense that there may not be any hope of well-established institutions being able to manage the multidimensional risk situation facing Bulgarian society. At least for the time being the substitute might be the numerous, powerful, active voluntary associations and movements. Unfortunately, this is not the case. Instead of becoming more influential in the course of democratic transformations, the environmental non-governmental organizations have lost their appeal and membership. Traditional party politics is taking the lead despite the wide-spread disenchantment with parties. The declining public pressure may free governments from the need to react in an unbalanced or hasty way. But the trend might also undermine the very social basis of democratic politics. Since democratic political traditions are not particularly strong in the country, the public mind can be persuaded that only a strong hand could handle the precarious situation effectively. Having in mind the complexity of problems one might only ask who can be so self-confident as to take the burden.

3) It is not the ineffectiveness of institutions themselves which makes the strengthening of democratic risk management so full of tensions and with unclear prospects. The crucial factor in risk management is and remains the individual. Facing economic uncertainty, political instability and cultural disintegration, individuals do not react by means of an increasing public activity but by retreat into their private lives. This personal strategy is deeply rooted in the national cultural tradition affected by

precarious circumstances. It has not been typical for Bulgarians to organize themselves for fighting risks. Moreover, facing intensive risks, Bulgarians tend to split their resources looking around for specific solutions thus putting their common good on trial. There is no sign that the current crisis situation is going to bring about a different pattern of personal behaviour.

CONCLUSION

Thus the prospects of democratic risk management in Bulgaria are not necessarily bright. However, as the country is quite dependent on international trends they will determine the success or failure of the current policies in the country. This will hold true for the policies aiming at sustainability in economic and political terms as well as for the attempts to manage environmental risks.

REFERENCES

Annual Report on the State of the Environment 1995. Sofia: Council of Ministers (in Bulgarian).

Genov, Nikolai (ed.). 1993. *Sustainable Development and Environmental Risk*. Sofia: Publishing House of Sofia University (in Bulgarian).

Genov, Nikolai (ed.). 1997. Bulagaria 1997. Human Development Report. Sofia: UNDP.

Hamm, Bernd and Ingo Neumann. 1996. Siedlungs-, Umwelt- und Planungssoziologie. Opladen Leske + Budrich.

Keating, Michael. 1993. *The Earth Summit's Agenda for Change*. Geneva: The Centre for Our Common Future.

Property Rights as a Tool for Desirable Development

Peter Marcuse

INTRODUCTION

The argument of this paper is simple: Property rights can be a very flexible instrument to affect many purposes: meeting basic human needs, distributing power democratically, achieving some desired level of equality, stimulating the accumulation of wealth, and providing for sound city planning.

To use property rights well:
— property must be understood as a bundle of many different rights, of which "owning" is just one;
— different things (land, houses, factories, tools, consumer goods) can be "owned" in different ways;
— "ownership" may be by different entities (individuals, coops, non-profits, private businesses, the state);

A systematic approach that "mixes and matches" different forms of property rights, as to different types of property, for different types of entities, must be used to achieve the best results.

The paper spells out this argument, and ends with a few examples of what a differentiated use of property rights might look like. The paper necessarily begins, however, with a somewhat theoretical examination of what "property" and "ownership" actually mean.

THE MEANING OF PROPERTY RIGHTS

The legal definition of "ownership" is clear, if complex: it is a bundle of rights, each of which is a relationship between persons as to a thing, not a relation between a person and a thing. Definitions are critical. What the forms of ownership and tenure imply can vary enormously within formal categories. The differences involve, in each case, different relations among people;[1] it is a fundamental principle of jurisprudence that ownership is a set of relations among persons and institutions with regard to a thing, not, as is often assumed in ordinary conversation, a relationship between a person or institution and a thing. The law of ownership is not a set of rules fixing what I may or may not do to a thing but a set of rules fixing what other people may or may not prevent me from doing to the thing, and what I may or may not prevent them from doing to the thing (Turner 1941). Such a definition of ownership is consistent both with traditional Western jurisprudence and the Marxist theory.

The analysis of ownership and the various tenure forms must then begin with a specification of exactly what relations among what persons each tenure form implies. This is the "bundle of rights" concept, well accepted at least in Anglo-Saxon law: that ownership or any other form of tenure is a collection of separate rights, and that each form of tenure can be defined by a specification of what rights it includes. I use the phrase "incidents of ownership" to cover those sticks in the bundle of rights that are most often associated with the"ownership" of a housing unit.

To help look at what kinds of rights, and by and against whom, are involved, I believe the most helpful as well as most rigorous approach is that developed by Professor Hohfeld (1966), largely followed in the standard legal discussion in the United States, who distinguishes among the benefits of ownership: rights, privileges, powers, and immunities, and among the obligations or limitations on ownership: duties, "no-rights," liabilities, and disabilities. The detailed scheme is too complex for a brief discussion, but the important point about it is that it is symmetrical: for every right by one person there is a duty by another, for every privilege on one person's part another person has "no-right", for every power one has, another has a liability.

PROPERTY RIGHTS IN HOUSING

Many different "sticks" make up the bundle of rights that is ownership; ten or so of these "sticks" make up the basic incidents of ownership of housing. Those characteristics that must be taken into account in trying to understand what form of tenure is desired, or what the consequences of a particular change in legal forms of ownership will be, include the following,

---

[1]I use "people" and "persons" here to include any type of legal entity, whether individual, corporate, governmental, or otherwise; see discussion that follows for the variety of entities that may be involved in "ownership".

which I would consider the key incidents of ownership: (See also Marcuse 1972):
— Privilege to occupy and have shelter,
— Privilege of broader uses, privilege not to have use restricted,
— Security, privilege of continued occupancy; immunity from eviction, right to protection in occupancy,
— Privilege of privacy, not to have other invade unit, right to exclude others,
— Privilege to modify, make physical changes to the unit, disposition,
— Rights to residential services, utilities,
— Privilege of transfer, as gift or inheritance (without profit), immunity from restrictions on disposition,
— Privilege of transfer, as sale or rental (with profit), immunity from restrictions on disposition,
— Duty of maintenance and repairs,
— Right to public subsidy or support, immunity from payments to the state. In addition, ancillary rights often are established for ownership, ranging from the right to vote to the receipt of various kinds of public benefits, subsidies, etc.

Obviously various combinations of these rights, privileges, powers, and immunities are possible; the extent to which each exists, who may have each, against whom, and as to what, makes up the range of possibilities that can be considered in defining a system of property rights. So let us look, next, as to why it might be logical to treat different forms of property differently, and then as to why it may make sense to treat different "owners" differently as to those forms.

SYSTEMS OF PROPERTY RIGHTS

Many different kinds of things may be "owned"; it makes sense to treat the "ownership" of some different kinds of things differently, for instance, agricultural land differently from urban, housing differently from stores or factories, consumer goods differently from producer goods.

All objects of ownership are not the same. Ownership of different kinds of property must be clearly distinguished from each other; a lot of mischief has been created by taking categories of ownership appropriate, for instance, to land, and applying them to housing units, or forms appropriate for consumption goods and applying them to machinery and tools for production. I believe very different concepts of ownership need to be distinguished (or developed, to the extent existing forms are inadequate), as they apply to:

1) Agricultural Land

This is the oldest form of private property, going back in uninterrupted lineage to the feudal systems.[2] The revolt against the feudal land owner-ship system was a necessary part of the transition to capitalism. In political development, the establishment of an independent yeomanry in England, the tradition of independent farmers and settlers in the United States, the failures to provide for individual farmer's land ownership in Russia (and in the South of the United States), the compromises preserving aris-tocratic land ownership in Prussia and much of the Austro-Hungarian em-pire, all were critical elements in determining the political as well as economic course of those countries into the twentieth century. By the same token, the misunderstanding (sometimes deliberate and certainly often self-serving) of this evolution, in which home ownership by city residents is equated with land ownership by independent working farmers, has plagued discussion of "tenure forms" for at least 100 years. It makes non-sense of such rhetoric as that of the president of the National Associa-tion of Real Estate Boards, for instance, when he says: "[The] far-seeing founders of our Republic... [visualized] a race of free men, made inde-pendent by individual ownership of the land. Life has indeed grown more intricate... but never has arisen any sound reason to question the ideal that goes to the heart of our economic existence—widespread home owner-ship..." (Dean, de Neufville and Barton). The easy substitution of "home ownership" for "land" conceals a fundamental historical shift: in the 18th century, individual ownership of land meant individual ownership by the farmer of his basic means of production, while today home ownership is an exclusively residential concept having nothing to do with production at all.

2) Natural Resources

Land is indeed only one of many natural resources, and the rules related to land might well be applied, by a parallel logic, to all natural resources.

3) Urban Land

The rules of law applied to agricultural land have been taken over to apply to urban land in all capitalist countries, and, surprisingly, in many socialist countries as well.[3] Yet the logic is entirely different, the interests affected

---

[2]The Roman system of property law was substantially more advanced than its feudal re-placement in Europe, but it remained a curiously alien system to at least the Anglo-Saxon evolution to this day.

[3]Agricultural land has indeed been specially treated, in some statutes, e.g. for the preser-vation of agriculture and the restriction of urban development, but always as a modification of

are different, the economic result is different. For productive activity, the rent paid to a landowner is a redistribution of value from producer to landowner, considered by many orthodox free market economists to be a parasitic drain on productive capital. Market prices for land as a method of allocating land among alternate uses and users plays an important role in city development in capitalist countries; it is however nowhere allowed free play in the planning of cities. A much more differentiated treatment of urban land would benefit cities in Western as well as Eastern countries.

Residential land may also logically be treated differently from land used for business purposes; or land used for single-family, owner-occupied housing differently from multi-family housing, which might be considered more similar to a business use, since "ownership" and use would be separate. Issues of residential land are involved in the treatment of housing, discussed later.

4) Means of Production[4]

Ownership here has traditionally meant, for Marxists, the right to extract surplus value from the labour of employees; the craftsman or craftwoman's tools are (sometimes with elaborate intellectual gymnastics) differentiated from the capitalist's machines. In capitalist countries, the costs of acquisition and the possibilities of financing are intimately connected with legal forms of ownership, and very sophisticated forms of leasing and pledging have developed to integrate ownership forms into a functioning economic system.

5) Consumption Goods

In developed capitalist systems, ownership here is again indistinguishable from ownership of other forms of property.[5] In most of the Eastern European countries, following both the orthodox interpretations of the Marxist theory and the example of the Soviet Union, "personal property", essentially goods for individual use and consumption, were the only kinds

---

a single system of rules governing all land. On the other hand, in Yugoslavia, urban land was nationalized in 1958, rural land not. Simmie 1991, p. 173.

[4]The distinction between ownership of the means of production and ownership of consumption goods goes back to the fundamental works of Marx and Engels; see Anti-Duhring, in Marx-Engels Werke, vol. 20, pp. 122–23.

[5]Particular rights and immunities attach to particular forms of personal property, e.g. in the United States exemption from certain forms of taxation, immunity from attachment under Homestead laws, etc., but these are again exceptions to an underlying uniformity of treatment, not a different category of ownership.

of private property allowed; their protection was generally, as in the former G.D.R., provided for in the Constitution itself.

6) Housing

Housing is both a particular form of a consumer good, a particularly large and expensive result of productive enterprise for others, and, particularly in its connection with land, a source of rent for sunk investment or for land owned. Because it differs from other "personal property" in these respects, specific rules had been developed in the countries of real existing socialism to deal with the "non-use" aspects of housing: prohibitions on private resale, for instance, or limitations on rent that may be privately charged, or public responsibility for production. Within the category housing, differences may also be made:

— Single-family housing is obviously the most easily adapted to purely individual ownership and responsibility;
— Multi-family housing, on the other hand, almost always needs some form of collective maintenance and mechanisms of collective decisions about the use of common spaces, etc., the kinds of decisions cooperatives facilitate.

Within multi-family housing, differentiations may be made by size. Yugoslavia, for instance, nationalized all buildings containing more than two units (Simmie 1991); rent control in New York City covers all buildings with six or more units.

7) Public Goods

Goods which either cannot be limited in their use (clean air), or as to which society as a whole benefits the more they are used (education), or the use of which is considered a fundamental right (health care) might also be considered a separate category of property, as to which public/state ownership is the only appropriate ownership form. It is so considered in most societies today, although the range of things or services as to which the concept applies (housing?) varies substantially from country to country.

Quite different forms of property rights can be provided for each one of these categories, and perhaps others; there is no reason why the same set of rules has to apply to all of them, and in fact in most countries important differences are recognized by law among them.[6]

---

[6]In the United States, a "homestead exemption" exempts owner-occupied housing and individually used tools from attachment by creditors, for instance; residential land is taxed differently than commercial; agricultural land often may not be built upon; environmental restrictions cover much use of natural resources; etc.

OWNERS

There are many different kinds of "owners": individuals, corporations, cooperatives, non-profit organizations, government. They can have very different kinds of tenures as to housing; "owning" and "renting" are just two of the possibilities, and they mean different things to different "owners". In many current discussions, it is assumed that there are only three, or possibly four, forms of "tenure": public ownership, private ownership, private rental, non-profit ownership. Such usage implies that "ownership" is a single and indivisible concept and that the distinction among tenures is a distinction based on who "owns" a given unit of housing: in private rental housing, a private person/entity other than its occupant "owns" the unit, in owner-occupancy the occupant is the "owner", in public rental housing the state is the "owner", in social or not-profit housing the "owner" is a social or non-profit entity. A focus on who has what incidents of ownership would be much more fruitful: a "tenant" of a unit "owned" by a non-profit organization, who cannot be evicted and whose family has the right to continue occupancy after his/her death, is more similar to the "owner" of a single-family house with restrictions on resale that to the "tenant' of a private landlord in an unregulated housing market. The forms of "tenure" can be listed by name, but the content of each will vary widely by economic system, historic tradition, constitution and statute, and judicial interpretation. As to a single piece of property, different tenures in the hands of different persons can also exist, separated by time, for example a unit can be publicly-owned for 15 years, then revert to private ownership.

The different forms of tenure can be as follows:

1) Individual ownership of detached single-family units;

2) Individual ownership of apartment units for the owner's own use, in multi-family buildings (called condominium ownership in the United States law), with collective control of common areas;

3) Cooperative ownership, within which many variations can be distinguished, the major line of difference being:

a) Cooperative private ownership, in which the individual's right of ownership can be sold privately for an unrestricted profit; and

b) Non-profit cooperative ownership (or limited equity cooperative ownership), in which the right to sell for a profit is limited or non-existent;

4) Non-profit organizational ownership, within which many variations can be distinguished, the major lines of difference being:

a) Publicly-owned (national, state, or municipal) corporations, or those a majority of whose directors are publicly appointed;

b) Charitable organizations;

5) Employer-established or controlled organizations;

6) Limited profit organizations, or organizations whose housing is non-profit only for a limited period of time, or whose dynamics otherwise are similar to those of profit organizations (e.g. high salaries for executives, speculation, etc.);

7) Direct public ownership, by a branch of local, state, or national government;

8) Private ownership for use by others than the owner, i.e., of rental units;

9) Collective, "social", "socialist", "people's" ownership, a category inherently antithetical to traditional capitalist concepts of ownership, whose closest analogy in Western law, judging from the experience of the German Democratic Republic in trying to reconcile ownership rights in Volkseigene Betriebe (people's own enterprises) with the legal system of the Federal Republic of Germany was the creation of a public trusteeship to take title of such enterprises, converting it essentially into state ownership. The concept was never satisfactorily developed in Eastern European societies either, however; Gorbachov, for instance, spoke of property in socialist ownership as being considered by many as being without any owner at all, and thus, by implication, available for exploitation by anyone so inclined.

Housing "classes", defined by "tenure", i.e. owners as one class and renters as the other class, seems a very clumsy approach to analysis, in this context. Leaving aside the question of whether classes are better defined by production or consumption cleavages, to the extent that consumption cleavages are invoked and housing consumption is made central, that consumption needs to be defined much more carefully than a simple "ownership-rental" duality does. As Alan Murie (1986) says, "The discussion about the interests generated by ownership refers to a set of historically specific circumstances rather than necessary attributes of the tenure".

USE OF THE PROPERTY RIGHTS CONCEPT

Different rights with relation to property, as to different types of property, for different persons, can be worked out; different rights, types of property, and persons, can be mixed and matched. A systematic and imaginative approach to property rights can serve a wide range of public policies very well. The range of alternatives that could be considered for ownership forms should systematically consider variations by:

1) What the present form of "ownership" of the property is—how are the various incidents of ownership, the rights, powers, privileges, and immunities, as to the property, divided up;

2) What kind of property it is—land, housing, in production, etc.;

3). Who it is that now "owns" the property—who has each incident of ownership, paying particular attention to who has the ability to use it, and who has the ability to make decisions affecting its future use; and

4) Who it is that it is. desired to "own" the property—who should be able to exercise each of the incidents of ownership connected with the property, paying particular attention (for housing) to who should be able to occupy it, who should have the right to profit from changes in its value, and who should have the right to make decisions as to its future occupancy.

As an example, and for purposes of discussion only, it might be sensible to differentiate between land and buildings, as different types of property. It might be desirable to give all rights of use to the present occupants of the housing unit within the building, and the land used in connection with it, and for life. The right to dispose of the unit could rest with the muncipality, with the exception of a right to dispose, for life use only, to the immediate family of the current occupant. The right to dispose of the land might belong to the municipality, but subject to the power in the occupant to require alternate residential accommodations. Distinctions might be made by who the owner is, and how large the unit is, with those having exceptionally desirable units as a result of a privileged position having fewer rights of continued occupancy than others. Obligations to maintain and repair might be placed either with a municipality or with a non-profit or resident-controlled entity. Duties to pay the costs of maintenance might be imposed on the occupant and/or the municipality, and might vary with who the occupant is, what type of household, what income, etc. Land not used in connection with housing and suitable for commercial and/or industrial use might be allocated to a trusteeship-type entity, for disposition at market prices in accordance with municipally-exercised privileges to determine permissible uses in accordance with a community plan, and so on.

As a concrete example of how a systematic "mix-and-match" approach might be used to further public goals of urban development, consider the following possibilities:

Central city commercial land might be rented out only, not sold, with title held by the municipality, with provisions regulating use included in the lease-for instance, jobs provided, environmental conditions. Only end users might be permitted to lease land; or, if a speculative builder is allowed to build, the duration and extent of the speculation allowed could be limited. Rights to assign leases could be severely curtailed, and require municipal permission. Financing might be provided by the municipality, and assignments to guarantee repayment if there is borrowing from private sources might be permitted of the right to collect rents. Rental payments to the municipality, perhaps based on a percentage of rents received by the primary tenant or of appraised value, could take the place of real estate taxes.

Single-family residential uses could permit life-long use secured to the occupant, with a payment based on some combination of value and income; thus for an established minimum quality of housing, no one might be required to pay more than 20 per cent of income, with payments going up as quality, space, and/or income rise, or family size goes down. Personal preferences could be expressed by permitting "bids" for occupancy based on payment of varying percentages of income. Assignment, by gift or inheritance, could be a guaranteed right of the occupant, but only to family members. Other assignment, i.e. sale to a third party, could be permitted, so as to recapture any investments in purchase or improvements, but without profit, and with priority to buyers certified from a priority list publicly established, based on need.

Multi-family housing could be held primarily by cooperatives, mutual housing associations, or community land trusts, forms in which collective "ownership" would be exercised by the democratic collectivity of those living in a building or buildings. Within that framework, rights and duties similar to those of single-family housing occupants could be provided. Large new residential developments could be transferred to democratic assemblies of their residents, including control over any commercial facilities or public space located within it. Property rights could be a way of guaranteeing neighbourhood self-government. The over-riding concerns of public policy, such as prohibitions against racial or ethnic discrimination, or maintenance of environmental standards, could be provided by law, as could equitable payment for supra-neighbourhood services among neighbourhoods.

These suggestions are only intended to be examples of what might be done through a flexible use of property rights; they are not detailed prescriptions recommended for immediate implementation anywhere. They should simply indicate the range of the possibilities. Other variations on property rights could also be imagined. Again, as examples, one could imagine:

1) Different permissible legal forms of private contracts for ownership and use of property;

2) Mechanisms for public (generally judicial) enforcement to different degrees or in different ways of private, personal, and public rights;

3) Taxation of various forms of property, and taxation of various forms of interest in (ownership of) property, varying by owner and use;

4) Protections of (and limitations on) rights of personal use of property, including regulation of eviction;

5) Different subsidies for different forms of uses;

6) Provisions for governmental, generally local, control of land uses in urban areas, including planning and zoning mechanisms;

7) Environmental regulations;

8) Provisions for taking by eminent domain, with procedures, payment, and permissible purposes varying by type of property and type of owner and use;

9) Provision for public decision-making regarding changes in any of the above.

Again, these are simply illustrative possibilities. Property rights, imaginatively defined and implemented, could thus provide an effective and flexible means of achieving a wide range of public policy goals. Accepting a conventional and restricted view of property rights, as being simply permitting unlimited private possession of all of the bundle of rights that "ownership" often is taken to mean, is throwing away a major tool for the governance of society according to the goals and desires of its members.

REFERENCES

Hohfeld, Wesley Newecomb. 1966. Fundamental Legal Conceptions as Applied in Judical Reasoning. New Haven, Yale University Press (first published 1916). 4. Restatement of the Law of Property, 1936. Adopted and promulgated by the American Law Institute. St. Paul, American Law Institute Publishers, May.

Marcuse, Peter. 1972. *The legal attributes of home ownership.* Washington, D.C.: The Urban Institute, April, Working Paper #209-1-1.

Murie, Alan. 1986. Social differentiation in urban areas: housing of occupational class at work?" in: *Tijdschrift voor Econ. en Soc. Geografie* 77(5): 345–357.

Quoted in Dean, Home Ownership: Is it Sound?, p. 3, and de Neufville and Barton, p. 5.

Simmie, James. 1991. Housing and inequality under State Socialism: an analysis of Yugoslavia. *Housing Studies*, July 6(3): 173.

Turner, J. W. Cecil. 1941. Some reflections on ownership in English law. *XIX Canadian Bar Review*, May.

The Future of Mega-cities: Planning Implication for a More Sustainable Development

Salah El-Shakhs

INTRODUCTION

It has become increasingly clear that one of the major consequences of the processes of development, modernization, and the integration of spatial, economic, and political systems has been an inevitable tendency towards increasing structural imbalances within settlement systems during the early stages of development (Friedmann 1973; Mera 1978; El-Shakhs 1972–1982). Among such imbalances are development disparities and inequities:

a) between rural and urban areas,

b) among cities within urban systems, and

c) between regions within the same country.

Thus the process of spatial polarization of development and the relative overconcentration of population, economic activities, and political power in one or a few core regions—indeed in one or a few primate cities—during the early stages of development became an important issue of public policy and a focus of explicit development strategies (Richardson 1977, Renaud 1981). Most developing countries perceived the spatial distribution of their population, and the resulting primate city patterns, as unacceptable and many governments have attempted to change such patterns through indirect national policies or explicit spatial development strategies. Such interest resulted from two major concerns: (1) the potential impact of unbalanced growth on the development and stability of the total system, and (2) the implications of the unprecedented growth of mega-cities for their own functional performance, manageability, planning, and sustainable development.

It is not surprising that mega-cities frequently receive a disproportionate share of government attention and planning activities. It is not clear, however, that such planning activities take full account of the uncertainties and dynamics of the long-range process of concentration/deconcentration within urban settlement systems. This paper is intended to focus attention on some aspects of this process and their general implications for the long-range planning of mega-cities, with a view towards creating more sustainable systems.

MEGA-CITY GROWTH PATTERNS

The thought that the population in the Third World's mega-cities could grow, given current projections (Table 1), to well over twenty million (Sao Paulo), or in excess of twenty-five million (Mexico City) became a nightmare for both policy makers and planners. The world's large cities (those with one million population and over) as a group are currently expected to increase their share of the urban population from 36 per cent in 1980 to 43 per cent by the year 2000. In the Less Developed Countries (LDCs) , their shares are 33 per cent and 45 per cent respectively. In terms of absolute numbers, the large cities of the LDCs are expected to house a population, by the year 2000, which is roughly equivalent to these countries' total 1980 urban population (0.96 compared to 1.01 billion), and more than the 1980 combined total urban population of the More Developed Countries (MDCs) (0.80 billion). Among this group, mega-cities (those with 7 million or more population) are expected to show the greatest growth by the year 2000 (218 per cent increase compared to 174 per cent for large cities as a whole) (United Nations 1993).

Whether such projections will in fact materialize is subject to question. The fact remains, however, that mega-cities in the LDCs are likely to grow rapidly in the foreseeable future. It is equally clear that the pressures, demands, and challenges facing urban governments and planners, particularly in mega-cities, and their capacity to respond to them are largely determined by national and international forces beyond their scope or influence.

Recognizing such unique relationships, many national governments directly took charge of the planning and management of mega-cities. Their efforts focussed primarily on counter-primacy measures aimed at restricting or slowing down the growth of primate cities. These range from "closed city" programmes and direct controls of population movement to redistribution strategies aimed at changing inter-regional development patterns. The success of such attempts during the early stages of development have at best been very limited, and at worst produced results opposite to those intended particularly in market and mixed economies (Findley 1977, Stöhr and Tödtling 1978, Renaud 1981). The reasons for such disappointing experiences seem to lie in the fact that they went against the grain of

Table 1: The World's Thirty Mega-cities by Rank in the Year 2010: Their Growth and Share of National Urban Populations

Rank	Mega-cities by rank in the year 2000	1990 Population (million)	per cent to National urban population	2010 Population (million)	per cent to National urban population	Average annual growth rate 1995–2000
1	Tokyo	25.0	26.24	28.9	27.14	0.82
2	Sao Paulo	18.1	16.16	25.0	15.08	1.77
3	Bombay	12.2	5.66	24.4	6.07	3.68
4	Shanghai	13.4	4.45	21.7	3.58	2.76
5	Lagos	7.7	20.29	21.1	20.91	5.41
6	Mexico City	15.1	24.6	18.0	18.64	0.80
7	Beijing	10.9	3.60	18.0	2.97	2.89
8	Dhaka	6.6	35.2	17.6	32.65	5.30
9	New York	16.1	8.54	17.2	7.23	0.39
10	Jakarta	9.2	17.35	17.2	15.77	3.49
11	Karachi	7.9	21.01	17.0	18.94	3.94
12	Metro Manila	8.9	33.32	16.1	32.24	3.25
13	Tianjin	9.2	3.06	15.7	2.59	3.04
14	Calcutta	10.7	4.97	15.7	3.91	1.65
15	Delhi	8.2	3.78	15.6	3.88	3.36
16	Los Angeles	11.5	6.09	13.9	5.84	1.16
17	Seoul	11.0	35.09	13.8	32.41	0.92
18	Buenos Aires	11.4	41.14	13.7	37.57	1.02
19	Cairo	8.6	37.48	13.4	33.38	2.17
20	Rio de Janeiro	10.9	9.76	13.3	8.05	0.95
22	Tehran	6.7	20.09	11.9	16.37	2.93
21	Bangkok	7.1	58.34	12.7	52.10	3.06
23	Istanbul	6.5	19.07	11.8	18.14	3.53
24	Osaka	10.5	11.0	10.6	9.95	0.00
25	Moscow	9.0	—	10.4	—	0.69
26	Lima	6.5	43.05	10.1	41.26	2.43
27	Paris	9.3	22.65	9.6	20.87	0.15
28	Hyderabad	4.1	1.91	9.4	2.34	4.48
29	Lahore	4.2	11.05	8.8	9.83	3.86
30	Madras	5.3	2.44	8.4	2.08	2.13

Source: United Nations. 1993. World Urbanization Prospects: The 1992 Revision; Estimates and Projections of Urban and Rural Populations and of Urban Agglomerations. New York: United Nations.

powerful national polarization processes and were subverted by the impacts of counter-policies and national integration efforts (El-Shakhs 1982).

Recent evidence, however, indicates that while most LDCs still have to cope with the urban explosion, particularly in their super-cities, many developed countries are already witnessing either relative or absolute decline in the population of their core regions (Vining and Kontuly 1978).

Such trends are no longer unique to the United States. The process of deconcentration within urban systems has been observed in Germany, Italy, Japan, and even in France, which has long been held as an example of unrelenting concentration. In fact, the Paris metropolitan area is estimated to have lost over 300,000 people between 1968 and 1975 (OCED 1979). In the metropolitan areas, central cities had experienced such trends of reversal or decline much earlier and to a greater degree. Philadelphia, Chicago, Detroit, Paris, and London lost population in the 1960s, and New York, Los Angeles and Tokyo in the 1970s.

POLARIZATION REVERSAL AND URBAN SYSTEMS

The process of "polarization reversal" (Richardson 1980) of more developed countries is beginning to occur in an increasing number both in the West and the East. While we do not yet fully understand the forces and timing of such a process, it does seem to be contingent on achieving a higher level of development and a more equitable distribution of budgetary, decision making, and political power. Indeed decentralization strategies have more success where local governments are strong (Stöhr and Tödtling 1978). Furthermore spatial deconcentration of urban population is either emerging or has already occurred in countries both with (Sweden, France, Poland) and without (United States, Japan, Republic of Korea) strong urban decentralization policies (Vining and Kontuly 1978).

Such trends suggest that the urban future is one of long range convergence in patterns. It implies that processes and problems of concentration inter-regionally (centred on core regions) and intra-regionally (focussed on central cities) would eventually give way to the reverse processes and problems of deconcentration and dispersion respectively. Regions within national spatial systems will tend to follow a similar pattern in which the most developed region (core) is likely to be the first to undergo a process of intra-regional deconcentration, followed by other regions as they reach appropriate concentration and development thresholds. In fact deconcentration within the core region (mega-city region) would likely precede and signal the onset of polarization reversal.

The process of polarization is predicated on continued economic growth and developments in transportation and technology, innovation diffusion, shifts in locational preferences and similar reversal pattern in the rates of national population growth. The ultimate result is the "total urbanization" of spatial systems in the form of vast interdependent "urban fields" or urban regions.

Countries undergoing the process of urban concentration are faced with the task of promoting national economic growth and full utilization of their resources, and at the same time, promoting regional equity and avoiding or reducing excessive development disparities and concentration. While these two objectives may not necessarily be in conflict, particularly in a long-range perspective (Stöhr, 1975), they require coordinated economic and spatial development policies at both the regional and national levels. Major spatial shifts in population and economic activities (international, inter-regional and inter-urban), whether they tend towards concentration or deconcentration, are likely to continue indefinitely to shape and reshape our urban system. An effective response thus requires a better understanding of the long-range patterns of change, the capacity to influence them through public policy, and a continuous national effort to equalize the levels and burdens of social welfare and of urban services and amenities.

The challenges to such policy and planning efforts lie in their ability to:

1) anticipate future spatial structures and, in the process of attempting to solve current problems, lay down the basis (in terms of both physical and institutional infrastructure) for their eventual emergence,

2) hasten the process of spatial transition and moderate the rates and impacts of extreme spatial shifts (first of concentration and later of deconcentration),

3) provide flexible and timely responses to the emergence of signs of change and avoid reinforcing the status-quo and current trends.

IMPLICATIONS FOR THE GROWTH OF MEGA-CITIES

Obviously the factors influencing the future of mega-cities and their regions will largely be determined by the development of their national urban systems and their places within the international hierarchy of "World Cities" (Friedman and Wolff, 1982). However, the nature of the impacts of the processes of polarization reversal (national or international) on the mega city and its region are in large part, a function of their current long-range planning and the resulting spatial and political organization. The preceding analysis raises several relevant issues and questions in this respect. Will current population projections for mega-cities turn out to be accurate predictions? It is already clear that the corner on the population explosion has turned much faster than anyone predicted (Abu-Lughod, 1982). Furthermore, projections not withstanding, several mega-cities (metro areas) already began to slow down, stabilize or lose population (New York, Paris, Calcutta). Given polarization reversal trends, several other mega-cities in the middle income countries may soon follow suit.

There is always a dangerous tendency to overbuild the centres of mega-cities during periods of concentration and rapid growth. The resulting rigidities in terms of capital plant, industrial infrastructure, production technologies, work patterns, and property and political interests may inhibit their responsiveness and ability to adapt to future economic shifts and processes of deconcentration. The incidence of physical and technological obsolescence would severely limit their competitiveness and capacity for renewal of their capital plant and employment base (Sternlieb and Hughes 1978).

Overbuilding mega-cities, within their currently defined boundaries, is a short-range response to the systematic overload on their infrastructure and supply of productive employment during periods of concentration. Such pressures however, often result in the expansion of the city's influence and functions over a much wider region, including other cities and rural settlements and a frequently uncontrolled and unplanned periphery. This requires a redefinition of what future mega-cities imply. Administrative and political boundaries and definitions effectively lose their meaning both under conditions of concentration and deconcentration. What is required is to establish meaningful and workable mechanisms for region-wide planning and administrative coordination and control of development. Such mechanisms and institutions should be flexible enough so that their authority and its boundary could be expanded to fit those of the phenomena.

While spatial polarization may be inevitable within the national urban system, this need not be the case within the core region. Appropriate long-range plans should anticipate and organize the spatial and economic differentiation of the core region's expansion. Unlike the conventional wisdom of attempting to forcibly limit core region's growth and physical expansion, this would call for recognizing and directing such expansion in ways which suit their particular spatial context. Such plans should provide an alternative to the excessive physical expansion of the large central city itself, to dispersed patterns which are expensive to serve and wasteful of energy, and to uncontrolled expansion into valuable farm land, ecologically sensitive areas or natural features worthy of preservation for better use.

LONG RANGE PLANNING IMPLICATIONS

Generally speaking, a more efficient spatial organization of mega-cities can be achieved through a set of consistent spatial planning policies whose aim is to articulate and redefine their internal structure in terms of an integrated hierarchy of interdependent activity centres and population settlements. Such policies include:

1) containing the horizontal expansion of central cities;
2) articulating the internal structure of central cities into identifiable communities around viable business subcentres;
3) restructuring peripheral developments into identifiable communities around activity subcentres and concentrated development nodes;

4) promoting and guiding the inevitable development of urban regions along corridors of intense interaction with other major cities;

5) promoting area-wide differentiation of functions and specialization of settlements and activity centres within the mega-city subsystem, whose boundaries are expanded to include those areas necessary for a balanced interdependent self-reliant development;

6) expansion and reorganization of administrative and planning functions to provide area-wide coordination, yet strengthen local autonomy, initiative, and identity both within and outside the central city;

7) containing the horizontal expansion of central cities.

One inevitable short-sighted response to the rapid growth of mega-cities has been the continuous incremental vertical and horizontal expansion of the main built-up area. Whether planned or not, such contiguous development is convenient and relatively more accessible to existing, utility and service systems, which are frequently over-extended. They are also more readily identifiable with living in the large city, compared to more distant areas. Such horizontal expansion often falls outside urban administrative jurisdictions and their planning and building controls and regulations. The consequences of such growth patterns are many: (1) unplanned rigid and long-lasting built environments with little or no limits or safeguards dictated by the natural environment, sustainability, or human scale; (2) extreme overloads on utility and transportation systems with frequent breakages which threaten the health and safety of the population; (3) decreasing accessibility to jobs, amenities and open space; and (4) increased levels of congestion and concentrations of environmental pollution among others. An alternative development pattern should attempt to spatially separate new urban expansions from the built-up area of the central city and reduce dependence on its utilities and service systems. They should, however, be made easily accessible to, and identifiable with, the central city if they are to become viable growth alternatives.

Such a multi-nucleated development pattern requires a two-pronged strategy of increasing the supply of accessible urban land in planned locations, on the one hand, and tightening land development and preservation controls on the other. The first requires transport expansion of convenient, and inexpensive and energy-conserving mass transit links to outlying development centres. Such links should be designed to leapfrog intermediate areas where development is to be discouraged or halted, to provide easy direct access to the designated areas. Land development and control concepts like regional zoning, designation of priority areas for development, greenbelts, land banking on the outskirts of central cities, acquisition of development rights, or outright public acquisition of existing and/or potential urban land, provide examples of the many tools available to planners for curtailing the sprawling horizontal expansion of central cities.

1) Articulating the Internal Structure of Central Cities

The sense of community within central cities themselves is often compromised or weakened by development pressures. The lack of identifiable boundaries or areas of transition, the loss of open and civic space, the general tendency towards more central control of local services, and the concentration of business and cultural activities and amenities in the city centre are all determined to local identity and pride. The usually rich heritage of diverse communities tends to disappear. Needless burdens are added to the transportation systems as a result of the increased dependence on the city centre. Frequently transportation projects respond to and reinforce such dependencies.

Planners should attempt to identify established communities and community centres and strengthen them through land use, transportation, and redevelopment plans. Decentralization of business, cultural, and governmental activities into secondary business subcentres can help reduce the extreme centrality and create a more balanced poly-nucleated pattern of viable communities. The boundaries of communities can be sharpened, for instance, by redevelopment of the often marginal uses at the edges (no man's land) into buffer zones and large passive open spaces, and right of ways of major high speed roads and limited access highways.

Such physical definition and articulation of a system or a hierarchy of communities and neighbourhoods should go hand in hand with a move towards governmental decentralization, specialization and greater local administration, initiative, and self-reliance.

2) Restructuring Peripheral Developments

Long range regional plans should anticipate and prepare for the eventual deconcentration or "counter-urbanization" within the mega-city region. Autonomous deconcentration and suburbanization processes are occurring in large metropolitan regions of most countries, both developed and less developed. Such unplanned, unregulated dispersal can be costly in terms of development and operational requirements, as well as in its indiscriminate use of valuable land resources.

It is estimated that roughly as much built environment as now exists will have to be constructed over the next few decades. Much of this is expected to take place in the LDCs, and more specifically in their exploding urban centres, particularly mega-cities. Thus the spatial distribution of urban population and activities within the settlement sub-systems of mega-city regions in LDCs becomes a crucial developmental and ecological issue.

Proper planning of such subsystems, especially during stages of rapid mega-city growth, would help spark a step-wise process of polarization reversal, and reduce growth pressures on the central city.

Such an approach would attempt to create an integrated regional settlement system through the promotion of a hierarchy of regional intermediate and small urban centres. The concept of new towns and expanded towns has proved more successful when they are developed as integral parts of mega-city subsystems. Additionally, the use of priority development zones and of industrial estates, to focus and synchronize development efforts, within large regions provides additional valuable experience in this context.

Spontaneous peripheral settlements and squatters should be recognized and stabilized as elements of any peripheral restructuring. Such communities which already exist should be integrated as far as possible into the envisioned settlement pattern and activity subcentres. Their inclusion in the plans and development strategies of the peripheral areas would in itself help stabilize as well as control such settlements. In the process, spatial relocations and adjustments may be inevitable but should be kept to a minimum in order to reduce potential social and economic costs.

3) Promoting Urban Growth along Corridors of Intense Interaction

In planning the development of mega-city regions particular attention should be given to the growth potential along intense transportation corridors linking them to other major cities, both within the national urban settlement system and between countries. A close look at the growth patterns of large cities would show that such a potential may have already generated major growth areas and created significant urbanization economies extending considerable distances out of such cities and at transport centres in between.

Experience indicates that the development of such urban regions is inevitable and is in fact under way in many LDCs. Locations along major corridors of interaction provide attractive alternatives for both basic and service industries as well as for migrants, and thus constitute rational choices for any decentralization moves out of the mega-city. They also enhance the potential for the development of intermediate cities and regional centres within the national settlement system.

4) Differentiation of Functions and Specialization of Settlements

The high degree of unity and interdependence and self-reliance within the mega-city subsystems allows for a significant degree of diversity and specialization among its constituent settlements. While a central-place type hierarchy of service functions is desirable or necessary, the same does not hold true for major economic, cultural, business, and governmental activities.

In fact, such groups tend to individually agglomerate within specific locations in and around mega-cities. This trend of spatial differentiation of major functions and specialization of settlement should become an important criterion in the planning for deconcentration of mega-cities.

Such an approach would help minimize the potential adverse impacts of deconcentration on the central city and allow for its orderly transformation through incremental conversion, renovation, and adaptive reuse programmes. It would help to redefine the functions of the main centre and of secondary centres, provide room for expansion and often badly-needed open space within the main centre, separate major non-compatible uses, and deconcentrate congestion and environmental pollution. Ports, manufacturing, warehousing, sports, resorts and recreation, wholesale animal and vegetable markets, universities and research centres, and national government offices provide a few examples of potential specialized settlement functions.

5) Promoting Local Autonomy and Initiative within Area-wide Coordination

In both growing and declining core regions, administrative and political boundaries have lost their meaning. In either case, a large and growing proportion of the mega-city region's population lives outside the city boundary. Yet this population frequently imposes major burdens on the city's economy and service systems without contributing to its resources or being influenced by its management. The processes of concentration and deconcentration within the super-city region, and their consequent pressures and conflicts, are not only inequitable and difficult to manage but could also be extremely wasteful and inefficient in the absence of planning and coordination at the regional level.

The first step, therefore, in facing the challenge of mega-city growth is to establish meaningful and workable mechanisms for region-wide planning and coordination and control of development. They should articulate a division of authority and responsibility that maximizes local participation while preserving integration at a regional scale (Bauhaus Seminar, 1991). Such mechanisms and institutions should be flexible enough so that their authority and its boundary could be changed to fit those of the phenomena. They should be designed to strengthen local identity and initiative within an expanded integrative framework of regional administration. Both autonomous and planned deconcentration within the mega-city region create higher levels of inter-dependency and intra-regional mobility. This tends to shift the focus of effective policies from the city or metropolitan level to both higher (regional) and lower (local) levels of government. The effective division of functions and authority between local and regional levels calls for more, rather than less, administrative coordination and government responsibility. Yet the local initiative and control at the small scale of towns and districts, in a spatially and administratively decentralized settlement system, would enhance self-reliance and sustainability for many urban functions. This would reduce the burden on the mega-city government and thus enable it to cope with the increasingly complex systems of interaction and regional functions.

CONCLUSIONS

This poly-nucleated spatial organization combined with a multi-level administrative approach provides a flexible strategy adaptable to future uncertainties. It would anticipate and minimize the adverse impacts of the likely long range trends of deconcentration. On the other hand, it would help organize urban regions along manageable and humane dimensions, were they destined to continue their unabated growth for long periods in the future. Such a spatial pattern would, at the same time, promote a more sustainable development process. It would help preserve human scale and promote a sense of identity, local initiative and control, self-reliance and access to nature. The efficient use of urban land and of energy resources through an optimum distribution of population within a balanced system of settlements would go a long way towards preserving natural capital.

REFERENCES

Abu-Lughod, Janet. 1982. The urban future: a necessary nightmare. In: *Tradition and Modernity*, J. Lutz and S. El-Shakhs (eds.). Washington, D.C.: University Press of America.

Bauhaus Seminar. 1991. '*Sustainable Development and the Future of Cities*. Bauhaus Dessau, Germany (September 7–14).

Dogan, M. and J.D. Kasarda (eds.). 1988. *The Metropolis Era*, Vol. 1: *A World of Giant Cities*. Beverly Hills, CA: Sage Publications.

El-Shakhs, S. 1972a. The urban crisis in international perspective: the challenge and the response. *American Behavioral Scientist* 15:4.

El-Shakhs, S. 1972b. Development, primacy and systems of cities. *The Journal of Developing Areas* 17:1 (October).

El-Shakhs, S. 1982. 'Regional development and national integration: the Third World. In: *Urban Policy under Capitalism*, Fainstein and Fainstein (eds.), Urban Affairs Annual Reviews, 22.

Findley, S. 1977. *Planning for International Migration: A Review of Issues and Policies in Developing Countries*. Washington, D.C.: Government Printing Office.

Friedmann, J. 1973. *A theory of polarized development*, in: *Urbanization, Planning and National Development*. Beverly Hills: Sage Publications.

Friedmann, J. and G. Wolff. 1982. Future of the world city, Paper presented at the Conference on Urbanization and National Development, East-West Centre, Honolulu (January).

Ghosh, Santosh. 1978. Regiopolis 2000: a study of intermediate urbanization in India. *Ekistics* 267: 82–87.

Hauser, Philip. 1982. *Population and the Urban Future*. Albany: SUNY Press.

Kasarda, J.D. and Dennis A. Rondinelli. 1990. Mega-cities, the environment, and private enterprise: towards ecologically sustainable urbanization. *Environmental Impact Assessment Review*, 10: 393–404.

Linn, J.F. 1979. *Policies for Efficient and Equitable Growth of Cities in Developing Countries.* Washington, D.C.: World Bank, SWP #342.

Mera, K. 1978. Population concentration and regional income disparities: a comparative analysis of Japan and Korea. Pages 155–75 in: *Human Settlement Systems*, N. Hansen (ed.) Cambridge, Mass.: Ballinger.

OECD. 1979. Population shifts and urban patterns. Unpublished report, Paris: Organization for Economic Cooperation and Development.

Park, S.W. 1979. City size distribution in Korea. Unpublished paper, Rutgers University Department of Urban Planning.

Perlman, Janice. 1989. *Mega-Cities Innovations in Urban Poverty and Environment: Towards Socially Just and Ecologically Sustainable Cities of the 21st Century.* Mega-Cities Project, New York University (November).

Perlman, Janice. 1990. A dual strategy for deliberate social change in cities. *Cities* 7:1 (February) pp. 3–16.

Rees, William E. and M. Roseland. 1991. Sustainable communities: planning for the 21st century. *Plan Canada* 313 (May), pp. 15–25 (also in this volume).

Renaud, B. 1981. *National Urbanization Policy in Developing Countries.* New York: Oxford University Press.

Richardson, H. 1977. *'City Size and National Spatial Strategies in Developing Countries.* Washington, D.C.: World Bank SWP #252.

Richardson, H. 1980. Polarization reversal in developing countries. The Regional Science Association Papers, 45.

Sternlieb, G. and J. Hughes (eds.). 1978. *Revitalizing the Northeast.* New Brunswick, N.J.: CUPR.

Stöhr, W. 1975. *Regional Development Experience and Prospects in Latin America.* The Hague: Mouton.

Stöhr, W. and F. Tödtling, 1978. An evaluation of regional experiences in market and mixed economies. Papes 85–119 in: *Human Settlement Systems*, N. Hansen (ed.). Cambridge, Mass.: Ballinger.

United Nations. 1979. *'Policies on human settlement in Latin America. Latin American Conference on Human Settlements.*, Mexico City (November).

United Nations. 1980. *Patterns of Urban and Rural Population Growth.* New York: United Nations.

United Nations. 1980. *Urban. Rural and City Population, 1950–2000 as Assessed in 1978.* New York: United Nations.

United Nations 1982. *World Population Trends and Policies: 1981 Monitoring Report*, Vol. 1: *Population Trends*, New York: United Nations.

United Nations. 1986–1991. *Population Growth and Policies in Mega-cities*, Series includes (Calcutta, Manila, Bombay, Dhaka, Bangladesh, Madras, Karachi, Jakarta, Cairo and Mexico City), New York, United Nations Population Division.

United Nations. 1993. *World Urbanization Prospects: The 1992 Revision; Estimates and Projections of Urban and Rural Agglomerations.* New York: United Nations.

Vining, D.R. and T. Kontuly. 1978. Population dispersal from major metropolitan regions: an international comparison. *International Regional Science Review* 3:49–73.

Walsh, A.H. 1969. *The Urban Challenge to Government: An International Comparison of Thirteen Cities.* New York: Praeger Publishers.

Part II
Regional Perspectives

The New Politics of Environmental Governance Environmental Sustainability and Life in the City: A Challenge for the Design Professions

Charles Middleton

INTRODUCTION

The rapidly escalating impact of human activity on the global environment is a critical issue for the foreseeable future. Population growth in less-advantaged countries is an obvious problem and an easy target. However, the lure of cities and their growth is every bit as problematic. They contribute massively to the growing influence of humanity on the biosphere. Consumer-oriented lifestyles of high income nations such as Canada are based on the extensive use of non-renewable resources, and are a primary source of environmental problems with global consequences. Car-oriented cities of the west, and the energy technologies that they rely on, result in heavy resource-consumption. But they are also emulated by cities in other countries, often with reliance on western technology, whereby compounding existing problems.

In order to attain sustainable development as a basis for the future of cities in both the more- and less-advantaged countries, it seems clear that conventional models for the built environment must be challenged by those who participate in design. Architects, planners and engineers, in new forms of collaboration, are in a position to undertake the development of innovative planning for cities that use fewer resources without reducing standards of living. The challenge is to seek alternatives that both improve the environment and the quality of life. Recent developments suggest that this is becoming increasingly possible, but much more needs to be done.

THE HUMAN ENVIRONMENT

Despite the development of technologies to control our environment, we human beings are still dependent on the same environmental conditions that support both ourselves and all other animal species on the planet. These include such life-sustaining requisites as gravity, the warmth and energy of the sun, atmospheric protection from cosmic radiation, air, water and food, to name but a few. These, along with innumerable other components, represent an integrated and balanced system on which we all depend. Through technology, human beings have developed the power to influence their environmental conditions, even breaking the bonds to the planet by space travel, or, here on Earth, by building cities. Both represent artificially developed environments, the former based on cutting-edge technology at an extremely small scale, the latter on established technology at a massive scale. They allow us to design our immediate surroundings. But this freedom is not without its price—that of altering the wider environment to some degree. If we wish to maintain its quality for our offspring, wisdom suggests that we may allow tampering to a limited extent—only to the point where our activities and life-styles do not threaten the integrity of the ecoystem and, by extension, the survival of all species, including ourselves.

Our technologies allow us to amass information, and to monitor change in the eco-system to an unprecedented degree. The results increasingly indicate that we humans are collectively overstepping the limits of the sustainability of the system, global warming and depletion of the ozone-layer being but two examples. It then seems imperative to develop ways to preserve the environment, and thereby safeguard the future of life as we know it.

Who is responsible? Perhaps we all are, but it is clear that average, cumulative effects mask inequalities in consumption and pollution. Not all are equally to blame. Those with the greatest responsibility must surely be those who have the greatest access to resources, who have the greatest control, and who coincidentally often generate much of the problem. This in turn raises issues for those who steer events, either by deliberately permitting market forces to prevail, or by other, more formal, means of planning and design.

1) Population Growth and Urbanization

The growth of population in less-advantaged countries is frequently targeted as the major problem affecting the impact of humanity on the environment. There is no question that the growth of the human population continues apace. But population is not the only parameter relating to human activity that continues to grow. There are even more direct, and escalating, impacts on sustainability. The last fifty years have seen pivotal change. This brief period is infinitesimal in historical terms, and has to be measured in relation to 150,000 years since the evolution of the *homo sapiens*. But it covers growth of explosive proportions in resource extraction and use. It is also sufficiently long to mould the understandings and expectations of three generations whose experience is of constantly increasing consumerism.

The growth of populations seems to be an ever-increasing problem for the ecosystem. Maximum growth rates are found in the less-advantaged countries, but are certainly not confined to them. They also continue in wealthy nations, even with low rates of natural population growth. World Bank indicators show annual urban growth rates in many low-income countries to be in the range of between five and ten per cent, while there is a much greater increase in large cities, with population of over 500,000. But even in the case of Canada, with a comparatively low overall population growth rate, the number of cities with over 500,000 population rose from 2 to 9, from 1960 to 1980, and this growth was from 31 to 62 per cent of the country's total (World Bank 1990, p.238).

The direct consequences of urbanization include increasing consumption of non-renewable resources used as fuels, or processed into building materials or consumer goods. In addition, the expansion of cities results in indirect pressures on their rural hinterlands—agricultural and forested regions, and in concentrated production of food and cash-crops, monocultures, and the use of fertilizers from petrochemical industries. This urban-centred cycle also generates wastes and pollution that further affect rural areas.

If anything has been learned from the comparatively recent interest in the environment, it is perhaps that all things are related and interdependent. No facet of development, or of the growing acceptance of urban lifestyles, can be separated from impacts on other components of the ecosystem. Cities, with their buildings and infrastructures, can no longer be designed in isolation. They generate many related problems in hinterlands that sustain them.

2) Technology

The advance of technology has made possible escalating urban growth. But choices as to which technologies are developed, and which are bypassed, are affected by what the United States president Ronald Reagan called "magic of the marketplace", with all its inadequacies and biases. Amongst the technologies that have thrived in the marketplace have been those of communications and transport. Together they have become influential in the growth of the built environment as we know it.

The currently accepted technologies of transport by road, rail, air and sea, allow the easy transportation of people and goods anywhere in the world, over long or short distances. Fossil-fuel products, with high energy-density and comparative ease of handling, are extremely convenient. Extensive infrastructures, industries and interests have grown up around their use. The system provides for a comparatively cheap and constant flow of fuel from distant sources to concentrated urban markets. But their convenience and availability encourage solutions in the building of cities that rely on technologies of artificial and energy-dependent heating, cooling and refrigeration for everything from comfort to food preservation and distribution. In addition, manufactured products increasingly employ synthetic materials, such as plastics, that are based on fossil-fuels, contributing to more exploitation of these substances as the never-ending search for new sources of oil shows.

The modern city cannot be divorced from energy consumption, a point recognized by the World Bank which uses this as one of its Indicators of Development.

Media technologies including television, film and radio, and other forms of communication, permit wide dissemination of knowledge. But most reflect an urban bias, familiarizing people, even those who cannot read, with the attractions of city life. Advertising is designed to stimulate expectations and aspirations for new consumer products and is most effective. Increasingly, in low-income nations as in the more affluent, the combined influence of the technologies of transport and communications facilitates rural-urban migration of young people, pushed by dissatisfaction over perceived problems in rural communities, and attracted by the "bright lights" of the cities (Middleton 1980). For many, attractions in the city quickly lose their charm as the realities of unemployment and urban poverty sink in. For the urban consumers, the only means of exchange is money, and everything, including food and shelter, must be paid for in cash. The cashless barter systems of sustainability of the rural areas are not available in cities. But once migrants move away from the country, few return, and they become hostages to the market forces of the city.

3) Consumerism

The growth of cities is paralleled, or perhaps driven, by increasing consumerism. Even language assists the process. People in the industrialized countries of the west seem generally comfortable in accepting the widespread notion that they are "consumers"—rather than with many other roles that they play as human beings. Almost by default, and apparently without much thought, they accept that their primary function in life is to consume, rather than to be providers for families for example, or to sustain or contribute to the social and ecological structures that support them.

A rough indication of the relationship between the growth of population, cities, and of consumer demand for energy can be seen in the following Table. Comparisons in growth for the period from the mid-forties to the mid-eighties are shown here.

Table

Parameter	mid-forties	mid-eighties	growth (per cent)
World population (billions)	under 2.5	over 4.5	200
Urban population (billions)	under 0.7	over 2.0	300
Energy demand (million tonnes of oil equivalent)			
Total, all sources	about 1,500	over 7,500	500
Coal/lignite	about 1,000	over 2,000	200
Oil/natural gas	about 500	over 4,500	900

(Times 1988, pl. 7)

The above Table was derived from a graphic representation and does not provide exact figures, but it is sufficiently useful to indicate the general picture. It clearly shows that the demand for energy has outstripped both the overall population growth, and urban population growth. The demand for oil and gas soared in the forty-year period, and at 900 per cent this is a clear cause for concern. These are resources the consumption of which is directly associated with cities, atmospheric pollution and global warming. City life-styles are not static but are generating further demands for energy. While the growth of urban population was 300 per cent over the forty-year period, the demand for energy grew by 500 per cent.

In relation to sustainability, the problems of consumer-oriented development of the western countries is twofold: (1) It is packaged as being attractive and within reach. The very purpose of advertising is to ensure that this message is clearly conveyed. Costs for individuals, for society, or for the long-term sustainability of the ecosystem are not on the agenda. (2) The affluence of the industrialized urban west has been achieved on the use of products from far-flung sources, whether oil from the Middle East or foodstuffs and other resources from the tropics. The combined populations of these same urban nations represents something in the region of one-fifth of the total world population, while they consume most of the available resources. The question must be asked what could happen when all others consume at the same level? The answer cannot be that they must curtail expectations that are driven by western advertising. One solution is obvious—the technological resources of the west be directed towards alternatives that consume less.

4) Resource Consumption

World Bank figures from 1988 show the following comparisons. They are based on the consumption of oil equivalent on a per capita basis

Country	Energy consumption (in kg)
(High income)	
Canada	9,683
United States	7,655
Sweden	6,617
West Germany	4,421
Singapore	4,464
Japan	3,306
(Low-income)	
China	580
India	211
Tanzania	36

(World Bank, 1990, p. 186)

The enormous difference between the high- and low-income countries is obvious. It can also be seen that the more affluent are the high energy-consumers that represent societies that are industrialized, urbanized and market-oriented. However, as their economies are largely based on non-renewable resources, it is clear that their directions of development are not sustainable over the long term. This raises the question of whether the comforts of western urban life-styles are necessarily founded on unsustainable energy consumption, and are therefore doomed, or whether they can be achieved with less impact. The range of energy consumption from 9,683 to 3,306 kg per capita in the high income countries, an almost threefold difference, suggests that comfort is not directly related to the consumption of energy.

North America's per capita energy consumption is around twice that of its industrialized competitors in Europe and Asia. Canada leads the world, and this rather dubious distinction includes the United States. Even Sweden, with a standard of living as high as, or higher than Canada, with a population concentrated well to the north of Canadian cities, and with a climate as cold, uses almost one-third less energy.

The differences between the less-advantaged and more-affluent countries are even more dramatic. The cases of Tanzania and Canada, with populations of almost equal size, can be used as an illustration. On the basis of World Bank figures, the Tanzanian population continues to grow at well over 3 per cent per annum. In this, it has one of the world's highest population growth rates and is typical of much of East and Central Africa. Canada with a rate of around 1 per cent is more typical of the industrialized countries.

Today Canadians, on an average, continue to be the world's greatest users of energy (Boyle 1990:249). They consume energy resources, per capita of over 250 times that of Tanzanians. Even allowing for some error in the figures, the discrepancies are so great that further questions arise in relation to the sustainability of life-styles: (1) Who, as a whole—the less advantaged people of Tanzania or the affluent of Canada—have the greater responsibility for pressure on the earth's resources. (2) On the basis of the above figures, is it valid to target high population growth of the less-advantaged nations as the primary cause of resource consumption, as often claimed? (3) Can Canadian life-styles, while undeniably comfortable, on any indicator of value, justify energy consumption 250 times greater than that of their Tanzanian counterparts, and if satisfaction could be usefully measured, would the Canadians be 250 times better off? Or, have they simply become accustomed to consumption and waste?

The figures published by such an authoritative source as than the World Bank, are not promising. Comparisons made below, with special reference to Canada as a consuming nation, indicate the connection between the consumption of resources as discussed above, and the consequent large-scale generation of waste and pollution.

5) Pollution

Industrial activity is all too often matched by contamination of the environment with toxic, chemical and nuclear residues, and overloads of less hazardous materials. The consumption of resources has resulted in wastes that are now polluting the globe as far as the Arctic and Antarctic. The combustion of fossil fuels and the production of materials based on them produce another damaging form of pollution particularly related to cities—excess heat. It is an issue that is not calculated in considerations of the normal measures, weight or volume, of waste.

In 1988, the U.S. generated 660 kilograms of garbage per capita, and Canada and the U.S. together produced roughly twice as much garbage per person as Japan or West Germany (Young 1991:44). Canada, however, has less than one per cent of the world population. If the rest of the world were to follow its present example of consumption and waste, the results would be catastrophic. The globe simply could not sustain the consumption, and the production of waste and pollution, by six billion people at the accustomed rates of urban consumers in North America. City form and life-style must be related to the consequences they have on the environment.

6) The Built Environment

The sprawling suburbs and roads that are so much a feature of North American cities, and increasingly of other parts of the world, aided by the subtleties of advertising and technical advice, go hand-in-glove with automobile-oriented transportation systems.

In a radio series on technology, Ursula Franklin made the point that although population growth and the resources needed to sustain it are rationally discussed, no "demograhic data base exists for the world's growing population of machines and devices." She went on to indicate that "although the support structures for the car population are in place, ... birth control for cars and trucks is not an important agenda item in any public discussion" (Franklin 1990).

In this, she touches on a central issue in any search for sustainability in cities, particularly if one reflects on rates of urban growth. The problem is one of mechanization, and the apparent lack of interest in challenging urban forms based on it. This is not to say that some devices, such as computers, cannot make life very much more comfortable and convenient without a high demand on energy. But there are other devices that consume much more energy than is warranted by the benefits they offer. Cars, and the individualized form of transportation they allow, are a prime example. Despite some convenience, for vast numbers of commuters blindly following the bumper of the car in front, they offer little amenity or pleasure. Yet the urban model, so widely advertised and accepted in the West, is based on this technology which cannot be considered sustainable by any standard. The built-environments of the post-industrial West continue to be designed around this out-dated model.

SUSTAINABLE ALTERNATIVES FOR CITIES

If the target is a sustainable future, it is fairly obvious that low-income countries such as Tanzania have something to offer. They are less dependent than the West on non-renewable materials, and are driven to use all resources to the best extent possible. In a post-industrial world, because of the cheap availability of energy, its consumption is of little concern. Big users such as industry are a major problem. But, for the high-income countries, this leaves two other parameters—our particular brand of urban living and laissez-faire market-orientation—as potential problems for sustainability.

The means to change these are available in the form of technology and specialized expertise. A new focus or direction for design effort is needed. If planning really had future sustainability as its primary goal, the results in the shape of the built-environment would be dramatically different. And if other nations followed the lead of the western countries as they have in the past, such new models could offer substantial moves toward more sustainable forms of urban development, to the benefit of all humanity.

Cities, by definition, represent concentrations of people. They have encouraged the development of appropriate specializations and technologies. For many urban dwellers, these result in a growing psychological distance from the natural processes of growth and regeneration upon which they depend. The example of city children whose understanding of the world is that milk comes from the boxes, rather than cows, is all too typical.

Cities, with few exceptions, stimulate a world-view that is based solely on the realities of those built environments, and not of the larger ecological systems within which the cities themselves are sustained. Survival is taken for granted. The capacity to understand change tends to become restricted to the specializations of urban life, and the buying or selling of consumer goods or services.

There is an associated lack of ability to comprehend or appreciate the cumulative impact of day-to-day activities on the ecosystem, and of the dangerous implications of continuous resource consumption on the planet.

A major problem in approaching sustainability in the cities of the future is that available data are not identified or correlated in such a way as to make the linkages between urban life-styles and the rate of consumption of resources on which they are based. This anomaly occurs despite very obvious, if recent, explosive urban growth based on industrial technologies. Many writings exist on the social ills of these cities. However, the assembly of data in such a way as to identify the problems of consumerism in relation to resource depletion is sparse.

This linkage can be seen in the structure of such documents as the World Bank's World Development Report, referred earlier. Of the 32 tables, which include information on population growth and urbanization on the one hand, and on energy, manufacturing and investment on the other, there is no correlation in the items that permit identification of the relationship between cities and the problems of their resource consumption.

For sustainable futures in the cities of the North and South, this information is critical and must be identified. It is essential for those who design, build or maintain cities to employ appropriate alternatives such as reduction, recycling, or re-use of resources on the basis of established data.

It is estimated that a serious commitment to conservation could reduce by 30 to 40 per cent our consumption while maintaining or even raising our standard of living (Morris 1982, p. 141). This appears a reasonable objective, not only for cities in the more affluent countries, but also in the less-advantaged. In both cases, planning and design based on reduction of consumption would result in better use of land and resources than in the present suburbs and superhighways of higher income nations, or the squatter cities or 'bidonvilles' of those with lower income.

The responsibility for change, however, must rest primarily on those consumerist societies where have not only generated majority of the problems, but also possess the technological, educational and economic resources to resolve the problems, particularly as they are also frequently called upon to act as consultants on the urban dilemmas of nations considered less fortunate.

RESPONSIBILITY FOR CHANGE

The above being the case, there is a responsibility on the part of architects, engineers, planners and others who determine the shape of cities in consumer-oriented countries to address, not so much aesthetics or convenience, but the central difficulty of excess consumption designed into the built-environments that they help create. In this, it seems that they will have to look beyond their traditional expertise and towards new collaborations with experts in such areas as ecology. The construction industry is conservative and slow to change, and in the field of safety rightly so. But in times of rapid consumption of irreplaceable resources, the response is not fast enough, and new initiatives are now becoming essential. These must come from professionals who have a broader vision than the perpetuation of the 'status quo'.

Fortunately, the work has already begun. New building materials are being developed that will conserve energy. Alternatives to conventional sources of heating and cooling buildings are coming on stream. Passive solar design is being refined. Research into the materials and methods of the building industry is being pursued. New and more efficient forms of transportation are being developed.

But all this is happening in a piecemeal fashion, while drilling for oil continues. Wars are fought in order to preserve access to inexpensive energy, which is inexpensive neither to the present-day consumer, nor to the environment of future generations. Again, the responsibility for change must lie with those in the professions who see it as their duty to change or who, like academics, may have some independence. There are precedents. In previous times of upheaval and change, alternatives were proposed by planners and architects for new forms of designed environment that would be responsive to changing conditions. Names such as Morris, Le Corbusier, and the Bauhaus come to mind, and the spirit and willingness to look anew at their environments could well be applied to the present.

If sustainability is accepted as the primary goal, there are plenty of resources to address the issue. However, in a period of history that has seen the triumph of capitalist, "laissez-faire" global markets, and the emergence of what is called the "new world order", it is timely to scrutinize the record of a system that has grown rich and powerful on advertising, consumerism and resource use, to see if its achievements fit the sustainable future we seek. At the same time it is also important to see, whether, with the pressuring of democratic socialism we may not be abandoning people, skills and commitments oriented to long-range planning and development that might be more advantageous to the peoples of the planet than the profit maximization for anonymous shareholders. Is this latter goal sufficient to achieve a sustainable future for all? Or are there other models that might combine the advantages of more than one approach, in the interest of a sustainable future. The questions are there for all, but particularly for those involved in design of the built environment.

CONCLUSION

The discussion above has drawn attention to some connections between consumerism in the post-industrial West and resource consumption. Such linkages should hardly be surprising. The concept that resource depletion is caused by population growth is a diversion from the real source of the problem, which lies not with the less-advantaged low-income countries but with the more affluent market-driven economies and their energy-consuming urban life-styles. If, indeed, this is where the problem lies, in high-income countries such as Canada that are rich in material, technological and educational resources, then it is important to look to the institutions of such countries to take a leading role in developing solutions to their urban problems that may in turn work to the benefit of others. By "thinking globally and working locally", as Hazel Henderson (1981) notes, it may be possible to show that lower consumption works while, with care, enhancing amenity.

Initiatives are already being taken to develop alternatives to high energy use in Canadian cities, but much more needs to be done, particularly by those professions that design towns and cities. Broader thinking and new collaborations with specialists in ecology and the environment hold the key to technologies for cities that are both more sustainable and pleasant to live in.

REFERENCES

Boyle, Patricia. 1990. Conservation and alternatives. In: *Energy in Canada*, Southam Energy Group, Don Mills.

Franklin, Ursula. 1990. *The Real World of Technology*. CBC Massey lectures series. Montreal: CBC Enterprises.

Henderson. Hazel. 1981. *The Politics of the Solar Age: Alternatives to Economics*. New York: Anchor Press.

Middleton, C. 1980. Migration and settlement planning in Tanzania. Unpublished research report for York University, Canada, and International Development Research Centre, Ottawa.

Morris, D. 1982. *Self-reliant Cities: Energy and Transformation in Urban America*. San Francisco: Sierra Club Books.

Times, 1988. The Times Atlas of the World. Seventh comprehensive edition. London: Times Books.

World Commission on Environment and Development. 1987. *Our Common Future*. Oxford: Oxford University Press.

Young, J.E. 1991: Reducing waste, saving materials. In: *State of the World, 1991: A Worldwatch Institute Report on Progress Towards a Sustainable Society*, Brown et al. (eds). New York: Norton and Co.

Local Self-Government
for Sustainable Development:
The Philippines

Alex B. Brillantes

INTRODUCTION

Development planning in the Philippines, both for the urban and rural areas, has been very lax over environmental issues. Urban planning has been primarily concerned with economic issues of increasing production and generating jobs rather than conserving the environment. Today however, a new perception of development is emerging. Planners in the Philippines now believe that to support an economic development strategy, although centred around the need to grow, has to be anchored on the principle of sustainable growth. These two meanings of sustainable development—one ecological and the other economic—have by now become conventional wisdom.

There is a third meaning to sustainable development, and that is to understand this concept also in a political sense. Models of political development everywhere have always been assessed in terms of their consequences on the social system's support. That is, where a development strategy leads to a widespread perception of a regime's ability to respond to and be responsible for its constituents, there is a tacit acceptance of its legitimate claim to power and authority. On the other hand, where there is curtailment of civil rights and human freedoms and where impositions are used as justifications to propel forward the development of society, then the strategy is said to be politically unsustainable. These are the major concepts that are currently being considered in the formulation of development strategies in the Philippines.

THE PHILIPPINE ENVIRONMENT: A SCENARIO

The Philippines initially had more than 20 million hectares of virgin forests. At present, less than a million hectares of virgin lands remain due to aggressive logging and encroachment of lowlanders into the uplands. The loss of forest cover has resulted in massive drought, flooding and impairment of vital sources of hydroelectric power, due to siltation. More than half of the land in 21 provinces is seriously eroded. Agricultural pesticides are not only killing pests but are also contaminating the food supply. Of the more than 5,000 varieties of rice, only a few dozens remain in the farmers' fields. Tons of mining wastes and silt are damaging irrigation canals in the lowlands and polluting rivers and marine life. The livelihood of coastal fishermen is also affected. Only less than 13 of the original mangrove forest remain in the coastal waters. Destruction of mangrove resources seriously affects the lifecycle of marine fishes. The welfare of nearly 70 per cent Filipinos, who depend on the products of the fishing industry, is put under stress. Most of the rivers snaking through Metro Manila are biologically dead, victims of extensive waste pollution. The same situation is prevalent in many urbanized areas and growth centres of the country.

Despite the infusion of billions of pesos of tax money into poor communities, more than 60 per cent of Filipinos are malnourished. About 55 billion pesos of the government's budget services the foreign debt of the Philippines. Twenty-eight billion pesos go to the military and only 4 billion to agriculture.

SUSTAINABLE DEVELOPMENT IN THE PHILIPPINES

The Philippine response to environment and development issues is basically embodied in the Philippine Strategy for Sustainable Development (PSSD) which was formally approved by the government in November 1989. Its goal is to achieve economic growth with adequate protection of the country's resources and its diversity, vital ecosystem functions, and over-all environmental quality. Soon after, Executive Order No. 15 formally created the Philippine Council for Sustainable Development (PCSD). This Council was established to provide the mechanism for implementing the principles of sustainable development and ensuring the integrating of these principles in national policies, plans and programmes that will involve all sectors of the Philippine society. The PCSD is unique in that it applies the principles of counterparting and consensus building in its structure. It includes the participation of the civil society as a counterpart to the state through the membership of non-government organizations (NGOs) and people's organizations (POs) in the council. The counterparting of decision-making that approximates consensus is exemplified in the Council. The

PCSD is a potent mechanism that will strengthen civil society and its role in sustainable development thereby giving flesh to the programme of people empowerment through the authentic participation of NGOs and POs. Guidelines were crafted and mechanisms to expand, concretize and operationalize the principles of sustainable development (SD) were created. They were anchored on four Categories of Action:
• Social and Economic Dimensions
• Conservation and Management of Resources for Development
• Strengthening the Role of Major Groups
• Means of Implementation

Social and economic dimensions: The strategy aims at ultimately combating poverty through economic and social reform programmes. Sustainable development, while anchored on improving productivity, has to ensure the equitable distribution of the fruits of production to the people.

Conservation and management of resources for development: The carrying-capacity of the country is currently being seriously looked at. This includes protecting the atmosphere, water and land; combating deforestation and drought; proper management of mountain resources; conservation of biodiversity; protecting and managing the oceans and fresh water; and managing wastes and safer use of toxic chemicals. It also focusses on the use of technologies and farming systems that conserve and rehabilitate land while increasing production.

Strengthening the role of major groups: This is to include women, children and youth, local people, workers and trade/labour unions, people from business and industry, scientists and technologists, farmers and fisherfolk and the local governments. These major groups serve as the cornerstones for the sustainable development of a country.

Means of implementation: These rely heavily on human and technology development through the enhancement of scientific knowledge which can support the prudent management of the environment and development for the daily survival and future of its people. A corollary to this is the need to identify environment and development problems and define solutions to these problems. This can only be done through education, training and the greater of public awareness.

LOCAL SELF-GOVERNANCE: A KEY TO SUSTAINABLE DEVELOPMENT

Quite significant is the passage of the Local Government Code of 1991 which further emphasizes the role of local government in achieving sustainable development as it assigns a number of relevant responsibilities to the LGUs like initiating and promoting environmental management programmes. Specific provisions of the Code are addressed at protecting the environment specifically Section 17 which mandates a municipality to provide basic services and facilities by implementing community-based forestry projects and for a Province to enforce forestry laws limited to community-based forestry projects, pollution control law, small-scale mining law and other laws on the protection of the environment.

Responsibility for sustainable development is likewise implied in the general welfare functions of local chief executives and legislators (sanggunians). Local Chief Executives have been mandated to perform environment and natural resources-related duties and functions. Village executives (Punong Barangays) shall "enforce laws related to pollution-control and protection of the environment" (Sec. 389). Mayors and Governors are called upon to "adopt measures to safeguard and conserve land, mineral, forest, marine and other resources of the municipality, city or province" (Sec. 444). The Local Legislative Bodies (SBs and SPs) have been assigned with the responsibility to "protect the environment and impose appropriate penalties for acts which endanger the environment.." (Secs. 447 and 468).

All these codal provisions provide the foundation for sustainable development because they transform local officials into development managers of their own municipalities. As such, local managers play a major role in all spheres of development—governance, economy, resource management, social services, etc.—which are all components of sustainable development. In the performance of their role as managers, they can be guided by the following principles, possible activities and strategies:

• A systems-oriented and integrated approach in the analysis and solution of development problems;
• A concern for meeting the needs of future generations termed as inter-generational equity;
• A concern for equity of peoples access to natural resources;
• A concern not to exceed the carrying capacity of ecosystems;
• Living on the interest rather than on the capital or stock of natural resources;
• Maintenance or strengthening of vital ecosystem functions in every development activity;
• A concern for resource efficiency;
• Promotion of research on substitutes, recycling, exploration, etc. from revenues derived from the utilization of non-renewable resources;
• A recognition that poverty is both a cause and consequence of environmental degradation;
• Promotion of citizens' participation and decentralization in implementing programmes.

The following have been identified as possible activities and strategies in pursuing the goals and objectives of sustainable development:

- Require Environmental Impact Assessment/Studies for development projects;
- Convene and operationalize the Local Development Council including the required sectoral representatives;
- Hold public assemblies/hearings before deciding on development projects and make sure that the affected groups are adequately represented;
- Create and implement projects such as:
    a) Forest stewardship contracts
    b) Small-holder timber concessions
    c) Contract reforestation
    d) Artificial reef licenses
    e) Community fishing grounds
    f) Mining cooperatives
- Facilitate the implementation of land reform; environment as well as their role in protecting the environment;
- Promote the conduct of studies about local resources—inventory, assessment, utilization, conservation;
- Encourage migration to less populated rural areas and discourage migration to densely populated urban areas by intensifying rural development, particularly through livelihood programmes;
- Actively support national government efforts towards responsible parenthood and family planning;
- Pass and enforce ordinances on the extraction and utilization of natural resources, particularly those considered endangered;
- Accelerate local government efforts in providing potable water and minimizing water pollution;
- Carefully plan and implement an environmentally sound waste disposal system (garbage dump site, sewerage system, etc.);
- Strictly enforce anti-pollution laws (industrial effluents, solid waste disposal from commercial and industrial establishments, exhaust from vehicles, etc.);
- Initiate efforts at cleaning up polluted rivers, creeks and other waterways in coordination with NGOs and POs;
- Formulate a land-use plan and strictly enforce it;
- Discourage the use of chemical fertilizers and initiate products for composting;
- Encourage energy conservation through public information campaigns and provision of incentives for innovations.

It is likewise important to point out that the Code encourages and lays the groundwork for direct and active participation of NGOs and POs in local government structures and processes. In fact, they occupy up to one-fourth of the local development councils and are allocated specific seats in the various local special bodies, ranging from the local health board to the local school board and the peace and order council. As such, they are provided with the opportunity to determine the various sectoral groupings in local legislative bodies and implement/deliver basic programmes and services. Hence, they are major participants in making democratic decisions in the development and maintenance of an ecological balance and in any environment-related efforts. Through collaborative efforts with the LGUs, they can integrate a comprehensive range of development interventions towards sustainable communities and ecosystem. These interventions may include, among other things, community organizing, information campaign programmes, research/situation assessment, environmental surveillance, contract reforestation and monitoring and environmental education. Interestingly, though, the Code does not specifically provide for the constitution of Local Environmental Councils, as it does for other LSBs that are sectorally oriented. However, this should not prevent local governments from creating such local environmental councils.

Through the Local Government Code, the golden opportunity for people empowerment and local accountability is becoming apparent as NGOs have the chance to operationalize their comparative advantage of having the capability to organize people. This advantage can probably be greater in mobilizing the people in cases of recall and petitions for initiative.

Sustainable Development further stresses that the maintenance and management of the ecosystem is a responsibility of all the concerned sectors of society. Therefore, through mandatory consultations and village (barangay) assemblies, the people can articulate their needs and sentiments which could influence the drafting of local development plans and programmes.

Finally, it is noteworthy that Sustainable Development is not limited solely to narrow environmental issues. It implies a new concept of growth—one that provides fairness and opportunity for all the world's people, not just the privileged few, without further destroying the world's finite resources and carrying capacity. As such, SD is designed to be an inherent process in the economic, fiscal, trade, energy, agriculture, industrial and all other policies of development. It also advocates that current consumption cannot be financed for long by incurring debts that others must pay, and that sufficient investment must be made in the education and health of today's population so as not to create a social debt for future generations. On top of all these, is that sustainable development is only possible if the results of development are equitably shared by the people. This, therefore, vastly expands the potential role of local governments as far as the general concern of SD is concerned.

CONCLUSION

Responding to the challenge for sustainable development in a developing country like the Philippines is not an easy task. This becomes more difficult in an environment where the economic and social disparity between the affluent and the underprivileged is remarkable. However, with the passage of the Local Government Code of 1991, the path of sustainable development has already been constructed. The Code has ensured not only economic and social sustainability but more importantly political sustainability as well. This is considered a major strategy to respond to the global battlecry for sustainable development. There remains, however, the continuing challenge to build on the hard-earned gains made during its first three years of implementation and sustain, if not accelerate, the speed to economic and social progress within the context of sustainable development by a highly empowered citizenry.

Sustainable Development in Developing Societies: The Case of Planning Sustainable urban Development under Post-Communist Conditions

Miroslaw Grochowski

INTRODUCTION

In Central and Eastern European countries, which were under communism, the approaches to the problems and concerns resulting from the urban processes were dominated by ideological principles. Cities and towns were treated predominantly as a space of production and a source of the labour force. Forceful industrialization policies prompted mass migration from the rural to urban areas and, under conditions of fiscal constraints and political priorities, resulting in underdevelopment of housing and social infrastructure. Procedures and techniques used to plan urban development were utilized to reinforce politically-motivated decisions. Lack of understanding on how the elements of the settlement system interact resulted in isolation of cities and towns from the surrounding areas. Functional links among them were rarely reflected in development plans since these plans were predominantly based on the "wishful thinking" principle and had negligible, if any, link with the plans of regional development.

The transformation policies started in Central and Eastern Europe after the political upheaval of the late eighties and the early nineties, have to address issues of the economic restructuring and building foundations for democratic political systems in the broad new context. One component of this context is a new paradigm of urban development. The new paradigm should incorporate elements like the sustainable development concept, impact of increasing dependencies within the system of global economy, and the new circumstances created through market-oriented changes, including those in the legal system of urban planning and management.

The goal of this article is to present issues related to planning for sustainable development under new systemic conditions in countries of Central and Eastern Europe. The article consists of three parts: Conditions and problems—urban development inherited from the communist era; Barriers and challenges—experience from the first years of transformation and Planning for the future—prospects for the future.

CONDITIONS AND PROBLEMS

The basic trends of urban processes in the communist countries were similar to those of Western democracies. The existing differences resulted from the specific regional conditions related to the implemented urban policies, the level of technological development and the level of control performed by the state/central government over processes of economic development. Both in the West and in the East one could find similar problems (Mercer 1983, Niessen and Peschar 1983) although the same results could be achieved through different reasons. The argument that different modes of production, consumption, exchange or settlement policy preclude any comparison (Castells 1977, Tabb and Sawers 1978) could be challenged since the spontaneous processes and social phenomena observed in communist countries were amazingly similar to the Western patterns. The main difference that existed between the two groups of countries was that urban policy was clearly interpreted in the Western countries. In the communist countries the urban policy was interchangeably called: spatial policy, territorial development policy, or settlement policy. Thus a question might be asked: did an urban policy ever exist in communist countries? Even if not called such was an urban policy executed as a part of the planning procedures. It is interesting that, regardless of the terminological difference, during the two first decades after World War II, most urban policies in Europe shared the same objectives (Bourne 1984). Among them were: balanced regional development, assisting peripheral and declining communities, developing the whole national territory, reducing congestion costs in large metropolitan areas, maintaining fiscal viability, improving housing, and equalizing the quality of urban infrastructure and services. After two decades of the rising economic disparities in developmental potential, significant discrepancies in the practice of urban development appeared. Communist governments were unable to continue intervening in the relationships between population processes, spatial structures and economic processes. The clear, logical and understandable rules for urban development were obviously lacking. To systemize the general conditions that determined urban development processes and problems to be solved the list of the following issues and dilemmas can be suggested:

1) Urban Areas, Rural Areas and Regional Disparities

A strong differentiation in terms of level of economic development and the standard of living between the rural and urban areas has always existed in the countries of Central and Eastern Europe. This differentiation results from the history of economic development and the processes of settlement systems development throughout the last three centuries. The first steps of macroeconomic reforms taken at the beginning of the nineties deepened the existing disparities. The implementation of systemic changes in the sphere of economy and politics was not accompanied by new mechanisms of administration and management that could address the issue of rising inequalities determined by location in space.

A city—an engine for development, home for workers and also an important agent of political change has always offered better access to goods and services in the Central and Eastern European countries. Urban areas still remain very attractive although, according to Western standards, they do not provide proper environment to live there (Bachtler 1991).

Although urban areas possess more human and capital resources, there is no indicator that these areas have enough potential to overcome their problems through measures focussed just on them. Therefore, a new strategy for urban development should be formulated as a part of a new policy of regional development. This is important to answer the question of what should be done first—reduce differences concerning the level of economic development between specific regions? Or, find solutions which may lead to new relations between rural and urban areas? The answer has many political implications. Looking for short-term solutions one may decide that it is more important to reduce differences between regions. In which case the negative trends will be continued. The second solution would mean preparing new urban policies.

A new approach to the regional policy must emphasize the fact that cities are not isolated islands, but parts of the socio-economic system. For used resources therefore, they should compensate the surrounding areas (Rees 1992). In other case it will not be possible to reverse the trends of migration and economic and social deterioration of areas located in the shadow of cities. The cities would start to grow as "defective growth poles" of the national economy.

2) New Urban Development Paradigm and Economic Growth Trends

Political integration within Europe will inescapably force post-communist countries aspiring to be members of the European Union to follow Western rules and standards (Hill and Zielonka 1990). The new urban planning paradigm will also have to embody aspects of development neglected so far. It seems that the changes that have taken place during the last five years would be a good starting point for a new paradigm design.

Among many factors that can help to develop the new paradigm of urban development, free flow of information seems to be crucial. Transfer of know-how is very essential. However, learning ideas and adopting others' experience may also create problems. It seems that this is the case with the post-communist countries.

After years of isolation the people of Central and Eastern Europe are exposed to the Western models of behaviour and consumption. This leads to on eruption of needs and stimulates huge demands for goods and services. The Western-solutions offer the shortest way to reach Western standards of life. Lack of criticism and objective evaluation of Western experiences is very dangerous (Grochowski 1992a). The market is perceived by many as a universal driving force of the healthy economy. Economic efficiency measured simply by the number of final products is the example of fixation on growth. This kind of approach may significantly impede the formulation of a truly new paradigm. Post-communist societies are not prepared to respond to new ideas in a constructive way as was the case of Western democratic societies that can better understand the concept of sustainable development going through the process of negotiations and looking for consensus (compare the chapter by W.E. Rees in this book). Paradoxically, the state (or central government) is still considered to be important, especially when the market does not fulfill all promises. Therefore, not only have new structures and mechanisms failed to replace the old ones, a new realistic and pragmatic thinking has not managed to replace the wishful thinking and naive perception, that a new system, which was supposed to supplant communism, would bring more efficiency and wealth and leave the same amount of social benefits.

There are two main obstacles in introducing the idea of sustainable development in post-communist countries. The first obstacle is that these countries deal with serious problems of economic nature. The rapid change of the structure of economy and technologies is not possible due to financial (foreign debt, lack of domestic capital) and technical reasons (the process of privatization is under way, and time is needed to introduce new technologies). The second obstacle is the social situation. Paradoxically: on the one hand these countries need more time to introduce the necessary changes, and on the other hand they do not have time, because the resources of social patience are running out. To avoid social unrest and protests which might paralyse the whole process of democratic reforms, governments have to find a "state of balance", a situation, when some solution can be shifted in time, while the others would be introduced at once.

In order to change the path of development post-communist countries must reach a kind of "turning point"—economic situation good enough that there is room to manoeuvre in terms of introducing principles of sustainable development policy.

Since the "turning point" cannot be reached unless the most urgent needs are met, the environmental costs of development would probably be considered less important for the next several years. Economic efficiency would be the main criterion of evaluation of measures undertaken to introduce reforms. This approach will influence the situation of cities that are treated as instruments and tools which may help the economy to fight recession. Thus formulation of sustainable urban development is an urgent and important task.

3) New Ecological Policy and Economic Efficiency

The concept of sustainable development is directly related to the issue of ecological policy. The extremely poor environmental conditions result both from the ideological principles adopted by communists in using the so-called free natural resources and from outdated and obsolete technologies. The primacy of economic growth and industrial production over development has brought ecological disaster in many regions in post-communist countries. The ecological conditions in cities, not only the centres of industry, are especially bad. The gap between the technology of life in Western cities and in post-communist countries is enormous. Although, as already mentioned, an improvement of the situation in cities depends on changes in a broader, regional and national context, cities may serve as a good starting point for these changes. Urban structures are the focal points of environmental problems but also of potential solutions (see the chapter by Weiland and Hitly in this book).

The concentration of production and consumption in cities is the reason that even small changes in their functioning may bring results on a large scale. At this stage of development the proactive protection of natural resources can and should take place primarily in cities. It gives a bigger chance that the implementation of the new ecological policy would also bring measurable economic results (urban areas are able to attract new firms and investors considering environment quality important). Measurable economic results might have important psychological meaning both for citizens and for those who make decisions. The experience of many countries proves that relationships between formal governing structures/decision makers and citizens are of great importance when innovative solutions are needed and when consensus is the first and necessary step to start designing development programmes (see the chapter by Lai in this book).

By concentrating the urban developmental pattern and confining new buildings to areas where technical encroachments on nature have previously taken place, and by utilizing each building site efficiently, considerable advantages can be achieved where the overall goals are to preserve nature and maintain environment (Naess 1993). Modern technologies open new possibilities to use urban space more intensely and efficiently (Owens 1986, Newman and Kenworthy 1989). To do this however, the environment cannot mean just open space and resources that can be used by people.

Planners in the post-communist countries will have to face a number of challenges since sustainable development requires environmentally sound planning. Conflicts are inevitable because the hierarchy of plans and solutions proposed do not necessarily meet the goals and expectations of specific communities (Naess 1944). Involvement in community life, participation of citizens in different phases of development, and preparation of plans will be the new exercise for planners, decision makers and citizens.

New plans will have to contain new ideas and solutions of how to implement them in the spatial context that was created under entirely different systemic conditions. Among these challenges are tasks like the reduction of energy consumption and emission of pollution, preservation of biological resources, preservation of landscape and cultural values. Environmental alternatives are new elements that should be included in the list of possible options and choices (Johnston 1989). In the planning procedures a new approach to provision of land for development will have to be worked out. In this context processes of re-privatization, privatization, restitution, compensation, etc., should be well prepared and must proceed much faster to foster development processes and to create mechanisms to supervise them (David 1993).

4) Economic Reforms—Political Reforms—Restructuring of Urban Areas

There is no doubt that the most important and urgent issues in the processes of reforms in post-communist countries are these of economic character. Achievements of newly elected authorities are strongly criticized. Because of the selective memory of post-communist societies and the very energetic activity of the followers of the former regime, positive opinions about the communist government are being formulated. New social and economic conditions are too tough for large proportions of societies. It results from the serious political mistake made by non-communist governments: comprehensive reports about conditions of the economy and society inherited from communists were not prepared.

In societies where people in power are usually perceived to be brought from "outside", new authorities are being accused of all failures in the reform processes and the deteriorating standard level of life. Thus, the room for political manoeuvre is becoming smaller (Grochowski and Kowalczyk 1991). In the broad national context, cities may become the engines moving the whole system forward. If the process is started, then the policy can be modified to include other areas and execute the mechanism of collaboration. The time needed to reach the first positive results of reforms is crucial for getting social support for further reforms. Any delay would have very serious consequences and impede the process which should lead to sustainable development.

The restructuring of urban areas should become a part of state/central government policy that leads to the restructuring of spatial structures. The policy should (in a proactive way—through sectoral projects and providing financial support) stimulate social and economic development (directly and indirectly). At this stage of reform a state/central government cannot limit its activities to the protection of traditional values (as recognized by the society) (Kulesza 1985).

5) Local Democracy Development and Social Participation

The decentralization processes that are under way in post-communist countries are changing not only relationships among different levels of governance, but they are also changing relations between local governments and urban development. Rebirth of the ideas of local-governance in Central and Eastern Europe will have a significant influence on the design and development of urban plans as well as on their implementation (Goverde et al. 1986).

The emergence of democracy has revealed the immense variety of interests of specific social groups. After years of one-political party domination, new political and social movements have appeared on the political scene. They articulate the interests of specific, sometimes very small, social groups. Basically, three main types of social groups might be distinguished using the following criteria: professional background, political affiliation, and spatial location. The criteria listed should be used separately. After almost five decades of communist regime, the social structure in the post-communist countries is amorphous. Its important elements were destroyed except for the family's structure on the bottom, and a powerful organization with strong social support—the Catholic church, on the top. The elements of social structure "from the middle" are very labile. It is not easy to define the social identity of these groups. Because of these facts not only are political events unpredictable, but they are also possible social reactions to new economic and social policy.

In the processes of the development of democracy, special attention should be paid to the question of local democracy. The mechanism of social participation must be worked out very carefully. New governments must convince the people, that improvement of their situation without giving any attention to national/global costs of changes is neither possible nor acceptable. Every step, goal, and measure should be related to much broader contexts. Only then is it possible to build a proper social background for sustainable development.

Social participation in the planning procedures, as mentioned before, is also needed. Planning under communism was limited to the production/drawing of plans by a group of professionals. Although theoretically possible, social participation did not exist in practice. Along with the self-organization of local communities the practice of social participation in the planning process should become a rule.

6) The Socio-Spatial Structure of Post-Communist City

The theory behind a model city of true socialism was that for enhanced productivity, large-scale industry was needed to be concentrated in the city and the necessary labour force was needed to be located next to the place of work. As a result cities were serving as places for the location of industry and providers of the necessary labour force and services.

Ideological principles determined the ways of the spatial development of cities. The idea was that homes would be collectively built and owned by the labour class (through established building cooperatives). Rents from shops and services located in these buildings would flow back to the collectivity and be redistributed. Interestingly enough, the idea of collective ownership never extended to factories. They were state-owned enterprises.

The socio-spatial structure of post-communist cities is a result of the objectives of spatial planning/urban policies implemented in socialist countries. These objectives were as follows (Kolipinski 1970):

1) Maximize within given external and environmental conditions, the efficiency of the production of goods and delivery of services,

2) Secure the highest possible consumption under given conditions,

3) Rationalize the use of natural resources in the interest of a given urban entity and its development.

The principles of cost minimalization and egalitarianism (equal access to urban goods) influenced planning and the implementation of plans in the following ways:

1) The search for an optimal city size and structure of a city resulted in administrative decisions concerning size and number of inhabitants:

2) City structure had been developed based on public transportation;

3) Strict segregation of urban land-use had been practised; and

4) Environmental policy had been realized predominantly through locational policy.

The tools used to implement these policies were basically administrative and were functions of political priorities. The socio-spatial structure therefore, was not a result of action of the main actors (local governments, interest groups, etc.) but administrative decisions and norms imposed by the planning authorities and decision-making centres.

Additionally, as mentioned before, city space had been shaped according to the needs of more efficient economic activity (usually industrial production). Under new systemic conditions the criterion of economic efficiency should get a new interpretation. The economic dimension of processes that influence the shape of social space of a city should also be revised. The social structure will depend to a large extent on results of the tough game between the influential actors of this process. Institutions responsible for planning must cope with the rising tensions between the actors, contradictory interests of specific social groups, conflicting goals of future-oriented and short-term plans. The future of post-communist cities therefore does not seem to be easy and optimistic. A lot of work should be done to reverse the negative trends to make urban environment more human and to incorporate cities into the socio-economic local, regional, and national systems.

7) The Role of the State in Planning Urban Development: Decentralization of Power versus Decentralization of Responsibilities

Decentralization promises a quick shift from a planned economy to a market economy through radical changes in the systems of political decision-making, policy-making and administrative control (Smith 1985). Decentralization is a kind of response to the social and economic crises. It is a search for alternative forms of distribution of power and resources and refers to change in the governmental structure whereby local government units obtain greater decision-making power with regard to articulating locally specific goals and delineating the desired means to achieve them (Hudson and Plum 1986).

It is still not clear whether central governments in post-communist countries plan to introduce decentralization or just think about simple deconcentration, that is terrritorial reorganization of governmental activity aimed at administrative rationalization and increased efficiency. If the latter is true, then local governments will be equipped with power just to execute decisions, not to make them. A simple change in the form, not allocation, of the power structure does not promise any real change in the processes and procedures (Scott 1980).

The institutional structure and the resulting urban pattern are determined in the first instance by the assumptions and constraints of the national political system. Liberal concepts bring, among others, the idea of self-sufficiency. The state as an institution planning, implementing, providing etc., and taking care of the citizens is losing its functions and dominant role. The liberal concepts were very popular at the beginning of the processes of political transformation. However, the design and implementation of urban policy take place within a specific environment, including economic conditions. All post-communist countries have to deal with enormous economic problems (among them is the outdated structure of the economy in many regions). The scale of the problems is so significant that without state intervention chances for economic restructuring are very problematic. Under existing conditions, without decentralized governing structures, a state, by definition, has to play an important role in most activities related to changes in the urban development policy. Further decentralization should change the contemporary situation. However, although the concept of strong central authorities is not popular in the post-communist countries any more, one should state, that the role of the central government is now even more important than it was in the past. The central government must play the role of a supervisor and moderator in the reform processes to avoid regional conflicts and to ensure that efficient cooperation between local, regional and national systems exists. In the other case, they may function as "spongers", using resources and giving in return spatial disorder and chaos, social conflicts, etc.

BARRIERS AND CHALLENGES

Among the main barriers for the planning for sustainable development are those of fiscal constraints, the lack of management skills and of understanding new conditions and challenges for urban development, and inertia of the spatial structure of settlement systems inherited from communism era.

Idealized settlements systems that were supposed to fit new political conditions were assumed to:

1) Reflect an abrupt shift in socio-economic politics from capitalism to socialism;

2) Provide people with material well-being and social, cultural, political milieu that is both fulfilling to individuals and constructive for societies; and

3) Reduce social and regional inequalities.

To achieve these goals new urban development policies were introduced that in fact damaged cities and developed them as industrial centres (Demko and Regulska 1987, Demko and Fuchs 1979, French and Hamilton

1979). The situation of post-communist cities after the first years of trans-formation reminds us of other cities in countries experiencing economic and political changes.

When economic and˙political crises emerge, a state usually responds with the reorganization of institutional arrangements at least in part, to maintain both state legitimacy and state control (Habermas 1975). This is manifested as a change in urban patterns resulting from evolving goals (Fainstein and Fainstein 1982).

Following the pattern from the first part of this paper a set of dilemmas representing experience from the first years of transformation can be proposed. These are as follows:

1) Relationships between Planners/Professionals and Citizens

The new political environment has a great potential to support the building of new democratic structures as well as working out new strategies for socio-economic development including urban development policies. The starting point is not, of course, favourable for systematic, comprehensive, and pragmatic activity (Przeworski 1991). After decades of communist regime societies of post-communist countries have lost the abilities to self-organization, articulation and presentation of their needs (Jalowiecki 1990).

The negative results of the first steps of economic reforms (unemploy-ment, increasing level of poverty, lack of social security) are not commonly perceived as costs of reforms, but as results of mistakes made by new governments. The division between society ("we") and govern-ment/authority ("they") turned out to be rooted very deeply. Tough condi-tions of every-day life and unclear economic future make people even more suspicious. In this social context a task to mobilize human resources is ex-tremely difficult (Jalowiecki and Swianiewicz, 1991, Grochowski 1992a).

Therefore, the implementation of the concept of participatory planning will be a very difficult task. Professionals dealing with the planning urban development not only face difficult technical issues to solve (such as ownership and environmental), but they also find themselves in a difficult situation because they are perceived as representing inefficient and unreli-able authority, ready to realize its self-interest instead of public-interest. Since plans of spatial development at the local scale have to be presented to, and consulted with, local communities new relationships between groups of professionals that deal with urban development and regular citizens are needed.

2) Politics and Urban Problems Solving

The first experience with newly created democratic political structures indi-cates that not all new people who are in power have brought new ideas and new styles of acting. In general, they do not assure proper/efficient working of political and administrative bodies. There are several reasons explaining this situation. The most important among them are:

- There is lack of democratic traditions and mechanisms for selection of government employees, negotiation among interest groups, reaching consensus by parties representing conflicting interests.
- New democratic institutions are being created from the very beginning in entirely new internal and external conditions—there is a lack of knowledge on how to act in the new legal and political framework.
- Very severe economic conditions of national economy and sophisticated socio-political aspects of its restructuring require specific skills and appropriate professional preparation and training to perform ascribed functions—these skills and preparation are still, in many cases, missing.

Referring these issues to the problem of planning for sustainable development one may conclude from the first years of systemic transformation that:

- One should expect disorder and chaos instead of cooperation in the field of planning for sustainable development.
- Clear dependencies between the level of power and responsibilities should be worked out early enough to facilitate the processes of planning.
- There are strong relations between the economic situation and social approval of political choices and technical measures used to create new conditions for development.

The transformation of post-communist countries might be facilitated through cooperation with countries of a well-developed market economy (Mync and Szul 1990, Szul 1990). This cooperation may help to create structures and mechanisms that would be compatible with and fit Western standards.

In the context of what has been said above, one should also add that intensive programmes of training for local leaders, planners, managers and politicians are still urgently needed. This training is required to enable them to define a "better future" for their localities, towns, cities and countries.

The issues which would crucially influence future development and particularly shape the policy of urban development are: privatization, reprivatization, character of taxation system, and investment policies.

The experience of Poland indicates, that these questions should be considered mainly from the "technical" and pragmatic perspective. Introducing a purely political dimension into procedures leading to their solutions would make existing situations even more complex and difficult.

PLANNING FOR THE FUTURE

Planning for sustainable development requires special conditions in the sphere of legislative framework as well as new tools and instruments for planning and changes in public awareness concerning environmental aspects of development. The following issues would need to be reconsidered:

1) limits to private ownership rights,

2) scope and coordination of plans developed for localities, regions and countries, and

3) extent of state administration control over behavior of agents of change.

Liberal approaches do not seem promising under unstable conditions where new structures and institutions are being created. It does not mean however, that the state should only play a role of restrictive supervisor that eliminates alternative behaviour. The state should rather be the advocacy-oriented agent coordinating efforts undertaken at different levels.

Under existing conditions, the development policy is determined by three main factors: (a) the ways in which the basis for a market economy is created, (b) the macro-economic situation and access to capital,and (c) legal framework for designing and implementing development plans. The influence of these three factors on development processes should be shaped by incorporation of the sustainable development concept as a superior principle for long-term political choices. It should be anticipated, that the introduction of policies focussed on the sustainability of development would sometimes violate the commonly-approved civil and political rights. Intensive education and establishment of the mechanism for participation in planning are urgent and are crucial for understanding the ongoing changes and their support.

Liberalism and theories of social learning had given the basis for incremental planning. The first period of systemic transformation in post-communist countries brought about a situation reminding of the practice of incremental planning. Rising disparities between regions and localities as well as urban and rural areas resulted in the formulation of conflicting development policies. The goals were not clear and not necessarily based on commonly accepted values. Post-communist countries ought to adopt different principles in planning procedures so as to have a chance to change directions of development that were worked out under entirely different political and economic conditions. One may argue that transactive planning that places emphasis on mutual learning and dialogue with those affected by the planning is a partial alternative (Klosterman 1985). Decentralized planning bodies can give population more control over the social process that are affecting their welfare. This type of planning may also influence people's self-esteem, values, behaviour, and general capacity for growth through cooperation. Different planning approaches and procedures offer specific advantages and disadvantages (Rittel and Melvin 1973, Scott and Roweis 1977, Camhis 1979). They should be revised carefully again before deciding what is really needed in countries experiencing intense transformation.

New planning approaches should be accompanied by innovative methods of urban management. In general, urban areas might be perceived in two ways: (a) as a place of location—a part of physical space, where certain functions are located; (b) as an element of dynamic system-generating innovations and playing the role of an important centre of political and economic life. The Polish experience indicates, that so far urban areas have served predominantly as a laboratory for reforms. These reforms do not necessarily fit the economic base for urban development. It seems that good, encouraging examples of new ways of management and economic reforms at the local level could be very helpful in promoting reforms and new methods used to design and implement these reforms.

Urban areas under post-communist conditions have become a scene where new actors play the game for a city. These new actors are: territorial self-government, entrepreneurs, corporations and firms, previous owners claiming their properties, interest groups, and central authorities responsible for strategic issues (development in the context of integration processes in Europe).

Urban space has again become a highly priced commodity and actors must compete for space to accomplish their goals. However, a clear mechanism and rules how to use urban space is still lacking. The structure of power within city borders is not clear. There are many conflicts concerning the formal capability of city administration and representative bodies. Territorial self-government has been introduced predominantly because of political not pragmatic/technical reasons. Although the idea of self-government is a very attractive one, to make it work local government employees should have proper skills and be trained to correctly use the new instruments of ruling and management. In this context prospects for the future of planning for sustainable development depends to large extent on the quality of human resources.

The development of urban areas is determined by directions of general reforms. After six years of reforms one may state, that they have not contained elements of a new urban policy. Old problems are being accumulated, although some attempts to change the situation through attraction of foreign capital have been made. However, all actions of limited character could not radically improve living conditions in cities, and contribute to the preparation and implementation of new development programmes for urban areas (Szul 1992).

The main barrier in further development of urban areas is the very bad shape of technical infrastructure. In fact, development programmes should start with projects that will lead to the replacement or improvement of existing obsolete and unreliable technical infrastructure. Then projects focussed on the revitalization of huge parts of old urban areas to restructure the economic base for future development should be designed. Both types of projects would be framed within the broader context of strategic development plans.

CONCLUSIONS

The processes of political decentralization and economic restructuring in post-communist countries have been started and are pretty advanced. This does not however mean, that the process of shifting power, competence and responsibilities from the centre to regions and counties or municipalities has been completed. This is just the beginning of the new organization of these states that eventually should bring into existence political, social and economic conditions that allow the development of new approaches to challenges resulting from a need to have sustainable concept present in development plans (Grochowski and Kowalczyk 1991). It is important to foster the processes of decentralization and economic restructuring to stop spatial chaos that will have long-term implications for future development plans (Kolodziejski 1991).

The still popular opinion that problems of cities can be solved separately, without structural changes to the national economy, is very naive. New leaders must be aware of this fact. Two barriers that ought to be overcome as soon as possible are: (a) traditional thinking about the blessing power of industrial development; (b) environmental awareness, which makes people believe that they still have time to improve conditions of natural environment, and use resources as to fulfil needs, without dangerous consequences. The existence of these barriers is to a large extent a result of action of political interest groups. These groups focussed on maintaining political power promote programmes of economic development aimed on immediate results. The programmes meet the social needs and expectations but do not meet criteria of rational use of natural resources and ecological behaviour in space.

A dynamic game for the new structures of society, economy and state is observed in post-communist countries. The game takes place in new internal and external conditions. Although the political situation is still not stable new political elites and new rules of the game assure that return to old communist reality is not possible (Hankiss 1990). The process of reform will take much longer than optimists believed some years ago. The good news is that the strong belief that there is no way back to the economy of shortages and to a centralized state governed by one party should help to mobilize human potential and force leaders to look for innovative solutions. The bad news is that the new authorities will work for years under permanent stress, because of many problems inherited from communism and which have to be solved immediately. It may force the authorities to choose "easy solutions" which make people happy in the short-time but which may further complicate the problems and make them more difficult to solve in the future.

Referring this issue to the problem of planning sustainable urban development one may conclude that a lobby supporting changes in the urban development policy is needed to articulate postulates and participate in the processes of transforming them into specific steps in programmes of economic, social and spatial restructuring.

REFERENCES

Bachtler, J. (ed.). 1991. *Regional Socio-Economic Development in the Countries of Central and Eastern Europe*. Glasgow: European Policies Research Center, University of Strathclyde.

Bourne L.S. 1984. Urbanization and Urban Policy. Research in Comparative Perspective: Pitfalls and Potentials, AAG, WDC;

Camhis, M. 1979. *Planning Theory and Philosophy*, London/New York: Tavistock Publications.

Castells, M. 1977. *The Urban Question*, London: Edward Arnold.

David, C-H. 1993: Provision of land for development in the New Federal States of Germany. In: *Proceeding of the Conference: Designing Markets*, University of Pennsylvania, Philadelphia.

Demko, G.J. and J. Regulska. 1987. Socialist Ideology and Its Impact on Urban Process. *Urban Geography*, 8: 289–292.

Demko G. and R. Fuchs. 1979. Geographic Inequality Under Socialism, Annals of the Association of American Geographers. 304–318.

Fainstein, N.J. and S.S. Fainstein (eds.). 1982. *Urban Policy Under Capitalism*, Beverly Hills. CA: Sage.

French R.A. and F.E.I. Hamilton. (eds.) 1979. *The Socialist City: Spatial Structure and Urban Policy*. Chichester: John Wiley and Sons.

Goverde, H., T. Markowski, J. Regulski, J. and J. Regulska. 1986. *Cross-national Comparison between East and West*. The Case of Local Government and Urban Development in Poland, Nijmegen: Kath. Universiteit.

Grochowski, M. and A. Kowalczyk. 1991. The Way Towards Democracy in Poland: The Question of Reorganization of Territorial Division of the State; Administrative Studies. *Journal of Finnish Association for Administrative Studies*, no. 2.

Grochowski, M. and A. Kowalczyk. 1992. *Eastern Europe in Transition—the Case of Poland*. University of Orebro, Sweden.

Grochowski, M. 1992a. Transformation of Post-Communist Countries: Chances or Threats for Cities in the Context of Sustainable Development. In: *Sustainable Development and the Future of Cities*, B. Hamm, G. Zimmer and S. Kratz (eds.), Center for European Studies, University of Trier;

Grochowski, M. 1992b: Strategies and Conflicts of the Local Development; Working Papers, Rutgers University;

Habermas, J. 1975. *Legitimation Crisis*. Boston: Beacon Press.

Hankiss, E. 1990. *East European Alternatives*. Oxford: Clarendon Press.

Hill, R. and J. Zielonka (eds.) 1990. *Restructuring Eastern Europe. Towards a New European Order*. Aldershot/Hants.: Edward Elgar.

Hudson, B. 1979. Comparison of current planning theories: counterparts and contradictions. *Journal of American Planning Association* 45: 385–398.

Hudson, R. and V. Plum. 1986. Deconcentration or decentralization? Local government and the possibilities for local control of local economies. In: *Urban Political Theory and the Management of Fiscal Stress*, M. Goldsmith and S. Villadsen (eds.). Brookfield, VT: Gower Publishing Company.

Jalowiecki, B. 1990. Narodziny demokracji w Polsce Lakalnej (Appearance of Democracy in Local Poland) series: Regional Development—Local Development—Territorial Self-Government, vol. 25, Warsaw: Institute of Space Economy, University of Warsaw.

Jalowiecki, B. and P. Swianiewicz (eds.). 1991. Miedzy nadzieja a rozczarowaniem. Samorzad terytorialny rok po wyborach (Between Hope and Disappointment. Territorial Self-Government One Year After Election), series: Regional and Local Studies, vol. 3 (36), European Institute for Regional and Local Development, University of Warsaw;

Johnston, R.J. 1989. *Environmental Problems: Nature, Economy and State*. London/New York: Belhaven.

Klosterman, R.E. 1985. Arguments for and against planning. *Town Planning Review* 56: 5–20.

Kolipinski J. 1970. Metody rachunku efektywnosci w miejscowym planowaniu przestrzennym w Polsce (Economic Evaluation Methods in the Polish Urban Planning), Studies KPZK , vol. XXXII, Warszawa.

Kolodziejski, J. 1991. O przyszly ksztalt polskiej przestrzeni (For the New Future of Polish Space); Warsawa: Ossolineum, Wyd. Polskiej Akademii Nauk;

Kuklinski, A., A. Mync and R. Szul. 1991. Warschau als eine Globalstadt; in: Stadtforschung in Ost und West. Perspectiven und Moglichkeiten der Kooperation der grozen Zentren in Europa, Berlin.

Kulesza, M. 1985. Administracyjno-prawne uwarunkowania polityki przestrzennej (Institutional Impact on Spatial Policy), Warsaw University Press.

Mercer, J. 1983. On the Necessity for a Comparative Urban Geography, West Point, N.Y.: MSDM, AAG.

Mync, A. and R. Szul. 1990. Private Economy in the Warsaw Region against the Background of Development of the Private Economy in Poland, Miscellanea Geographica, Warszawa;

Naess, P. 1993. Can urban development be made environmentally sound? *Journal of Environmental Planning and Management*, 36 (3):

Naess, P. 1994. Normative planning theory and sustainable development. *Scandinavian Housing & Planning Research* 11: 145–167.

Newman, P.W.G. and J.R. Kenworthy 1989. Cities and Automobile Dependence: An International Sourcebook, Aldershot, Gower.

Niessen J. and P. Peschar (eds.) 1983. *International Comparative Research: Problems of Theory, Methodology, and Organization in Eastern and Western Europe*. Oxford, UK: Pergamon.

Owens, S. 1986. *Energy, Planning and Urban Form*, London: Pion.

Przeworski, A. 1991. The "East" becomes the "South"? The "Autumn of the People" and the Future of Eastern people. *Political Science and Politics* March 1991.

Rees, W.E. 1992. Understanding sustainability. In: *Sustainable Development and the Future of Cities*, B. Hamm, G. Zimmer and S. Kratz (eds.), Centre for European Studies, University of Trier.

Rittel, H.W. and M.L. Melvin. 1973. Dilemmas in general theory of planning. *Policy Sciences* 4: 155–169.

Scott A.J. and S.T. Roweis, 1977. Urban planning in theory and practice: a reappraisal. *Environment and Planning* A 9: 1079–1119.

Scott, A.J. 1980. *The Urban Land Nexus and the State.* London: Pion, Ltd.

Smith, B.C. 1985. *Decentralization: The Territorial Dimension of the State.* London: Allen and Unwin.

Szul, R. 1992. Stolica Rzeczypospolitej Polskiej w krytycznej dekadzie mijajacego wieku (The Capital City of Polish Republic in the Critical Decade of the Passing Century); Ratusz, Biuletyn Urzedu Miasta st. Warszawy, Maj, 1990.

Szul, R. 1990. *The Spatial Structure of Poland's Industry.* Osteuropa Wirtschaft, Stuttgart, 4/1989;

Tabb, W.K. and Sawers, L. (eds.). 1978. *Marxism and Metropolis; New Perspectives in Urban Political Economy.* New York: Oxford University Press.

Sustainable Development or Loss of Cultural Urban Identity?

Ljubinko Pusic

CAN SUSTAINABLE DEVELOPMENT BE A PARADIGM OF CULTURAL-URBAN PLURALISM?

The most attractive idea within the scope of the present considerations of global future is the planning for sustainable development. The basic concept of this type of planning has hardly gone beyond the limits imposed by natural resources but rather it has treated the environment in such a way as to secure prosperity for the generations to come. The recent treatments of this idea have established a new paradigm of urban and territorial development. Presently, however, the thesis on sustainable development is acquiring negative connotations because it is being exploited for various manipulations with the projections of future development.

To be able to fully demonstrate its value in the sphere of urban projecting, the theory of sustainable development should include a clearly expressed component of cultural-urban pluralism. In other words, the global strategy should protect the important local characteristics, to a measure and in a way that would contribute to the coherence of the (European) urban system. In an urban-cultural context, sustainable development implies a satisfying of social needs at a higher level than is the case in a vulgar interpretation of the economic and ecological assumptions of sustainability for a community. In this paper it is assumed that the natural and necessary needs of the individual have been previously met. A holistic concept of sustainable development cannot be based only on strategies which insist on a full stomach for the world population, on normative approaches to the economic measuring of growth and development of a society, or on the premises of ecological purism. The main idea within the framework of general concern about the urban future may be condensed to the following two questions:

a) How much are the social upheavals which characterize the modern world and which involve all European cities a prearranged framework?

b) How much are they a conceivable framework for urban future?

Despite the holistic concept of sustainable development, reduction of the problems of the prospective city to geopolitical, cultural, and other planes is not only possible and reasonable, but also necessary. This, however, does not mean that the apparently narrower view will make the search for possible answers any easier. The urban reality operates with a widely accepted syntagma about a large set of specific but unessential social and spatial characteristics of the East European city. But the reality is that these cities deserve all attributes that make them a full-fledged factor of the European urban milieu. At this point, their specific cultural and historical characteristics should be considered as definitely positive influences. The above statement is based on the fact that the development of most cities east and south of the Alps followed the patterns of the historical process of urban development of the West European cities.

The main attitudes toward the method of urban development planning includes those facts which may be characterized as speculative. Perhaps the single most important attitude is the one which draws the equal sign between the needs for a coherent European urban future and universal egalitarianism. Concerning the prospectives of the "non Western" urban areas in the prevailing conditions, the main question seems to be: What prerequisites are needed to minimize the uncertainties associated with the prospectives of the city in this cultural zone? In seeking an answer two alternative approaches may be taken: (1) the global circumstances for human living in this geopolitical area, and (2) the specific characteristics of each individual social reality and urban milieu.

The first approach to the global social changes that provides room for considerations about a transformation of the city in the former East Europe, is concerned with a question: what happens to the city after the social stage, in which the city had taken part, has toppled the political scene? Francis Fukuyama (1989), in his article "The end of history", claimed that the wave of reforms in the Soviet Union and East Europe and the expansion of consumerism is in a way "a triumph of the West and the Western ideology"—the end of history that we know: the ultimate accomplishment of the ideological evolution of mankind and the universalization of Western liberal democracy as the final social "form". If this apocalyptical version of civilization development is taken as a standard of measure, i.e., if the end of history is in fact "the end of human deliberations about the primary principles", then where can we place the ideology of urban reality/future of a relatively insignificant cultural-urban area such as the East European city? Does it mean that the course of its future transformation has been predestined by the fate of the capitalist city of Western civilization? Perhaps, everything is not as simple as Fukuyama forecasts. It is an irrefutable fact that the main civilization course runs right through the centre of the city. Today, this is clearer than ever before, maybe because we are carried by the swiftest of its currents. There is also no doubt that social relations, having a firm foothold in institutional relations, control the process of urban transformation. However, it is a historical fact that the complexity of transformation of the city exceeds the scope of transformations dictated by global changes. No matter how radical and sudden, even when reality turns into its own inverted mirror image, these changes are incapable of inducing automatic transformation of the city. Urban transformations recognize innumerable nuances of gradation and adaptability which defend the historical self-sustainable substance of the city.

The second approach to the global social changes falls within the realm of political speculations about the urban future. Recognizing the need for different avenues of cultural development in different parts of Europe, Johan Galtung asks a belated question: What is going to happen, after the vehement political changes that have taken place, when Europe becomes dominated by the junk civilization in all segments of the society? Obviously, the focal point of this phenomenon is in the city. We should be concerned about the pervading concepts of globalization which threaten to cover all Europe—the false thesis which says that the planning of sustainable development is more important than cultural-urban pluralism. A form of resistance to the indiscriminate globalization are various forms of nostalgia for the social security and cultural identity of the past. It may be expected that these sentiments will escalate into specific forms of urban unrest which the "non-Eastern" Europe will try to hide through special social programmes. Also, there is no doubt that urban movements, oriented either left or right, will be invariably caused by the process of social change for the emergence, development, and escalation of ideological ideas. It is obvious that the shadow already covers "the rest of Europe", in the form of peripheral capitalism (a variant of the Third World neocapitalism adapted for Europe). Social diversification is more than obvious in the East European city. But processes of stabilization and coherence are still out of fight as the cities are presently passing through the period of adopting peripheral capitalism.

If the planning of sustainable development does not establish itself as a paradigm of cultural development, the future of the "non-Western" cities is also open to other speculative variants. The possible scenarios of urban changes would in fact be subvariants of the transformation of the postindustrial/capitalist city. Nevertheless, it appears that such variant of urban transformation will not be a complete incarnation of M. Castells' thesis, which says that "the global society and its predominant production method are the factors which determine the character of living in an urban community", simply because the dynamism of changes imposed in front of the modern society functions on the principle of ascending time spiral, i.e., calls for global changes in the urban sphere will repeat over and over. It would not be realistic to expect the forms of social organization in some of the former socialist countries to be in perfect harmony with the requested capitalist post-industrialization. It is very likely that the discrepancy will be most evident in the sphere of the cultural urban transformation. Just like any globalism in the social or ecological sphere, Europe will have to grant legality to the cities east and south of the Alps for a number of specific characteristics. On the other side, these cities will have to realize that in the long run, they have nothing to regret. In order to become full-fledged members of the European urban network, Belgrade does not have to strive to adopt the cosmopolitanism of Amsterdam or Brussels. Conversely, Bucharest may not try to regain its image of "Little Paris" without having to share the teletopic vision of future with Paris itself.

To be in tune with the "contemporary" forms of transformation, the "non-Western" cities are expected to transform into full-fledged members of the European urban network practically overnight, i.e., in a period which is too short when compared with the period that gave them their present social profile. In this context, there exist at least four major problems: (1) Their spiritual transformation into the cosmopolitan environment that would be attractive to the modern man will not be feasible for an extended period because of the non-cosmopolitian heritage bestowed on them by the past half century; (2) Time is required for their institutions, economies, and finally, citizens to establish a continual active relationship with the process of dynamic urban changes (the so-called "continual urban progress"); (3) A need for establishing a stable urban network: each city within the network should have a clearly defined regional role and a stable and differentiated economic position; and (4) A need for defining a new model of urbanization which would replace the worn-out patterns of unbridled demographic and territorial expansion.

Any of the possible concepts of urban development in the Eastern and/or Central European context must necessarily involve information of political processes which are going to rule the fate of the people and the territory. The possibility of adhering to indigenous cultural and historical models is bound to be an accepted direction of urban development. Endeavours to rapidly adopt Western European urban models will be limited by the pace of social transformations. The city is a phenomenon which changes much slower than is the case with global social or technological transformations. Urban changes take a roundabout way. Considering the

European integrating process, what may be expected to happen to the city which we have recognized up to yesterday as a Eastern European city?

The first prerequisite for a possible future of "non-Western European cities" is to solve major conflicts which determine their present situation. Most conflicts result from the typical lack of political foresight and willingness of people (including urban planners and decision makers) to take an active part in solving these problems.

To be able to face the European challenge of integration in and harmonization with its urban network, "non-Western" European cities must solve the problem of their *internationalization*. Is it possible at all, and if it is, what degreee of internationalization is needed for their future prosperity? Extreme policies of self-sufficiency and ethnocentrism, which have led to their provincialization, have been devised at the expense of traditional culture which has been a predominantly positive potential of these cities. Hopefully, this attitude is very likely to be quickly abandoned. It is clear that internationalization is an inevitable part of the scenario inherent to the development of western cities. To take part in such a scenario "non-Western" European cities should respond positively to questions like the following: Are we ready to become an integral part of the world? Are we capable of attaining a position which will be acceptable to the world? Although the components of this scenario of possible urban development seem to be a series of general statements, the fact remains that many cities in yesterday's Eastern Europe pass through an imitative phase misinterpreting international forms by organizing uneconomic and culturally debatable events.

Some western models of future urban development insist on *communicational* performances of the city. This scenario has recently attracted much attention because revolutionary communication technologies play a fundamental role in urban transformations. Unaccustomed to the challenge of the information future, inhabitants of yesterday's Eastern European city are sceptics whose experience says that novelty does not necessarily imply improvement.

The negative effects of a long-continued indoctrination of urban planners, decision makers, even scientists, may be seen on the fronts of practically all large and medium-sized yesterday's Eastern European cities. From the advent of modern trends in architecture and urban planning, i.e., for some six decades, the urban entity in its material and spiritual sense has been steadily corrupted. Therefore, it is reasonable to expect that *reconstruction* will be an important direction of future urban development. The following prerequisites are needed for this to happen: evolution of political consciousness untill the concept of "socialist city" is recognized as an ideological blunder; evolution in attitudes of urban planners who must accept that the city is no mere agglomeration of houses; rediscovery and reaffirmation of the lost architectural and planning context founded on regional values; and finally, decades of patient waiting to perceive improvement in the material and spiritual qualities of the city.

It is a grave fact that the networks of urban centres in Central and Eastern Europe reflect a situation in which the territory is sharply divided between the centre and the periphery. This is a consequence of the political idea that people, assets and territory are efficiently controlled by methods and techniques of strict centralization. To be rational, the city should accept to operate within a *decentralized regional network*. To realize this model, it is necessary to reconsider and transform the ruling political doctrines and to decentralize the political power to equitably distributed regional centres. In other words, it implies a rationalization of management. When talking of concentration , it is essential to keep in mind that this is not a mere physical concentration of people and assets. Out of several important components of concentration we mention only two components which are important for the urban system of Eastern Europe, and which may govern the development of regions in a wide vicinity of an urban centre: (1) concentration of status and power, i.e., politics, management and information; and (2) cultural concentration which may be a powerful tool in developed and underdeveloped regions alike. Only after these two categories comes the physical concentration as a technically and technologically preferable framework of the urban way of life.

The reviewed hypotheses of future urban development of the Eastern and Central European city obviously follow a line of indispensable changes of the currently prevailing mental processes and make room for a more social approach to sustainable development.

WHAT COULD BE THE EFFECTS OF THE TRANSFORMATION OF AN URBAN SOCIETY IF IDEAS ABOUT THIS ARE DERIVED FROM ENVIRONMENTS WHICH DO NOT UNDERSTAND THE CULTURAL CONTEXT OF THE COMMUNITY?

If it can be considered that the idea of social transformation, as the framework for sustainable development, has been ostracized on the supranational level (as in the case of the European Community or in any other case when there is a formal equalization of cultural regions for the purpose of economic and political unification and integration), the effects for different areas of these regions vary quite extensively, but they are always very significant and inevitably painful. All the effects manifest themselves on the following common levels:

1) Changes in the Economic Structure

One of the basic assumptions for realizing the concept of sustainable development concerns adapting the economic structure of society to

greater efficiency and utilization of resource potentials, in all of its segments. As a rule, an urban society is an aggregate which most quickly,
powerfully and extremely sensitively reacts to every outer and inner
demand for social change. Finally, all the elements of the economic performance of a society such as production, consumption and ecological conditions derive to a great extent from the demands of the urban environment.
Urban systems and cities in the Third World and East European countries
are very telling examples of the extent to which supranational demands for
an egalitarian application of the liberal capitalism and market economy
model strongly affect the reshaping of traditional cultural models of urban
living, the urban and urbanistic identity of the community. The economic
models of the western world, often to imaginary levels and forms of well
being, follow paths which irremediably undermine the distinctive traits of
autochthonous urban (and not only urban) cultures. Economic efficiency
and progressive economic growth need not necessarily be prerequisites for
the culturally and urbanly sustainable development of a community.

2) Changes in the Social Structure

The social structure of society is one of its most dynamic factors and, at the
same time, exponent of the greatest number of traits of a society. Despite
this fact, the stability of a society is also measured by the steadiness of its
social structure. When external demands are made for social change, this
automatically also calls for such changes in a society's social structure
which are profiled in a long-term process. It could be claimed that the
"urban profiles" of most of the urban centres in Europe (in all its regions)
were developed over a long period of time. In addition to this, in each
European country the dominant segment of the social structure is constituted by the middle-class layer of society. This is the layer toward which
the social challenges are addressed and, at the same time, it is a "trans-
former" toward the other layers of society. The quantitative and qualitative
challenges of sustainable development in the spheres of production, consumption and utilization of space are most extensively realized in this middle layer. The spaces and functions of every city are, in the largest number
of cases, adapted to the requirements and demands of this layer: housing
(manifested as the distribution of forms of housing, the structure and
quality of houses), the network of institutions (education, health, culture,
administration), employment positions, transportation infrastructure (for
this is the layer from which greatest number of the work force is recruited
and which has a need for daily mass migrations within the city or area),
outdoor and indoor spaces for recreation, and so on. It is clear that
demands for social change induce changes in the way of life of this most
numerous portion of urban society. In periods of widespread social transi-

tion, such as, in the nineties, the countries of former Eastern and partly Central Europe are undergoing, this erosion of social structure is best visible. Whole social layers are disappearing (primarily the middle class), and some new ones are taking shape, which will eventually play a dominant role in contouring the urban profile of the whole society. The decomposition of a society's social structure need not necessarily also imply an advancement toward a better form of community, since a society's traditional social structure is an essential factor of its stability. When a system of values has been established, and when, in the meantime, another one is not developed through evolution, what then happens is that the gaps created by transition are filled by an ad hoc system. The sudden entrance of a market economy and market thinking into the everyday life of urban societies in transition is causing gaps in their social structure. One of the most important effects is that traditional forms of urbanality are being decomposed at the same time.

3) Changes in the Urban Structure

Through the focus on social and urban reality of new social structures created by transition, in most of the large cities of the former political East, dramatic changes are taking place in their inherited urban structure. This means that the urban-morphological matrix, which is an important identification demarcation in the life of the maximum number of citizens (and of other inhabitants as well), is being altered. New rules of the game in the planning and utilization of space are being adapted to the social layer which holds the levers of political and economic power. In this case, these two are most often overlapping. The face of the city which takes shape in such conditions results from the current redistribution of social wealth, which is passing into private hands. In countries of the former socialist order, this is what is termed "the selling of the state", in which speculations with urban real estate are the most attractive, that is, most profitable. Since the right to ownership is one of the fundamental values and impetuses for western democracies, this is what countries in transition are tending toward. This right, linked with organized urban regulations in a process of evolution (where the monetarization of society and administrative and legislative trends are concurrent), it is well known, has given rise to the recognizable and functionally differentiated cities of western society. Many cities in Western Europe are examples, in the general case, of "desirable and good" urban structures. It cannot, however, be expected that in the process of social transition such a transformation can take place without serious effects for urbanality. The larger and medium-size cities of the European east and especially their central parts are today being deconstructed. Appearing on the scene is a great European wave of "osmanization", which is rapidly erasing the marks of former times. The concept of sustainable development must be based on strategies which respect the patterns of urbanality originating in the long process of the historical constitution of the urban morphology. This does not mean (nor is it possible) that there should be an obligatory and required return to or insistence on "authentic" architectural forms, such as we have in Berlin today, which is attempting, at any cost, to return to the look it had in the thirties, by remodelling some of its central areas. What shape can, in the simplest case, this attack on established values of urban culture take? For instance, in cities whose traditional centres of marketing are bazaars or open air markets (cities in the Mediterranean region or those in the East), when there is a new approach and insistence on large indoor markets, whose economic efficiency is measured by a quick turnover of money and a consumer mentality of the western type. Or, when in the construction of new traffic communications across old city centres, the network of historical urban patterns is disrupted. This also occurs when the construction of new housing projects (usually on the outskirts) establishes no organic link with the important morphological features of the urban past or when patterns established by tradition are not raised to an adequate semantic level.

4) Changes in Living Patterns

If the thesis that "urbanism manifests itself as a way of life" (L. Wirth) is correct, then the urbanality of any space is given by the patterns it is being lived through. Since patterns of living are exponents of certain cultural and social features of a society, changes in them also affect the acquired values of the community. Sustainable urban-cultural development has to take into account the actual differences which exist in various geographical and cultural-genetic zones. The patterns of urban living in a Mediterranean city and in one north of the Alps are essentially different. The homogenization of the "urban mass" of Europe (or of any other space characterized by differences) should not simply be a process of unification.

The urban identity of a community is an exceptionally valuable component of sustainable urban-cultural development. The wealth of a civilization is measured by the variety of its manifest forms; the wealth and vitality of an urban civilization is expressed by the multitude of its different forms of urbanality. The urban identity of a community can be expressed by the term *city-making*. Some of the fundamental elements of its complexity can be considered to be: the manner of social organization within the community (which can be inefficient in the economic sense, but is always typical), the temporality of the community, the characteristics of its urban structures (its urban morphology), the atmosphere of the city/community as a quality of its historical duration, a specific form of its social structure (which need not mean that it is also the desired one), the retaining of a certain type of social segregation and spatial differentiation (which cannot be obliterated by any model of social and urban development, and so, in the social concept of sustainable development one should not even insist on their elimination), etc.

The notion of maintaining a certain level of urban identity in a community is not, however, without dangers which are opposed to rational forms of social development. Some of the most important ones are: romanticization and emphasized exclusiveness of one's own culture; separation from other urban communities of the broader region or continent; withdrawal into the shell of a national state, that is to say, state-national egotism; the seeking of development patterns in nostalgic historicism which transforms an idealized past into dogma; the dominance of political ideologies and religious exclusiveness which employ traditional values in order to promote conservativism, nationalism, ethnocentrism and intolerance. The spiritual categories which are the very essence of the urban identity of a community cannot be valued by material criteria, and should not be too close to the growth of other authentic cultural values of another provenance. Sustainable urban-cultural development is, in one of its essential aspects, urban pluralism. (This should not be equated with so-called multicultural society which, some believe, is the future of global development and which is, supposedly, the marker of the degree of a society's democracy.) It is certain, however, that value relations in urban communities/cities, which are established only within the framework of given cultural patterns and the spiritual quality of the accumulated past, should not be closed to innovated (enriched) but also authentic cultural patterns. In any case, this is what constitutes the positive difference between, for instance, the southern, central and western regions of Europe.

Part III
Local Answers

Sustainable Urban Management: Opportunities and Risks of Information Technology

Ulrike Weiland and *Lorenz Hilty*

THE NEED FOR SUSTAINABLE URBAN MANAGEMENT

The world-wide urbanization process is a challenge to urban planning and information technology. Recent forecasts predict that up to 90 per cent of the increase of world population will take place in urban agglomerations. In the year 2025 the average number of inhabitants of the largest 36 cities in the world will be about 9 million, and in the year 2035 six out of eight billion people will live in urban areas (Hahn 1991). At the same time, cities and urban areas have become a symbol for, and a product of, the careless treatment of scarce and vulnerable environmental resources. Most of worldwide energy and raw material consumption as well as waste production is due to industrial technology, the urban lifestyle and the spatial separation of urban functions. Present concepts of urban planning and technology are inadequate in solving the basic urban crisis. In order to develop sustainable urban areas, we need concepts, techniques and measures which allow us to combine environmental policies with social and economic policies.

"Sustainability in an urban setting ... describes the potential of a city to reach qualitatively a new level of socio-economic, demographic and technological output which in the long run reinforces the foundations of the urban system, although its evolutionary path may exhibit various stable or unstable temporary fluctuation. Thus urban sustainability ensures a long-term survival of the urban system" (Nijkamp 1990, p.8, see also Hamm et al. 1992). Urban planning should be replaced by the new concept of Sustainable Urban Management (Weiland 1994a). Sustainable Urban Management has to "include the minimization in the use of non-renewable resources, the achievement of the sustainable use of renewable resources, staying within the absorptive capacity of local and global waste absorption limits and meeting basic human needs" (Choguill 1993, 3).

Sustainable Urban Management must meet four criteria: urban policies must be ecologically, economically, socially and technically sustainable (Choguill 1993). Key issues are the protection of habitats and resources necessary to humans and wildlife. This requires high resource efficiency by means of value-preserving transformation processes in production, consumption and recycling as well as the minimization of ecotoxicological and health risks. One of the most important goals for urban areas is the reduction of transportation demand (see also Hahn 1991).

APPROACHES TO SUSTAINABLE URBAN MANAGEMENT

Implementation of Sustainable Urban Management requires more and different information than is available today. Starting from a systems approach to urban areas, prognoses and scenarios of alternative planning measures and effects have to be worked out, giving special attention to long-term and side effects. Explicitly stated goals of environmental quality should set the level of aspired and consensual environmental precautions and serve as scales for planning decisions. Ideas, norms and goals of a Sustainable Urban Management should be formulated in a strategic plan, which should incorporate a plan for the management of material and energy flows. The four instruments outlined below can serve as approaches to Sustainable Urban Management (Hilty and Weiland 1994). Some of them are directly applicable, others need to be transformed for use in urban management. The list is not comprehensive.

1) Environmental Impact Assessment

An Environmental Impact Assessment (EIA) contains the prognosis and evaluation of environmental impacts of planning measures. It can be used as a decision support instrument at different planning levels; EIAs for plans should be supplemented by EIAs for projects. Computer support for EIA comprises database systems for the management of environmental data (e.g. EQUEL by Plank 1994), specific forms of Geographical Information Systems (GIS, e.g. SAMBA by Boman et al. 1994), atmospheric and hydrologic models and simulation tools for the prognosis phase and expert systems such as EXCEPT. The EXCEPT system is a generic expert system shell for evaluation tasks in the field of environmental planning. The basic idea of the system is the separation of formal, methodological and objective aspects. A generic representation of evaluation methods is necessary for the representation, processing and comparison of many different evaluation approaches. Evaluation methods are built up in modules. The system consists of a knowledge acquisition component for the maintenance of knowledge bases, an inference mechanism for the generation of environmental evaluations and a document-generating component. Included are user-definable strategies for handling incomplete or inconsistent knowledge (Weiland et al. 1993, Weiland 1994b).

2) Life Cycle Assessment

Life Cycle Assessment (LCA) is a general methodology of investigating the environmental impacts of anthropogenic objects (consumer products, buildings, infrastructure) during their whole life cycles, beginning with resource extraction and ending with waste disposal. Today, LCA is most frequently applied to consumer goods (Pedersen Weidema 1993). For Sustainable Urban Management, this approach is relevant at two different levels. At the level of consumer goods, it has an indispensible function in combating the overwhelming waste treatment problems in a sustainable manner. It also serves as an early warning system of future waste treatment problems. At the level of buildings and infrastructure, LCA can help reduce the burden we put on the shoulders of future generations, because the problems of maintenance and demolition are taken into account from the beginning. There are a number of software tools that support the LCA methodology (for an overview, see Miettinen 1993). However, these tools usually lack a mathematically consistent formalism for modeling the underlying mass and energy flows. A first approach with a clear theoretical background is outlined by Schmidt et al. (1994), where the formalism of Petri Nets is used.

3) Eco-logistics

Modern logistics is concerned with systems of material, energy and information flow. The goal of logistics is to structure and to control these systems optimally, that is to maximize logistical performance (providing the right objects in the right condition at the right time and place) while minimizing logistical cost. Optimal solutions for eco-logistical systems are different from those for conventional logistical systems. Computer simulation is an important tool of logistics, since the complexity of most logistical systems is beyond the scope of analytical methods.

The concept of eco-logistics, as outlined by Hilty et al. (1994), is an extension of logistics that integrates secondary material and energy flows into the system under consideration. An example of a secondary material flow is the flow of carbon dioxide (CO_2) from road traffic into the atmosphere, the primary material flow being the freight. The physical mass moved by secondary flows often reaches or excels the scale of the primary flows. New methods of computer modelling and simulation have been developed to meet the requirements of eco-logistics (Hilty et al. 1994). The models can help to find sustainable logistic structures and strategies in a dynamic environment. Therefore, they are well-suited for Sustainable Urban Management.

4) Material Flux Analysis

This approach, as introduced by Baccini and Brunner (1991), shares the paradigm of "material, energy and information flow" with the eco-logistics approach. However, its special quality is the view of regional economies as complex living organisms. This metaphor leads to a methodology of material flux analysis that allows to qualify and quantify the metabolism of anthropogenic systems. Such analyses usually show that the material and energy efficiency of anthropogenic systems is extremely bad compared to the efficiency of natural systems. Therefore, material flux analysis can reveal the primary problems and help to find the most effective measures to improve ecological efficiency, for example, in the field of regional material management. Besides controlling regional material fluxes, this approach leads to the development of cybernetic strategies for the metabolic evolution of the anthroposphere. Supported by a simulation system for the assessment of such strategies, this approach should be a basic building block of Sustainable Urban Management.

AMBIVALENCE OF INFORMATION TECHNOLOGY IN SUSTAINABLE URBAN MANAGEMENT

One of the most striking examples of the ambivalence of Information Technology is found in the traffic sector. This example is of special importance because urban traffic is one of the hardest problems to be solved on the way to sustainable cities. Mokhtarian (1989) introduced a widely used typology of relationships between telecommunication and transportation:
— Substitution: Telecommunication substitutes physical traffic
— Induction: Telecommunication induces traffic
— Optimization: Telecommunication helps to optimize traffic systems
— Flexibilization: Telecommunication allows for more flexibility in the choice of traffic means and paths.

While the (limited) substitution effect of telecommunication arising from telecommuting and various forms of tele-services (e.g. tele-banking, tele-shopping) can reduce the environmental load imposed by urban traffic, the induction and 'just-in-time'-logistics due to telecommunication networks clearly leads away from the path to sustainability. Optimization and flexibilization can have different impacts depending on the specific form and economic conditions of their implementation. Another example that shows the ambivalence of information technology in the urbanization process is 'Artificial Intelligence' (AI). On the level of life-styles and societal value systems, AI systems can have a negative influence because of the implicit paradigms and misrepresentations that are deeply embedded in them (see Brunnstein 1991). On the other hand, expert systems can be useful in urban management, if they meet the specific needs of user groups and if they are combined with Geographical Information Systems (Weiland 1994c).

CONCLUSION AND OUTLOOK

The instruments for a Sustainable Urban Management listed earlier require completion and integration. It is a challenge to urban management and computer science to find a consistent methodological basis for the wide spectrum of methods and the corresponding computer support. Moreover, we suppose that these approaches—even if integrated in a holistic and consistent framework—are not sufficient to bring about the paradigm shift from conventional urban planning to Sustainable Urban Management. New ideas are also needed on the level of the models and theories behind the instruments, for example:

- The concept of fractal urban form which relies on a cellular modelling approach to the evolution of urban land-use patterns (White and Engelen 1993).
- The Sequential Interindustry Model (SIM) for examining transient processes (Romanoff and Levine 1993), and
- The dynamic economic-ecological models for sustainable development by Van den Bergh and Nijkamp (1993).

Sustainable Urban Management requires a deeper understanding of the evolution of ecological, social and economic structures and, based on this understanding, the construction of instruments that help to approach sustainability. For both steps, information technology can offer various forms of support. Approaching the vision of sustainable urban areas will be a decisive test of the problem-solving potential of information technology.

REFERENCES

Baccini, P. and P.H. Brunner. 1991. Metabolism of the Anthroposphere. Berlin: Springer.

Boman, J., M. Olsson and M. Sundholm. 1993. *SAMBA—A Way to Deal with GIS*. In: *Computer Support for Environmental Impact Assessment* (CSEIA) Guariso et al. (1994), pp. 3–13 Amsterdam, London, New York: North-Holland.

Brunnstein, K. 1991. Human Intelligence and AI. Pages 136–142 in: *Proc. Intern. IFIPConference—Opportunities and Risks of Artificial Intelligence Systems*. Hamburg: University of Hamburg.

Choguill, C.L. 1993. Sustainable Cities: Urban Policies for the Future. *Habitat Intl.* 17(3): 1–12 (Editorial), Pergamon Press Ltd.

Guariso, G. and B. Page (eds.). 1994. *Computer Support for Environmental Impact Assessment* (CSEIA). Amsterdam, London, New York: North-Holland.

Hahn, E. 1991. Ecological Urban Restructuring. Theoretical Foundation and Concept for Action. FS II 91-402, Berlin: Wissenschaftszentrum (WZB) Berlin.

Hamm, B., G. Zimmer and S. Kratz. (eds.). 1992. Sustainable Development and the Future of Cities. *Proceedings of an International Summer Seminar* held at the Bauhaus Dessau, 7 to 14 September, 1991. Trier: Centre for European Studies, University of Trier.

Hilty, L.M., D. Martinssen and B. Page. 1994. Designing a simulation tool for the environmental assessment of logistical systems and strategies. In: *Computer Support for Environmental Impact Assessment* (CSEIA). Guariso and Page (eds.) (1994), pp. 187–198

Hilty, L.M. and U. Weiland. 1994. Sustainable Cities—Opportunities and Risks of Information Technology. Pages 613–618 in: *13th World Computer Congress 94*, Volume 2, K. Brunnstein and E. Raubold (eds.): North-Holland: Elsevier Science B.V.

Miettinen, P. 1993. Software Tools in Life Cycle Assessment. Pages 93–104 In: *Environmental Assessment of Products*. Helsinki: UETP-EEE.

Mokhtarian, P.L. 1989. A typology of relationships between telecommunications and transportation. *Transportation Research* 22A: 283–289.

Nijkamp, P. 1990. *Sustainability of Urban Systems. A Cross-National Evolutionary Analysis of Urban Innovation.* Avebury: Aldershot.

Pedersen Weidema, B. 1993. *Environmental Assessment of Products.* Helsinki: UETP-EEE.

Plank, T. 1994. EQUEL—A database system for the management of environmental data. Pages 61–73 in: *Computer Support for Environmental Impact Assessment* (CSEIA). Guariso and Page (eds.).

Romanoff, E. and S.H. Levine. 1993. Information, interindustry dynamics and the service industries. *Environment and Planning A.* 25: 305–316.

Schmidt, M., J. Giegrich and L.M. Hilty. 1994. Experiences with Ecobalances and the Development of an Interactive Software Tool. In: *Proc. Umweltinformatik 94—Environmental Informatics 94*, L.M. Hilty, A. Jaeschke, B. Page and A. Schwabl (eds.). Hamburg. Metropolis Verlag. Marburg

Van den Bergh, J.C. and P. Nijkamp. 1993. Aggregate Dynamic Economic-Ecological Models for Sustainable Development, pp. 1409–1428.

Weiland, U., J. Pietsch and M. Hübner. 1993. The EXCEPT-Projekt: Expert System for Computer-Aided Environmental Planning Tasks—Methodology of Computer-Aided Evaluation. Pages 358–367 in: *Proc. IFIP Working Conference on Computer Support for Environmental Impact Assessment (CSEIA)*, Como.

Weiland, U. 1994a. Der Beitrag der Stadtökologie zu einer ökologischen Stadterneuerung und entwicklung—Konzeption einer Umweltplanung für Stadtregionen. Pages 87–94 in: *Stadtökologie—Versuch einer Standortbestimmung.* R. Wittig and H.-C. Frnd (eds.), 11, Frankfurt/Main: Geobot. Kolloq.

Weiland, U. 1994b. Strukturierte Bewertung in Umweltverträglichkeitsprüfungen—Ein Konzept zur Rechnerunterstützung am Beispiel der UVP in der Bauleitplanung. Pages 224–226 in: *UVP-report 4/94.*

Weiland, U. 1994c. Strukturierte Bewertung in der Bauleitplan-UVP—Ein Konzept zur Rechnerunterstützung der Bewertungsdurchführung. UVP-spezial 9. Hg.: Verein zur Förderung der Umweltverträglichkeitsprüfung. Dortmunder Vertrieb für Bau- und Planungs-literatur. Dortmund.

White, R. and G. Engelen. 1993. Cellular automata and fractal urban form: a cellular modelling approach to the evolution of urban land-use patterns. *Environment and Planning A.* 25: 1175–1199.

Sustainable Communities: Planning for the 21st Century

William E. Rees and Mark Roseland

INTRODUCTION AND PURPOSE[1]

"Sustainable development" has become the rallying cry of dedicated environmentalists and trenchant industrialists alike. While this unifying power is to be admired, any concept with such broad appeal across the political-ideological spectrum merits a closer look. Is there objective meaning in sustainable development? What is the rational basis for significant changes in our approach to economic and community development? Based on a reassessment of certain key assumptions of macro- and neoclassical economics, prevailing environmental trends, and ecological theory, we develop an ecologically realistic framework for planning sustainable communities and explore some of its implications for Canadian communities in the 21st century.

DEVELOPING SUSTAINABLE URBAN COMMUNITIES

"Strong sustainability" has serious implications for the urban form, for the material basis of urban life, and for community social relationships that must be expressed as practical measures in planning Canadian communities. These measures must emphasize the efficient use of urban space, reducing the consumption of material and energy resources, improving community livability, and organizing administrative and planning processes which can deal sensitively and comprehensively with the attendant socio-economic and ecological complexities.

---

[1]For the theory of sustainable development, see the contribution by William E. Rees at the beginning of this volume.

The Unsustainable Community

Most North American cities were built using technologies which assumed that abundant and cheap energy and land would always be available. Communities therefore grew quickly and inefficiently, and became dependent on lengthy distribution systems. Cheap energy influenced the construction of our spacious homes and buildings, fostered our addiction to the automobile, and increased the separation of our workplaces from our homes (Environment Council of Alberta, 1988).

Urban sprawl is the legacy of abundant fossil fuel and our perceived right to unrestricted use of the private car whatever the social costs and externalities. Per capita gasoline consumption in the U.S. and in many Canadian cities is now more than four times that of European cities, and over 10 times greater than Asian cities such as Hong Kong, Tokyo, and Singapore. The biggest factor accounting for these differences in energy use appears to be not the size of cars or the price of gasoline, but the efficiency and compactness of land-use patterns (Replogle 1990). One conclusion of a study prepared for the U.S. Government was that "'sprawl' is the most expensive form of residential development in terms of economic costs, environmental costs, natural resource consumption, and many types of personal costs.... This cost difference is particularly significant for that proportion of total costs which is likely to be borne by local governments" (Real Estate Research Corporation 1974).

Other local and regional consequences of sprawl, such as congestion, urban air pollution, jobs-housing location "imbalance", and longer commuting times are now recognisable. Yet, until recently, few researchers acknowledged that the land-use pattern of North American cities also has serious global ecological ramifications. For example, residents of most Canadian cities annually produce about 20 tons of carbon dioxide per capita, placing Canada among the top three of four nations in terms of per capita contribution to potential climate change. In contrast, citizens of Amsterdam produce only 10 tons of carbon dioxide per capita per year. Sprawl, exclusionary zoning and low density account for much of this difference.[2] According to recent research at the International Institute for Applied Systems Analysis, if North American cities modelled future development on cities like Amsterdam, future carbon dioxide emissions here would only be half as much as current gloomy projections now indicate (Alcamo 1990).

---

[2]Other factors have also influenced the compact development patterns of the world's Amsterdams, for example, historically higher energy prices, more efficient automobiles, lower rates of automobile ownership, and a tradition of support for public transit and bicycle transportation. These factors certainly reinforce compact development patterns; however, they are more likely to result from compactness rather than cause it.

The Sustainable Community

The post-war pattern of Western urban development is ecologically inefficient and socially inequitable. In contrast, sustainable development implies
that the use of energy materials be in balance with such "natural capital"
processes as photosynthesis and waste assimilation (Rees 1990a, b). This in
turn implies increasing community and regional self-reliance to reduce dependency on imports (RAIN 1981; California Office of Appropriate Technology 1981; Morris 1982). The benefits would be reduced energy budgets,
reduced material consumption, and a smaller, more compact urban pattern
interspersed with productive areas to collect energy, grow crops, and
recycle wastes (Van der Ryn and Calthorpe 1986, p. ix).

Cities with low "automobile dependence" are more centralized; have
more intense land-use (more people and jobs per unit area); are more
oriented to non-auto modes (more public transit, foot traffic and bicycle
usage); place more restraints on high-speed traffic; and offer better public
transit (Newman and Kenworthy 1989). This suggests a new approach to
transportation planning and traffic management in Canada. Transportation
planning in the past several decades has been a largely reactive, dependent
variable, driven by increasing congestion and resulting in the low-density
outward expansion of the city. Transportation planning must become a
determinant force, one that induces the needed change in urban form
(Replogle 1990).

The ideal urban form for a particular locale will depend to some extent
on the nature of the energy-supply options: for example, higher densities
make most efficient use of district heating and public transport networks,
while lower densities may make solar energy more viable. The location,
gross density and form of new development should therefore be determined in conjunction with programmes for energy supply and conservation technologies (Owens 1990, pp. 78–79). This principle is illustrated by a
recent study from San Jose, California, which compared development pressures with or without a "greenbelt". Without it, 13,000 ex-urban homes
would be developed, which, compared with an equivalent number of units
downtown and along the transit corridor, would require at least an additional 200,000 of auto-commuting plus an additional three million gallons
of water every day, as well as requiring 40 per cent more energy for heating
and cooling (Yesney 1990).

Another study from Montgomery County, Maryland, found that continued growth in an automobile-dependent pattern would produce traffic
congestion levels high enough to choke off economic development. However, an anticipated doubling of population and employment could be
accommodated without excessive traffic problems if most new growth
were clustered in pedestrian- and bicycle-friendly centres focussed on an

expanded rail transit and busway system. Through such strategies, the share of County work trips made by non-auto alternatives could double to 50 per cent resulting in only half the level of energy use and air pollution compared with the sprawled, automobile strategy (Replogle 1990).

Such studies demonstrate that the pattern of growth is more important than the amount of growth in determining the level and efficiency of resource use and traffic congestion.

LOCAL INITIATIVES FOR A SUSTAINABLE FUTURE

Although "environmental concerns" currently top the polls, resistance to changing specific behaviours and development practices may be formidable, as is evident by the global debate over whether to adopt, and how to implement, a 20 per cent reduction in carbon dioxide emissions (Rees 1990d). The U.S. Environmental Protection Agency has estimated that merely to stabilize atmospheric concentrations of carbon dioxide at the current level, carbon emissions must be cut by 50–80 per cent. Scientists and policymakers meeting in Toronto in June 1988 offered a short-term goal: cutting them 20 per cent by 2005 (Toronto Conference Statement 1988, Flavin 1990). Meanwhile, Canada is considering whether merely to freeze emissions at 1988 levels by 2005.

International bodies and national governments struggle to formulate policies to achieve this goal, but it is at the community level where most of these initiatives will have to be implemented. Many local governments have therefore started taking action singlehandedly (see City of Vancouver 1990). They recognize that net fiscal, economic, and ecological benefits will accrue to those who get their environmental house in order. For example, most energy dollars leave the local community. Shifting purchases from energy to retail sales, for example, is more likely to result in the retention of dollars in the local economy and produce a larger multiplier effect.

In Tables 1 through 5, we outline several kinds of initiatives which could be adopted or adapted by municipal and other governments in Canada to satisfy the criteria of land-use efficiency, reduced consumption of resources, and improved community livability. We also indicate implementation mechanisms and jurisdictions in which these initiatives are being practised or proposed.[3] In countries where federal initiatives have resulted in several local government responses, the names of the countries are given.

---

[3]The jurisdictions are cited as examples: these are not intended to be comprehensive listings.

Summarizing Actions and Directions: From Tables 1 and 2, we determine that land-use planning and controls must be created or strengthened (see Richardson 1989).[4] Energy-efficient land-use policies must be developed to reduce the need for transportation (Federation of Canadian Municipalities 1990). Grants and loans for transportation investments should be tied to compliance with requirements for regional land-use planning and growth management. Sprawl should be attacked by setting maximum expansion limits and favouring growth near transit stations. Metropolitan planning should shift from access by transportation to access by proximity (City of Vancouver 1990).

Automobile trip-reduction bye-laws, road pricing, preferential parking, regional carbon dioxide taxes, street redesign and traffic calming, and all measures to encourage public transit and bicycle transportation, should be actively encouraged. Governments, investors, and banks should require analysis of alternative long-term least-cost strategies for transportation and land-use investments. Long-term least-cost strategies would tend to give pedestrians, cyclists, and public transportation priority over the automobile. They would favour the building of surface light rail and bikeway systems connecting higher density pedestrian-friendly city and suburban centres. They would favour the building of bicycle parking garages. They would lead to policies that slow down car traffic to improve conditions for pedestrians and cyclists (Replogle 1990).

From Tables 3 and 4, we determine that energy efficiency should be increased in all sectors to reach specific targets, e.g., 20 per cent by 2000. Energy conservation retrofit ordinances and renewable energy technologies should be encouraged and financially supported. Packaging restrictions should be adopted, along with ambitious goals to reduce, reuse, reprocess and recycle waste.

Initiatives cited in Table 5 demonstrate efforts to fulfil human needs, improve social equity, and provide for social self-determination, can and must be pursued in concert with initiatives to maintain ecological integrity (Gardner and Roseland 1989a). Many of today's health problems—cancer, heart disease, emphysema, car accidents—have lifestyle and environmental causes. Reducing these threats involves traditional preventive measures that parallel and reinforce environmental objectives (see e.g., Mathur 1989, Boothroyd and Eberle 1990).

---

[4]Oregon's system of Statewide Planning Goals is a good model for comprehensive land-use planning. The State sets mandatory goals (e.g., to provide for widespread citizen involvement; to preserve and maintain agricultural lands; to conserve energy), which are general standards for land-use planning. Planning remains the responsibility of city and county governments, but it must be done in accordance with these statewise standards (Rohse 1987).

Table 1: Efficient Use of Urban Space: Transportation Planning and Traffic Management Initiatives

Initiative	Purpose	Mechanisms	Practised/Proposed
Trip reduction bye-laws	To reduce peak hour trips and increase the ratio of people to vehicles.	Require employers to implement a program, including appointment of a transportation co-ordinator and any reasonable combination of commute alternatives designed to achieve the required target.	Vancouver, Bellevue, WA; Montgomery County, MD; 37 California cities and counties
Automobile restrictions	To reduce urban air pollution, traffic congestion.	Prohibit automobile use one or more day per week; fuel taxes.	Florence; Budapest; Santiago; Mexico City
Road pricing	To reduce car traffic in urban centres; also being used to fund public transit.	All drivers entering the city centre are required to display a valid monthly transit pass or other sticker.	Singapore; Hong Kong; Holland; Stockholm; Vancouver
Parking measures	To favour high-occupancy vehicles over single-occupancy vehicles.	Preferential parking, parking pricing, parking offsets.	Ottawa; Vancouver; Portland, OR; Seattle, WA; Montgomery County, MD; Sacramento, CA
Free or inexpensive transit	To encourage use of public transit.	Transit is free, at least within the downtown core.	Portland, OR
Bicycle transportation	To make bicycling a better transportation alternative.	Car-free bicycle routes; bicycle parking; shower and locker facilities in all new developments.	Palo Alto, Davis, Berkeley, CA; Bordeaux (France); Groningen (Holland); Toronto; Vancouver
Street redesign and traffic calming	To slow traffic speeds, reduce noise and exhaust, and make streets safer for pedestrians, children, seniors and bicyclists.	Woonerfen, or "slow streets," with narrow lanes, curves, speed humps, shrubbery, slow speed limits, etc.	Holland, Saarbrücken (Germany); Berkeley, CA
Telecommunications	To encourage alternatives to commuting.	Determine tasks/jobs, provide training and/or equipment.	Portland, OR; Vancouver

Table 2: Efficient Use of Urban Space: Land-Use Planning and Housing Initiatives

Initiative	Purpose	Mechanisms	Practised/Proposed
Proximity planning	To make access by proximity rather than access by transportation a central focus of city planning.	Developing policies and incentives.	Vancouver
Residential intensification	To create new residential units or accommodation in existing buildings or on previously developed, serviced land.	Creation of rooming, boarding and lodging houses; creation of accessory apartments; conversion of non-residential structures to residential use; infill; redevelopment.	Kingston, St. Catherines, Metro Toronto
Co-housing	Participatory, intentional neighbourhood design.	Extensive common facilities; developments are organized, planned, and managed by the residents themselves.	Denmark, Holland, Sweden, Norway, France, Germany; Winslow, WA
Community land trusts	To hold land for the benefit of a community and of individuals within the community.	A democratically structured non-profit corporation, with an open membership and an elected board of trustees.	Philadelphia, PA; Burlington, VT; Atlanta, GA; New York City, Greenfied, MA; Providence, RI; Franklin, NH; Norwich, CT
Rural area protection	To compensate for damage to natural areas.	Land reconstruction rules in the landscape plan.	Enschede (Holland)
Co-management agreements	To provide for a high level of user-group participation in resource decision making.	Detailed provisions for rights, obligations and rules for decision makers and resource users, plus a structure to co-ordinate decision making.	Quebec, Wisconsin, Washington

Table 3: Reducing Consumption of Resources: Energy Conservation and Efficiency Initiatives

Initiative	Purpose	Mechanisms	Practised/Proposed
Energy efficiency targets	To increase energy efficiency in all sectors of the city by, for example, 10 per cent.	Municipal policy.	Portland, OR; Toronto; Vancouver
District heating and cogeneration	To combine heat and power production, reducing energy consumption and fuel emissions.	District-wide system of underground low-temperature hot water pipes supply space heating and domestic hot water to residential, commercial and institutional users.	Helsinki; Saarbrücken; Cornwall Country (UK)
Municipal energy conservation campaign	To conserve energy.	Infrared photos of energy leakage sent to each home in town by municipal utility.	Osage, IO
Energy conservation retrofit ordinances	To conserve energy.	Requires all existing buildings to be brought up to an energy conservation standard at the time of sale.	San Francisco
Solar oven cookbook	To promote solar cooking; to reduce air conditioning in overheated kitchens.	Municipal utility	Sacramento, CA
Local energy supply concept	To reduce dependence on fossil fuels; encourage renewable resource use.	Promote direct solar, photovoltaics and district heating.	Saarbrücken
Energy-efficient neighbourhoods	To conserve energy through urban design, site planning, development controls, and energy-efficient land-use planning.	Solar orientation of streets, cluster development, neighbourhood-level services and facilities, increased densities, natural drainage, narrow roads, energy conservation programes; traditional neighbourhood development ordinances.	Davis, CA; Eugene, OR; Seaside, FL

Table 4: Reducing Consumption of Resources: Waste Reduction and Recycling Initiatives

Initiative	Purpose	Mechanisms	Practised/Proposed
Waste reduction goals	To recycle, compost, or avoid production in 10 years (1998) of 60 per cent of the total combined residential and commercial waste which would otherwise be generated within the city.	Public education, curbside collection of recyclables and yard waste, commercial and apartment recycling, mixed waste processing, and possibly developing a food waste composting facility.	Seattle
Packaging restrictions	To encourage a recyclable and compostable waste stream.	Ordinance restricting non-degradable, nonreturnable and non-recyclable food and beverage packaging—including national brands—originating at retail food establishments.	Minneapolis
"Precycling" campaigns	To educate consumers to consider waste before they buy.	Media, public events, etc.	Berkeley
Municipal composting	To reduce yard wastes and to sell dry sewage sludge as a soil amendment.	Centralized composting programme for 60,000 tons of yard waste per year.	San Jose
Polystyrene plastic foam bans and restrictions	To prevent one-time use of polystyrene plastic foam by restaurants and retail food vendors.	Municipal bye-law.	Portland, Berkeley
Integrated reclamation/recycling centres	To recover and reprocess everything from glass, metals, paper and waste oil to cotton, animal bones, chemical fibres and human hair.	State complex employing 29,000 full-time and many more part-time employees through a network of purchasing stations, integrated recycling centres, sales departments and retail shops selling reclaimed products.	Shanghai
Constructed wetlands	Sewage treatment	Treat sewage effluent through a series of natural marshes and restored wetlands.	Arcata, CA
Solar aquatics waste treatment facility	Septage treatment.	Greenhouse marshes to purify wastes.	Providence, RI

Table 5: Improving Community Livability

Initiatives	Purpose	Mechanisms	Practised/Proposed
Citizen participation	To build a united, broad-based political coalition for progress on sustainable community development.	A 49-recommendation platform for the future of the city's environment agreed to by over 200 local organizations.	New York City
Noth-South partnerships	To cooperate on municipal environmental assessment; to promote "municipal foreign policy"; to support development education, liberation movements, and renewable energy use in developing countries.	"Twinning" or "linking" with sister cities; a local elected officials project; *The Bulletin of Municiapal Foreign Policy*; an overall partnership development programme.	Federation of Canadian Municipalities; U.S. Local Elected Officials Project; Bremen (Germany)
Gender equity	To respond to the special needs of women crime victims, and to create new career paths for women.	"Delagacias da Mulher," all-female police stations.	Sao Paulo (Brazil)
"Disassembly" line	To integrate environmental and social policy.	Apprentice shop for unemployed young people where discarded but serviceable equipment (e.g., refrigerators) is repaired and sold, and polluting substances are removed.	Zutphen (Holland)
Public-community partnerships	To work with the nonprofit sector to meet community needs.	Municipal leadership in establishing a community land trust; "linkage" programme to provide funds for affordable housing, job development and day-care.	Burlington, VT; Boston, San Francisco
Healthy communities projects	To promote community health.	WHO, CIP, CPHA, FCM	Canada; Rouyn-Noranda, PQ: Seattle, WA; Liverpool, Sheffield, Oxford (UK)

From a fiscal perspective, the policies and public programmes described above will save city operations thousands or even millions of dollars annually. Several of these are fee fundable, and so do not compete for general revenues. These policies and initiatives are proving effective. As a result of a 1989 CFC bye-law, the City of Irvine, California reduced local emissions of ozone-depleting chemicals by 46 per cent in just one year. Within the first year of Mexico City's 1989 "Hoy No Circula" (Day Without A Car") programme, the city recorded a 23 per cent reduction in air pollution emissions. As a result of bicycle transportation incentives, bicycle commuters now account for more than 40 per cent of passenger trips in some Dutch cities. As a result of integrated transportation and land-use planning, most people in Curitiba, Brazil prefer mass transit for routine urban travel, despite one of the highest rates of motor vehicle ownership per capita in the country (United Nations Environment Program 1990, Bleviss and Walzer 1990).

EQUITY AND SOCIAL FACTORS

Planners and policy analysts are rightly concerned about the dislocations, economic costs and potential inconveniences associated with the above measures and their distribution across society. Polls do suggest that the public is willing to make some sacrifice to achieve ecological stability. However, both the gain and the pain of adjustment should be shared fairly by community members. Participation in the decision-making process by affected groups "can help make the attendant redistribution of costs and benefits fairer and more widely understood. Democratic mobilization is essential to the achievement of such policies in the face of the opposition [by vested interests they] inevitably engender" (Paehlke and Torgerson 1990, pp. 50–51). The employment impacts of sustainable policies are a frequent concern and highly variable. For example, mandatory container reuse and recycling, many energy conservation measures, and enhanced public transportation may involve more rather than fewer job opportunities, while energy efficiency standards for appliances and automobiles may be employment-neutral. Where there are significant dislocations, special job training programmes and new forms of social nets may have to be implemented to serve those people in transition from unsustainable forms of employment.

Many other sustainability measures are inherently positive in their distributive effects. For example, more efficient land-use and tax policies to discourage land speculation will increase the affordability of housing in the city and enable people to live closer to work. Shifting some of the public subsidy from automobile use to improved public transit will improve access to the city for lower income groups while attracting more riders from all social strata. All such effects are much in need of further research. However, in the final analysis, to the extent that improving the health, access, and livability of our cities contributes to the long-term survival of society, we all benefit in equal measure.

ADMINISTRATION FOR SUSTAINABILITY: REINVENTING THE WHEEL OR JUST SPINNING IT?

Administration for sustainability includes environmental commitments and legislation, investment and purchasing/procurement policies, environmental education, environmental enforcement, environmental management practices, sustainable community planning processes, and cooperative research. Table 6 presents our findings on these aspects.

While progress in environmental management appears to be the order of the day, a look at even recent history gives cause for concern. For example, in 1990 Toronto made headlines around the world by becoming the first city to commit itself to reducing its 1988 level carbon dioxide emissions to 20 per cent by 2005. Included in its "call for action" was a goal of "significantly reducing the number of commuting autos" and a strategy to "promote significant reductions in the energy intensity of transportation in the city" by promoting public transit, bicycling and walking (City of Toronto, 1989, pp. 6–9). Yet ten years earlier the Toronto City Council had passed an energy conservation bye-law designed, among other things, to encourage development and redevelopment that would contribute to energy-efficient urban form, reduce the need for transportation, discourage automobile use and encourage public transit and bicycle transportation (Lang and Armour 1982, pp. 63–65).

Another example of the purported progress is the recent mushrooming of municipal and local government environmental departments, coordinators, task forces, staff committees, and citizen boards. At one level this is certainly deserves applause. Yet a major survey of environmental management in nearly 3,000 North American local governments in 1973 found that 20 per cent had staff environment committees, 40 per cent had designated environmental coordinators, and 24 per cent had citizen environmental boards. Inadequate funding, uncertainty and delay in programme administration, inadequate communication with senior levels of government, and inadequate technical assistance were all perceived in the mid-1970s as major impediments to adequate local responses to environmental problem-solving (Magazine 1977, pp. 17–31, 67). Nearly 20 years later, this list sounds all too familiar.

The concern that we may be both reinventing and spinning our wheels is clearly not unfounded. Conventional wisdom considers the environment as an administrative problem, to be solved by better management. Better

Table 6: Administration for Sustainability

Initiatives	Purpose	Mechanisms	Practised/Proposed
Environmental commitments and legislation	To, for example, reduce the threat of atmospheric change.	Targets and bye-laws to reduce or eliminate emissions of carbon dioxide, CFCs, etc.	Toronto; Irvine, CA; Vancouver
Investment and purchasing/procurement policies	To favour environmentally sound business practices; to encourage or create markets for recycled materials.	Procurement policies; codes for environmentally sound business practices, e.g., the Valdez Principles.	Ottawa, Vancouver, Los Angeles, New York City, Pasadena, Philadelphia; California, New Jersey, New York, Minnesota.
Eco-Counsellors	To review the environmental impact of all municipal practices.	Recommend environmentally sound practices to various government departments.	Germany, Sweden, Switzerland, Austria, Italy, Spain, UK, France, Luxembourg, Belgium
Environmental enforcement	To improve the effectiveness of environmental policies and legislation.	Police department enforces environmental laws; environmental officers and investigation teams.	Weert and Apeldoorn (Holland); Richmond and Los Angles, CA
Municipal Environmental Impact Assessment (EIA)	To review the environmental impact of all municipal practices; "ecological self-control" of local government.	Draft bye-laws; propose grants and subsidies; build projects; review procurement policies, development and waste disposal plans.	Germany: Freiburg, many other towns
Municipal environmental management	To monitor and coordinate environmental management; to transcend the administrative mindset.	Ecosystem planners, environmental managers and programme administrators, energy conservation offices; hiring Greenpeace activist; national programmes.	Burnaby, Vancouver, Toronto; Portland, OR; Irvine, CA; Gothenberg (Sweden); Norway, Finland, Holland
Sustainable community planning processes	To encourage cooperation in the formulation of effective policies.	Local round tables on environment and economy.	Canada: Burlington, Guelph, Kitchener, Muskoka, Peterborough, Skeena
Networking and cooperative research	To share experience in the formulation of effective policies.	International Council for Local Environmental Initiatives.	Chartered 1990 by local officials from 45 countries, United Nations.

management is understood, in this context, as cutting the environment into bite-size pieces, an approach which appears increasingly unable to deal effectively, sensitively and comprehensively with environmental complexities.[5] Rather than the environment as an administrative problem, it would appear that administration is itself an environmental problem (Paehlke and Torgerson 1990, p. 113).

PUBLIC-COMMUNITY PARTNERSHIPS

The alternative to conventional urban administration is an emerging form of what has been called "environmental administration". It can be characterized as non-compartmentalized, open, decentralized, anti-technocratic, and flexible (Paehlke and Torgerson 1990, pp. 292–299).[6]

Like other levels of government, the institution of local government has many limitations, not least among them resources, jurisdiction, inequitable representation and the reductionist administrative mindset. It will take a great effort over a long time to turn the system of local government into a paragon of environmental administration, though try we must. In these transition decades, however, an effective and popular way to implement sustainable community development is urgently required. One attractive option for this is what we call "public-community partnerships" between government and decentralized, flexible, locally-controlled, democratic and open community institutions to implement sustainable development at the community level.

Community land trusts may be the best examples of such sustainable community development institutions. A community land trust is an organization created to hold land for the benefit of a community and of individuals within the community. It is a democratically structured, nonprofit corporation, with an open membership and a board of trustees elected by the membership. The board typically includes residents of trust-owned lands, other community residents, and public-interest repre-

---

[5]One exception to this might be California's South Coast Air Quality Management District (SCAQMD), a powerful agency with the responsibility for comprehensive air pollution control and the duty to represent the citizens of the South Coast Air Basin (SCAQMD 1989). However, it must also be noted that the context for these powers is that the South Coast Air Basin has the most serious air quality problem in the U.S.

[6]The sustainable development "round tables" now underway in several Canadian jurisdictions could become a leading example of environmental adminstration if: (1) they actually had significant decision-making powers, and (2) the people most affected by such decisions (e.g., workers, community residents) participated in those decisions. The prospects, however, are not good. The model for these round tables, the CCREM National Task Force on Environment and Economy, was an advisory body that completely excluded representatives of organised labour.

sentatives. Board members are elected for limited terms, so that the community retains ultimate control of the organization and of the land it owns (Institute for Community Economics 1983).

There are now many successful community land trusts in both rural and urban areas in the United States. The model is being used both by neighbourhoods concerned with affordable housing and by organizations concerned with the plight of agricultural lands and wilderness. However, for these kinds of institutions to have an appreciable effect on developing sustainability, public powers and public funds will be required for their creation and expansion. Supporting legislation and programmes of start-up funding and technical assistance from any or all levels of government could enable these institutions to flourish, as they are in some New England cities and states (Seidman 1987). With such public-community partnerships, these community-based institutions could become an effective, decentralized, locally controlled and politically popular way to implement sustainable community development (Gardner and Roseland 1989b).

CONCLUSION

Sustainable development means looking ahead to the opportunities and constraints that will face us tomorrow, not merely those that face us today. In the 21st century, the single greatest change in our collective consciousness may well be the redefinition of our concept of security. Security is no longer the exclusive domain of economists and generals: environmental threats to security are as serious as economic challenges and military conflict in the new global order, and they require as much political and civic attention. In the final analysis, we are only as secure as the ability of the planet to provide us and our children with healthy air, water, food, energy and other life-support essentials.

Planning for the 21st century means developing communities to be sustainable in global ecological terms. The kinds of initiatives we have described here are sometimes perceived as economically costly and socially disruptive. However, if the logic of "strong sustainability" is correct, they are not only essential to maintaining civilization, but will also improve the quality of urban life. Sustainable communities will be cleaner, healthier, and less expensive, they will have greater accessibility and cohesion; and they will be more self-reliant in energy, food and economic security than our communities now are.

With their relatively wealthy and well-educated populations, Canadian communities have a moral obligation to demonstrate leadership in (and consequently benefit from) developing the knowledge, technologies, and processes which the world requires for sustainability in the 21st century. The models and strategies exist for innovative provincial planning programmes, for local government initiatives, and for public-community partnerships with the nonprofit sector. More than ever before, public interest and political will are supportive. Planners have an special obligation and ability to frame issues, assume leadership, champion initiatives, and demonstrate sustainable alternatives in their everyday practice. With creative leadership we may yet be able to leave our children a legacy of which we can be proud.

REFERENCES

Alcamo, J.M. 1990. Compact city design as a strategy to cut dangerous air pollution. Paper presented to the First International Ecocity Conference, Berkeley, California, March 30.

Bleviss, D.L. and P. Walzer. 1990. Energy for motor vehicles. *Scientific American*, 263(3), September: 103–109.

Block, W. 1990. Environmental problems, private property rights solutions. Page 304 in: *Economics and the Environment: A Reconciliation*, W. Block (ed.), Vancouver: The Fraser Institute.

Boothroyd, P. and M. Eberle. 1990. *Healthy Communities: What They Are, How They're Made.* Vancouver: UBC Centre for Human Settlements.

California Office of Appropriate Technology. 1981. Working Together: Community Self-Reliance in California, Sacramento, California Office of Appropriate Technology.

Canadian Council of Resource and Environment Ministers (CCREM). 1987. Report of the National Task Force on Environment and Economy, Ottawa: Canadian Council of Resource and Environment Ministers.

Canadian Healthy Communities Project: 1990. *A Conceptual Model for Winnipeg.* Winnipeg: Institute of Urban Studies.

City of Toronto. 1989. *The Changing Atmosphere: A Call To Action.* Toronto: City of Toronto.

City of Vancouver. 1990. *Clouds of Change. Final Report of the City of Vancouver Task Force on Atmospheric Change.* Vancouver: City of Vancouver.

Dasgupta, P. and D. Heal. 1979. *Economic Theory and Exhaustible Resources.* London: Cambridge University Press.

Environment Council of Alberta. 1988. Environment by Design: The Urban Place in Alberta. ECA88-PA/CS-S3. Environment Council of Alberta.

Federation of Canadian Municipalities. 1990. *A Guidebook on Transportation Energy Management.* Ottawa: Federation of Canadian Municipalities

Flavin, C. 1990. Slowing global warming. Pages 17–38 in: *State of the World* 1990: *A Worldwatch Institute Report on Progress Towards Sustainable Society.* Brown, Lester R. et al. New York/London: W.W. Norton & Co.

Gardner, J. and M. Roseland. 1989a. Thinking globally. the role of social equity in sustainable development, *Alternatives* 16.3 (October/November): 26–34.

Gardner, J. and M. Roseland. 1989b. Acting locally: community strategies for equitable sustainable development. *Alternatives* 16.3 (October/November): 36–48.

Heilbroner, R. 1989. The Triumph of Capitalism. *The New Yorker*, 23 January, 1989.

Herfindahl. O. and A. Kneese. 1974. *Economic Theory of Natural Resources.* Columbus, Ohio: Charles E. Merill.

Institute for Community Economics. 1983. *The Community Land Trust Handbook.* Emmaus, PA: Rodale Press.

Lang, R. and A. Armour. 1982. *Planning Land to Conserve Energy: 40 Case Studies From Canada and the United States.* Ottawa: Lands Directorate, Environment, Canada.

Magazine, A.H. 1977. *Environmental Management in Local Government: A Study on Local Response to Federal Mandate*, New York: Praeger Publishers.

Mathur, B. 1989. 'Community planning and the new public health". *Plan Canada*, 29:4 (July).

Morris, D. 1982. *Self-Reliant Cities: Energy and the Transformation of Urban America*. San Francisco: Sierra Club Books.

Nelson, J. 1990. Deconstructing Ecobabble, notes on an attempted corporate takeover. *This Magazine* 24(3): 12–18.

Newman, P.W.G. and J.R. Kenworthy. 1989. *Cities and Automobile Dependence*. Brookfield, VT: Gower Technical.

Nikiforuk, A. 1990. Sustainable Rhetoric. *Harrowsmith*. October 1990: 14–16.

Owens, S.E. 1990. 'Land use planning for energy efficiency. Pages 53–98 in: *Energy, Land and Public Policy*, Cullingworth, J. Barry (ed.). New Brunswick, N.J.: Transaction Publishers.

Paehlke, R. and D. Torgerson (eds.). 1990. *Managing Leviathan: Environmental Politics and the Administrative State*. Peterborough: Broad View Press.

Perry, D., M. Amaranthus, J. Borchers, S. Borchers and R. Brainerd. 1989. Bootstrapping in ecosystems. *BioScience* 39(4): 230–237.

RAIN (ed.). 1981. *Knowing Home: Studies for a Possible Portland*. Portland: RAIN.

Real Estate Research Corporation. 1974. *The Costs of Sprawl*, Volume I: *Detailed Cost Analysis*. Washington, DC: US Government Printing Office.

Rees, W. 1989. Defining sustainable development. *CHS Research Bulletin*, May 1989, Vancouver: UBC Centre for Human Settlements, V6T 1W5.

Rees, W. 1990a. Sustainable development and the biosphere. concepts and principles". *Teilhard Studies* No. 22, Chambersburg, P.A. Anima Books for the American Teilhard Association.

Rees, W. 1990b. The ecology of sustainable development. *The Ecologist* 20(1): 18–23.

Rees, W. 1990c. Why economics won't save the world. Paper presented to The Ecological Economics of Sustainability, a conference sponsored by the International Society for Ecological Economics, Washington, DC: The World Bank (21–23 May, 1990).

Rees, W. 1990d. Atmospheric change: human ecology in disequilibrium. *International Journal of Environmental Studies* 36: 103–124.

Replogle, M. 1990. Sustainable transportation strategies for world development. Paper presented to the World Congress of Local Governments for a Sustainable Future, United Nations, New York, September 7.

Rohse, M. 1987. *Land Use Planning in Oregon*. Corvallis: Oregon State University.

Richardson, N. 1989. *Land Use Planning and Sustainable Development in Canada*. Ottawa: Canadian Environmental Advisory Council, Environment Canada.

Seidman, K. 1987. A new role for government: supporting a democratic economy, 1987. In: *Beyond the Market and the State: New Directions in Community Development*, Bruyn, T. Severyn and James Meeham (eds.), Philadelphia: Temple University Press.

South Coast Air Quality Management District (SCAQMD). 1989. Summary of 1989 Air Quality Management Plan. El Monte, CA: SCAQMD.

Toronto Conference Statement. 1988. The changing atmosphere: implications for global security. Toronto: Environment Canada, June 27–30.

United Nations Environment Program, International Union of Local Authorities, and Centre for Innovative Diplomacy. 1990. *The World Congress of Local Governments for a Sustainable Future*. New York: United Nations Environment Program.

Van der Ryn, S. and P. Calthorpe. 1986. *Sustainable Communities: A New Design Synthesis for Cities, Suburbs and Towns*. San Francisco: Sierra Club Books.

Yesney, M. 1990. The sustainable city: a revolution in urban evolution. *Western City*, 66(3) (March): 4–44.

REFERENCES

Association of Netherlands Municipalities and the Ministry of Housing, Physical Planning and Environment. 1990. Municipal Environmental Policy in the Netherlands: Setting out for Sustainable Development. The Hague: Association of Netherlands Municipalities.

Bjork, Sven and McLaren, Nadia. 1990. Environment and health: the Norwegian response. Paper presented to the First International Ecocity Conference, Berkeley, CA, March 30.

Boston Redevelopment Authority. 1988. *Linkage.* Winter.

Bulletin of Municipal Foreign Policy. 1990. 4:3 (Summer).

California Department of Transportation. 1990. A Directory of Trop Reduction Ordinances. Second Edition. Sacramento: Division of Transportation Planning Canadian Broadcasting Corporation. 1990. *The age of ecology. IDEAS.* Toronto: CBC Ideas. Part Five, June 25.

City of Portland Energy Office. 1990. Draft Portland Energy Policy. *City Heat* 2:1, Winter 1– 8.

City of Seattle. 1988. Resolution 27871 (Waste Reduction, Recycling and Composting).

Ciudad de Mexico. 1990. *Ciudad de Mexico.* Mexico City. Departmento del Distrito Federal Community Economics. 1989. 18 (Summer).

Cornwall County Council. 1988. Energy Considerations in the Structure Plan. Truro, Cornwall, UK, Cornwall County Council.

Environment and Public Health Administration. 1990. *A Summary of the Stockholm Environment Plan.* Stockholm: City of Stockholm, Environment and Public Health Administration.

Ernst, Rainer W. 1990. Integrated urban and transport planning in Saarbrücken. Paper presented to the World Congress of Local Governments for a Sustainable Future. United Nations, New York, September 7.

Federation of Canadian Municipalities International Program. n.d. Africa 2000: The Municipal Response. Ottawa: Federation of Canadian Municipalities Federation of Canadian Municipalities International Program. n.d. International Office. Ottawa: Federation of Canadian Municipalities.

Foulds, David W. 1990. Environmental and economic sustainability go hand in hand. *Municipal World.* 100(7) July: 5.

French, Hilary F. 1990. You are what you breathe. *Worldwatch* 3 (3) May–June: 27–34.

Giese, Jo. 1990. A communal type of life with dinner for all and day care, too. *New York Times,* September 27, p. B1.

Gunnerson, C. G. Resource recovery and utilization in Shanghai. 1987. UNDP/World Bank. Global Programme of Resource Recovery. Cited in: United Nations Centre for Human Settlement (Habitat). 1989 Urbanization and Sustainable Development in the Third World: An Unrecognized Global Issue. Nairobi: United Nations Centre of Human Settlement (Habitat).

Helsinki Energy Board. 1989. District Heating. Helsinki: Helsinki Energy Board Jalkanen, Pekka. 1990. "The Role of Finnish Municipalities on the Way Towards the Sustainable Future". Helsinki, Finland: Environmental Department, The Finnish Municipal Association (Unpublished paper) August 17.

Knack, R.E. 1989. Repent, ye sinners, repent. (Neotraditional Town Planning) Planning August.

Leonhardt, Willy. 1990. Local concepts for the reduction of CO_2. Paper presented to the World Congress of Local Governments for a Sustainable Future. New York, September 7: United Nations.

Local Government Commission. 1990. *Model Ordinances for Environmental Protection.* Sacramento, CA: Local Government Commission, March.

McCamant, Kathryn and Durrett, Charles. 1988. *Cohousing: A Contemporary Approach to Housing Ourselves.* Berkeley: Habitat Press.

Metropolitan Toronto Planning Department. Policy Development Division. "Housing Intensification". 1987. Metropolitan Plan Review Report No. 4. Toronto Planning Department.

Ministries of Municipal Affairs and Housing. 1989. Land use planning for housing. Toronto: Ministry of Government Services.

Minneapolis Code of Ordinances. 1989. Amending Title 10. Adding a New Chapter 204. "Environmental Preservation: Environmentally Acceptable Packaging" Norwegian Ministry of Environment and Norwegian Association of Local Authorities. 1989. Development Programme for Municipal Environmental Protection in Norwegian Local Authorities (MIK). Oslo: Kommunenes Sentralforbund.

Norwegian Ministry of Environment, Norwegian Association of Local Authorities, and Local Authorities of Fredrikstad, Norway. 1990. Environmental surveillance and international cooperation between local authorities in Norway, Poland and Zimbabwe. Paper presented to the World Congress of Local Governments for a Sustainable Future, United Nations, New York, September 5.

Office of Environmental Management, n.d. "The Sustainable City: San Jose, California". San Jose, California: Office of Environmental Management Otto-Zimmermann, Konrad. 1990. "Environmental Impact Assessment on Local Level in the European Countries". Paper presented to the World Congress of Local Governments for a Sustainable Future. United Nations, New York, September 6 Public Broadcasting System. 1990. The Race to Save the Planet. Boston: WGBH, Parts Five and Eight.

Register, Rischard. 1987. *Ecocity Berkeley: Building Cities for a Healthy Future.* Berkeley, CA: North Atlantic Books.

Rotterdam Public Works. n.d. *Rotterdam's Policy on the Environment. Rotterdam:* Rotterdam Public Works.

Skinner, Nancy. 1990. Ecocity legislation. Paper presented to the First International Ecocity Conference. Berkeley: California, March 31.

Solis, Manuel Camacho. 1990. Meeting the environmental challenges of the mega city, Paper presented to the World Congress of Local Governments for a Sustainable Future, United Nations, New York, September 6.

South Coast Air Quality Management District (SCAQMD). 1989. *Summary of 1989—A Quality Management Plan.* El Monte, CA: SCAQMD.

Stockholms Gatukontor. 1989. Traffic Master Plan 89 Summary. City of Stockholm, December.

Tietel, Rainer. 1990. Eco-counselling. Paper presented to the World Congress of Local Governments for a Sustainable Future, United Nations, New York: September 6.

Totten, Michael. 1990 (in press). Energywise options for state and local governments. a policy compendium. Washington, D.C., National Centre for Policy Alternatives, November 1989 draft.

Towns and Development: Local Initiatives for Global Development. n.d. Getting to know towns and development. The Hague. Towns and Development.

UK One World Linking Association n.d. Linking with 'Third World' communities. Oxford. UK: One World Linking Association.

United Nations Environment Programme 1990. Mexico City: polluted metropolis takes radical steps for environment. New York: United Nations Environment Programme. September 6, Press Release.

Sustainable Development in Developing Societies: The Case of Isfahan Region

Asghar Zarrabi

INTRODUCTION

Many developing countries have experienced unbalanced spatial development. This is due to the emphasis on overall growth and neglect of regional
disparities and inequalities (Yang 1986). Such disparities and inequalities
have occurred between rural and urban areas, among cities within urban
systems, and between regions within the same country (El- Shakhs 1997).

In most cases, the strategy of overall economic growth has drained
capital and labour from rural hinterlands to urban areas and from small
cities to large urban areas, particularly to primate cities (Rondinelli 1980,
Gilbert and Gugler 1982). Therefore, the population of most of the developing countries has become more concentrated in large and primate cities and
changed the structure of settlement systems of the countries. The concentration of economic activities and population in large cities has created
several problems at the macro and micro levels.

At the macro level such concentration of population in large cities: (1)
inhibits the development of rural areas and the growth of smaller towns
and cities; (2) increases regional and personal inequalities and heightens
conflicts and political instability; (3) increases the consumption of cultivated land for housing and infrastructure; and (4) causes natural and environmental disasters (El-Shakhs and Amirahmadi 1984).

At the micro level the concentration of population in large cities: (1) increases overloads on the functional, services and the organizational
capacity of large cities; (2) leads to rigid inappropriate land-use patterns; (3)
reduces residential mobility and inflates demand for transportation and increases cost and use of peripheral and marginal land as cities grow; (4) increases unemployment and underemployed and depresses wages all of

which unfairly impact the urban poor; (5) increases slums and squatter settlements; and (6) increases congestion and decreases commitment to environmental concerns (Ibid.).

As a result of growing disparities in the levels of economic development and wealth among geographical regions and problems of large cities,
it became a crucial problem for government planners and an important
concern of international assistance agencies such as the World Bank (Rondinelli 1980, 1985).

In the light of these problems, development was redefined in terms of
reduction or elimination of poverty and inequality and unemployment
within the context of a growing economy (Todaro 1981) and solving the
problems of large cities. Therefore, spatial equity or the reduction of spatial
disparities of living conditions became the key objective of most national,
urban and regional development policies (Stöhr and Todtling 1977). As
Muttagi (in this volume) has noted, "Developing countries must achieve
economic growth with equity first and then strain for sustainable development. There is no shortcut."

Iran is among the developing countries that has gone through this
development process. Early emphasis on economic development has led to
extreme regional disparities.

The main purpose of this paper is to examine the extent of such disparities at subnational level, particularly in the Isfahan Region, and finally
an attempt will be made to suggest an appropriate spatial development approach for more sustainable development of the region and particularly Isfahan, a large city.

THE ISFAHAN REGION

1) General Setting

The distribution of benefits of economic development in Iran like many
other developing countries is unequal. There are large disparities in living
conditions between the urban and rural populations generally, and substantial differences in the levels of development and rate of growth between provinces and within provinces among urban areas. One research
project by the World Bank (1974) found that more than half of the
households in Iran are poor. There are high disparities between the capital
city Tehran and the rest of the country whether measured in term of income, unemployment, net migration, or industrial structure (Kiannejad
1975).

The spatial distribution of resources in Iran is also unbalanced. For example, the province containing the capital city, Tehran, with less than one-
fifth of the total population, produces over a third and consumes more than

two-fifths of the national output, accounts for more than half of the national investment and manufacturing production, and completely dominates social services and facilities more among 50 to 60 per cent of the total (Richardson 1975). The national settlement pattern is also unbalanced. According to the new census, the population of Tehran in 1985 was nearly 6 million, which was more than that in nine big provinces of the country. The Central Province, which includes Tehran had one-fifth of the total population (Javan 1988).

The socio-economic disparities in Iran are manifest in the following: three dimensions: (a) between rural and urban areas; (b) between provinces; and (c) between the capital city Tehran and the rest of the country.

Jabbari (1981) in his study of rural-urban disparities in Iran has found them very high, for example, the ratio of urban to rural average total monthly expenditures varies between ranges of 2.966 for Central Province and 1.118 for West Azarbaijan which is one of the underdeveloped regions. It is obvious that such disparities between rural and urban areas are the result of concentration of economic activities, social services and welfare facilities in urban areas, particularly in large or primate cities such as Tehran.

Analysis of "socio-economic variables that are drawn from the 1985 censuses and other publications reveal the existence of extreme disparities among the provinces (Zarrabi 1991). The finding of the study highlighted that the disparities are particularly wide between some of the developed regions such as the Tehran, Isfahan and the rest of the provinces. Such disparities are very high between Tehran, a large city in Iran, and the rest of the country.

2) The Case Study

Here the economic and social disparities which exist in Isfahan province are described. The study included urban areas with more than 5,000 population. By national definition, there are towns which have municipality status, and are considered urban areas. The reason why urban areas were selected is that most cities perform the central functions which serve people living outside their boundaries. They serve as channels for the flow of goods and services (Rondinelli 1983). In the Isfahan province there is a high primacy between Isfahan city which is the capital city in the region and has more than one million people, and the second largest city, such as Kashan, which is a secondary city with more than 100,00 population. Therefore, in terms of population Isfahan stands alone among the urban areas in the region. Table 1 shows the Pearson Correlation Coefficient between 20 socio-economic variables. As shown there is a strong correlation at 0.01

significant level between percentage of annual population growth and number of residents born in other urban areas (0.82).

There is also a significant correlation at the 0.05 level between annual population growth and number of residents born in rural areas (0.38), but it

Table 1: Pearson Correlation Coefficients Matrix

	v01	v02	v03	v04	v05	v06	v07	v08	v09	v10
v01	1.00	.11	.13	.14	.29*	−.22	.09	.16	.01	.80**
v02	.11	1.00	.82**	.38**	.12	−.39**	−.05	.39**	.16	.15
v03	.13	.82**	1.00	.52**	.17	−.35**	−.11	.48**	.12	.17
v04	.14	.38**	.52**	1.00	.38**	−.45**	−.04	.50**	.00	.18
v05	.29*	.12	.07	.38**	1.00	−.24	.48**	−.12	.02	−.07
v06	−.22	−.39**	−.35*	−.45**	−.24	1.00	−.40**	−.59**	−.12	−.35*
v07	.09	−.05	−.11	−.04	.48**	−.40**	1.00	−.43**	.00	.03
v08	.16	.39**	.48**	.50**	−.12	−.59**	−.43**	1.00	.03	.03
v09	.01	.16	.12	.00	.02	−.12	.00	.03	1.00	.01
v10	.08	.15	.17	.18	−.07	−.35*	.03	.30*	.10	1.00
v11	.04	.15	.15	.10	−.01	.23	−.10	.26	.07	.33*
v12	.11	.23	.41**	.37**	.03	.35*	−.27	.58**	.10	.19
v13	.26	−.01	.09	.39**	.50	−.22	−.17	.36*	.00	.21
v14	.43**	−.02	.06	.41**	.12	−.29*	−.19	.46**	−.04	.21
v15	.31*	.54**	.58**	.57**	.11	−.64**	.02	.66**	.04	.37**
v16	−.06	.20	.00	−.27	.20	.21	.24	−.41**	.14	−.21
v17	−.13	.38**	.22	.03	.26	.04	.27	−.25	.20	−.13
v18	−.12	.36*	.26	.03	−.19	−.02	−.11	.21	.15	.19
v19	.21	.12	.12	.26	.10	−.21	.12	.09	.02	.07
v20	.50**	.39**	.55**	.36*	.02	−.33	−.23	.54**	.01	.20

	v11	v12	v13	v14	v15	v16	v17	v18	v19	v20
v01	.04	.11	.26	.43**	.31	−.06	−.13	−.12	.21	.50**
v02	.15	.23	-.01	-.02	.54**	.20	.38**	.36**	.12	.39**
v03	.15	.41**	.09	.06	.58**	.00	.22	.26	.12	.55**
v04	.10	.37**	.39**	.41**	.57**	−.27	.03	.03	.26	.36*
v05	−.01	.03	.05	.12	.11	.20	.26	−.19	.10	.02
v06	−.23	−.35*	−.22	−.29*	−.64**	.21	.04	−.20	−.21	−.33*
v07	.10	−.27	−.17	−.19	.02	.24	.27	−.11	.12	−.23
v08	.26	.58**	.36*	.46**	.66**	−.41**	−.25	.21	.09	.54**
v09	.07	.10	.00	−.04	.04	.14	.20	.15	.02	.01
v10	.33*	.19	.21	.21	.37**	−.21	−.13	.19	.07	.21
v11	1.00	.15	.09	.07	.16	.04	.14	.04	.04	.17
v12	.15	1.00	.48**	.28	.53**	−.41**	−.19	.15	.12	.66**
v13	−.09	.48**	1.00	.52**	.37**	−.34*	−.24	.04	.10	.34*
v14	.07	.28	.52**	1.00	.31	−.35*	−.47**	−.19	.01	.35*
v15	.16	.53**	.37**	.31	1.00	−.28*	.02	.22	.25	.55**
v16	.04	−.41**	−.34*	−.35*	−.28*	1.00	.54**	−.03	.05	−.29*
v17	.14	−.19	−.24	−.47**	.02	.54**	1.00	.19	.15	−.19
v18	.04	.15	.04	−.19	.22	−.03	.19	1.00	.05	.21
v19	.04	.12	.10	.01	.25	.05	.15	.05	1.00	.13
v20	.17	.66*	.34*	.35*	.55**	−.29*	−.19	.21	.13	1.00

* significant at the .05 level, ** significant at the .01 level. For the list of variables see Table 2.

Table 2: List of Variables

Demographic Indicators
1. Population size
2. Percentage average annual population growth (1976–86)
3. Number of residents born in other urban areas as percentage of total population
4. Number of residents born in rural areas as percentage of total population
5. Population density

Economic Indicators
6. Primary employment as percentage of total employment
7. Secondary employment as percentage of total employment
8. Tertiary employment as percentage of total employment
9. Number of industrial electricity users per 100,000 population

Housing Availability and Living Condition
10. Percentage of dwelling units with electricity
11. Percentage of dwelling units with piped water
12. Percentage of dwelling units with telephone

Health care Indicators
13. Percentage of hospital beds per 100,000 population
14. Number of physicians per 100,000 population

Education Indicators
15. Percentage of population which is literate
16. Pupil/teacher ratio in primary schools
17. Pupil/teacher ratio in secondary schools
18. Pupil/teacher ratio in high schools

Transportation Indicators
19. Number of buses and minibuses per 100,000 population
20. Number of taxis per 100,000 population

is not as strong as the former one. These two correlations indicate that the growth of cities particularly the Isfahan city is influenced by the migration from other urban or rural areas. This argument is supported by Rondinelli (1983) who explained that "about half of the urban population increase in developing countries is attributed to rural migration". It is also supported by Todaro (1981) who has noted that "Rural-to-urban migration was the most prominent factor contributing to urban growth." Table 1 indicates that the annual population growth is also positively related to tertiary employment and literacy. It is also statistically correlated with the pupil/teacher ratio in secondary and high schools. These data show that the growth of cities, particularly Isfahan, is dependent on education facilities and employment situations. The two migration variables (v3, v4) are significantly associated with the percentage of population engaged in territory employment (v8). This indicates that migration to urban areas increases because of the expansion of commercial and service sectors.

In other words, migration to urban areas in the region is in search of jobs. The economic opportunities are the main factors that attract the rural people to urban areas. These two variables are strongly related to the percentage of population which is literate. This may indicate that the migration to urban areas is influenced by education. Most of the migration to urban areas is to find better jobs and education facilities. Furthermore, it could be explained that most of the migrants from small towns and rural areas to urban areas, particularly to a large city like Isfahan, are educated people. These two migration variables are also significantly related to housing and transportation facilities. This indicates that migration to urban areas may be influenced by increases of housing stock and the availability of transportation facilities.

To sum up, from analysis of the correlation matrix (Table 1) it is found that in Isfahan province urban growth is greatly influenced by migration from rural and other urban areas and such migration is due to the search for jobs and a better quality of life. Among the 48 urban areas in the Isfahan region, the Isfahan city stood alone as the most urbanized urban centre in the province. In 1986 it had nearly one million population which is more than seven times than the second largest urban centre in the province, Kashan, with 138,309 people. Isfahan is the second largest city in Iran.

In terms of socio-economic activities Isfahan stood alone among the 48 urban areas in the region . Most of the industrial factories and economic activities are located near Isfahan. The existence of extreme disparities among the urban areas particularly between Isfahan city and the rest of settlements in the region created several socio-economic problems for the government.

This strategy for development followed the "growth pole" and "growth centre" strategies which encouraged the concentration of socio-economic activities, particularly large capital-intensive industries, in or around a few major cities (see Kuklinski 1970, Stöhr and Taylor 1981; Rondinelli 1985). The Iranian government hoped that such policy could spread the benefits of development to backward areas through the 'trickle-down' effect. Unfortunately, such a policy had a marginal effect on the backward areas and development could not spread significantly through the whole of the region and gap between the settlements, and particularly between the Isfahan city and the rest of the settlements in the region widened.

The concentration of socio-economic activities in Isfahan, made more opportunities for rural people who were searching for jobs and a better quality of life. Therefore, such a policy increased rural-urban migration, particularly to Isfahan, a large city. One of the main problems of the growth of Isfahan is environmental, such as deterioration of the physical environment, congestion, and the pressures against the limited water resources of Isfahan which is located near the desert. It was estimated that 80 per cent of air pollution in Isfahan was caused by industrial factories around the city and by the transportation.

The concentration of population in Isfahan may make it difficult to provide urban services such as telephone, water and electricity. Another problem of Isfahan city is social alienation. There are high levels of underemployed among the recent migrants which maintain these people in poverty. Finally, it is very difficult to extend and maintain the existing sewer, water and drainage systems, and the indequacy of utility and services often creates health and sanitation problems in densely populated areas and puts a strain on existing social, health and education services which in any case become more strained with population growth (Rondinelli 1984). These problems create instability in the region and particulary in Isfahan. Most of the migrants tend to move to Isfahan from economically-depressed environments in order to find a chance for improvement. Recently the over-concentration of population, economic activities in Isfahan city, became an important issue for the government for sustainable development.

SUGGESTIONS

In order to reduce the regional disparities which exist in Isfahan province, the Islamic government should pay more attention to the backward areas, particularly to strengthen the middle-sized cities which can distribute the benefits of development to more people in the hinterland. They should invest in productive jobs and urban services in potential urban areas. This policy may reduce the pressure on Isfahan city. The improvement of small- and labour-intensive industries in small- and middle-sized cities would create economic opportunities for the rural people who are seeking jobs. Such jobs can either be developed by the government or by the informal sector (see Todaro 1981, Rondinelli 1990).

The transportation linkages are weak in the Isfahan province. It is necessary to stretch the roads to small towns and rural areas, particularly to those that have the potential for development. It is necessary to adapt the comprehensive spatial planning and more investigation needs to be carried out into the formulation of the problems in backward areas and about what people really want in these poor areas. It is obvious that by reorganizing existing financial and technical assistance programmes, by relocating them to small- and middle-sized cities, and by upgrading such urban areas and creating a strong network between them, it would be possible to distribute the benefits of urbanization to more people and to absorb a larger number of migrants who migrate to Isfahan. This would also help to finally reduce regional disparities which exist in the region and create more sustainable development, particularly for Isfahan city, which is one of the largest cities in the central part of Iran.

REFERENCES

El-Shakhs, S, 1997. The future of mega-cities; planning implications for a more sustainable development, in: Bernd Hamm and Pandurang K. Muttagi, (eds.), this volume.

El-Shakhs, S. and Amirahmadi. 1984. Population growth, urbanization and Third World spatial development. *Journal of Asian-Pacific and World Perspective*, 8. (l): 27-49.

Gilbert, A. and J. Gugler. 1982. *Cities, Poverty and Development: Urbanization in the Third World*. New York: Oxford University Press.

Jabbari, A. 1981. Economic factor in Iran Revolution: poverty, equality and inflation, In: *Iran: Essays on a Revolution in the Making* A. Jabbari and R. Olson (eds.) Lexington: Asia Publication.

Javan, J. 1988. *Population of Iran and Spatial Setting*. Iran: Ferdowsi University Press.

Kiannejad, H. 1975. Policies of Spatial Discrimination in Promotion Development in Iran. In: *Growth Pole Strategy and Regional Planning in Asia*, pp. 157–163.

Kuklinski, A. 1970. Regional development, regional policies and regional planning, *Regional Studies* 4: 269–278.

Richardson, J.A. 1975: Regional planning in Iran. *Growth and Change* 6: 16–19.

Rondinelli, D.A. 1980. Regional disparities and investment allocation policies in the Philippines: spatial dimensions of poverty in a developing country. *Canadian Journal of Development Studies* Fall, pp. 262–287

Rondinelli, D.A. 1983. Dynamic of growth of secondary cities in. developing countries. *The Geographical Review* 73 (4): 42–57.

Rondinelli, D.A. 1984. Small Towns in Developing Countries; Potential Centres of Growth, Transformation and Integration. In: *Equity with Growth: Planning Perspectives for Small Towns in Developing Countries*, H.D. Kammeier and P. Swan. (eds.). Bangkok: Asian Institute of Technology.

Rondinelli, D.A. 1985. Equity, growth, and development: regional analysis in developing countries. *Journal of the American Planning Association* 51: 434 –448.

Rondinelli, D.A. 1990. Policies for Balanced Urban Development. In: *Asia: Concepts and Reality in Regional Development, Dialogue*, 11 (1) Spring: 23–47.

Stohr, W. and F. Todtling. 1977. Spatial equity some anti-theses to current regional development doctrine. In: *Papers and Proceedings of the Regional Science Association*, 38: 53.

Stöhr, W. and F. Taylor, 1981. *Development from Above or Below? The Dialectics of Regional Planning in Developing Countries*, New York: John Wiley and Sons Ltd.

Todaro, M.P. 1981. *Economic Development in the Third World*. New York: Longman.

World Bank Group. 1974. *The Economic Development of Iran*, Vol. l: The Main Report, Report No. 378a, Washington.

Yang, S.C. 1986. *Regional Development and Multi-Level Planning*. UNCRD, Working Paper No. 85-5, Nagoya, Japan.

Zarrabi, A. 1991. Regional Disparities in Iran: The Case of Isfahan Province, unpublished thesis, Department of Town and Regional Planning, University of Sheffield, U.K.

Sustainable Development in Urban Design: A Northern Aspect

Aarne Tarumaa

INTRODUCTION

There are three factors which differentiate the north from the rest of the world and which are common to all Arctic areas. Nature is particularly sensitive and vulnerable to all human activity, and its capacity for regeneration is both limited and slow. Wide areas are sparsely populated, the overall population is small, and settlements are widely dispersed. The options for earning a living are very few; the primary occupations are linked to nature—forestry and agriculture. These factors have determined the traditional patterns of life in the north. Tradition in building, until broken apart by modern ideas in the 1960s, was closely tied to such conditions. The mass movement into the large cities which took place in the same decade was a catastrophe for the eastern and northern parts of Finland. Environmental issues gained importance in the 1980s. However, when environmental damage was clearly visible to all, The principle of sustainable development became part of the Finnish Building Act in 1990. Environmental Impact Assessment (EIA) has long been a question of great interest, and ecology-based planning is currently one of the fundamental questions in building.

Architects' talk about sustainable development in planning seems to focus on ecological solutions. To planners, on the other hand, ecology mainly means the use in practice of technologically workable operations.

The three case studies presented here are different in terms of their approach and aims:

1) *Case Rovaniemi* represents ecology-based planning. The aim was to find a new model for a residential area, based on different planning ideologies; the final solution combined the so-called Winter City ideology with ecology-based planning. The city's location on the Arctic circle gives the plan a character of its own.

2) *Case Pudasjarvi* is a study of EIA-related master-planning, based on the project of building a peat-fuelled power station. The solution, difficult in terms of ecology, has been analysed at the land-use level in order to determine the advantages that are to be weighed against the disadvantages, without forgetting the latter.

3) *Case Sotkamo* represents a sustainable development-based communicative planning procedure in which the inhabitants are actively involved from the outset. Plans for individual farms form the whole, toward which new construction in the village can be oriented.

On the basis of the case studies, we can conclude that the understanding and application of local tradition to the present is one of the basic prerequisites for a good solution. Acceptance of environmental awareness as the starting point in every planning process is essential, both from the ecological and the human comfort points of view. Strategic planning is necessary in times of recession too, since everything cannot be based purely on growth. One of the basic principles in sustainable development is to develop the bottom-up planning method, so that proposals coming from residents are as important a part of the planning as the general "isms" and official regulations.

Typical features in recent societal development have been fast and sweeping changes. The system that reigned in Eastern Europe for 50 years collapsed almost overnight. At the same time in the western world the basic institutions of society are being privatized with increasing speed. The financial recession of many years is putting to the test those systems which were created in order to ensure people's income in times of unemployment or ill-health. While people, goods, culture and capital cross borders very faster, more and more people are feeling insecure in the midst of these rapid changes.

A large homogeneous culture is being born in the world. But in contrast to this global culture, people are becoming more aware of their own cultural background. Local "mosaic cultures" are arising, which are homogeneous in nature, closed communities, reacting negatively to outside influences (Naisbitt and Aburdene 1990). These groups are arising everywhere, but especially at the outer boundaries of areas of domination, such as the far north, which are very favourable to their formation.

THE NORTH

1) Harsh Conditions

Clear seasonal changes are typical in the northern areas. Each season is clearly differentiated, which means that people's activities and hobbies also change with the seasons. The winter is, however, the dominating season.

Problems arising from the planning circumstances can be crystallized into three basic climatic facts: (1) taking advantage of solar warmth, (2) problems relating to the cold, and (3) protection from the wind.

Finland belongs to a zone which has wet and cold winters. Features of this zone are that the average temperature of the warmest month, July, is above +10°C and that of the coldest month, February, is below –3°C. The climate is damp and in each month it either rains or snows. The length of the winter can be defined according to the duration of snow-cover, that is, about half of the year in Finland. At the Arctic Circle there is snow on areas of open land for 190 days on an average, and in forests even longer (Hautamäki 1989:79). On the other hand, the whiteness of the snow reflects light in a completely different way than does dark soil, so the snow is instrumental in increasing the amount of light. Therefore the typical winter city scenario is a white ground, a black sky, and in between an illuminated cityscape.

The sun shines round the clock in summer, and in winter it is almost permanently hidden below the horizon. The sun's warming effect in summer is, however, relatively little because of its low angle; it shines from near the horizon. It is to be noticed that in mid-winter in latitude 65°N, the lowest angle of the sunlight is 1° 30', which means that the sun is visible for one hour. In contrast, the angle of sunlight in mid-summer is 48.5° (Hakanen 1993: 30).

Because it is essential for the full use of the sun's warming effect, a certain openness is demanded in building. The demand for sunlight creates specification on the distance between buildings, heights of buildings, the size of yards and their proportional relationship to the street space, all of which lead to a low and dispersed physical structure. Taking advantage of the topographical features such as south- and west-facing slopes is also common in planning. The sun has an important psychological significance for people in the north.

The cold imposes several additional demands on the technology of planning and building. Technical solutions concerning heat-insulation, frost-proof foundations, district heating, winter traffic, snow-shifting and other problems caused by winter have been perfected, but they demand high energy consumption and the use of unrenewable natural resources. Energy consumption, for example, increases in the sub-zero temperatures, in the form of additional heating costs and higher fuel-consumption in traffic; also the exhaust fumes stay hanging in the air, causing breathing difficulties.

Wind protection improves comfort, but it also affects energy consumption and the accumulation of snow to a substantial degree. In severe frost the wind increases the risk of freezing and feeling cold. In buildings, the wind factor causes an increase in energy consumption, deterioration of the microclimate, and the inconvenience of snowdrift formation. It has been seen that in 9 m/s wind, the heating required in an unprotected building is 2.4 times more than in one protected on three sides (Zrudlo 1988:100–101). Wind has been extensively researched, especially in towns. The structure and shape of a block, the height and massing of the buildings, and their location on the site, provide the starting points for good planning. In Arctic conditions the planner needs to know where the snow will accumulate most. The height of the snow-drifts in cities is not of great significance, but the places where snow will gather need to be known. In traffic-route planning too, a good solution can decrease the extent of snow-drifting problems (Börve 1990).

Out of the various planning recommendations published by winter city researchers in different contexts, we can form a crystallized manual of winter city ideology. Essentially, it is urban planning practices which aim at climate awareness and decreased energy use, in which the central elements are getting sunshine and making use of its energy.

In the northern areas people are living on the extreme edge of western culture. Large uninhabited areas, fragmented and dispersed habitation, low population figures and harsh natural conditions are common defining features in descriptions of the northern living culture. Here, mankind has traditionally been a part of nature. Modern technology has, however, obscured the inhabitants' relationship with nature, giving the impression that the dependence on nature has disappeared. An "error in perspective" has been produced, since the relationship still in fact works today, although now through the medium of the great technological institutions.

2) Ecological Aspects in Urban Design

From the architect's point of view, sustainable development in planning focusses on ecological solutions. The planner focusses on technologically workable operations. A large Congress dealing with city ecology was held in Ankara in 1992. On the basis of the Congress it seems that city ecology can be interpreted in at least three different ways (Pakarinen 1993:10–12):

a) The town forms its own ecosystem with its own material and energy flows.

b) Recognizing the way nature appears within the city; green belts, protected areas and the multiplicity of the natural ecosystem.

c) Protecting the living environment in the city, preventing of pollution.

In all of these points of view we can choose whether or not to highlight the human and societal aspect. Northern researchers seem to be almost u-nanimous as to what constitutes a sustainable development-based community. They generally include the following characteristics (Hakanen 1993:14):

- the exploitation of solar energy and renewable energy sources, and the avoidance of fossil fuels
- the prevention of ill-effects
- the saving of unbuilt areas
- the saving and protection of functional nature areas
- recycling of material
- minimization of material transfer between systems
- making cycles as short as possible
- maximum possible local self-sufficiency.

The characteristics mentioned above place an emphasis on ecology. In practice, the requirements mean compacting the structure of society . This compacting involves infill development, i.e. building on empty sites, adding extra structures to sites—often in business use, for example—where there are few buildings, and starting to use non-traditional building areas like wasteland, land-fills, dumps, traffic areas, etc. It is also permitted to build above traffic areas. Nature areas should not be built on, but left as recreation areas and the "lungs" of the city. The free spreading of urban areas and urban sprawl in construction must be restricted.

The shape of the urban area needs to be given more attention than in the past. The form of the sustainable development-based city is concentrated. The satellite-based solution is in contradiction to the general aim of sustainable development, although some consider this "island" model possible. The island model is based on separate independent cities for 10,000 to 30,000 inhabitants, which all together form a city archipelago. It is questionable how such small units can maintain their independence (Lahti and Harmaajärvi 1992:72). In some cases the question of the linear city-plan is raised. This model, developed in the 1800s, achieved its greatest success to date in the general plans for Soviet industrial cities in the 1930s in the shape of N. A. Miljutin's zone-city plan. Otherwise the zone principle in city-planning structure has caused unnecessary traffic needs, so it should be dropped in favour of an integrated city structure.

When we compare northern views to those put forward by the European Union for the improvement of the urban environment, we find them to have almost identical content (Green Paper 1990). The density of cities in Europe, however, is in a completely different class than in the north, where the population is scattered and close to nature. The importance of historical protection perhaps bears more weight in the EU. Favouring public transport and decreasing the use of private cars are common to both views.

In a more detailed check on ecological planning aims, comes the enlivenment of residential areas with new activities, which at the same time means the more effective use of the building area. A common suggestion is the building of low blocks of flats, where the vital closeness to nature is preserved, but a more economic outcome is assured in terms of energy and municipal engineering. Social interaction with the use of communal services is also easier to arrange in areas of greater residential density. Large single-house sites in urban areas do not represent sustainable development (Lahti and Harmaajärvi 1992:12).

An ecologically sustainable city is an unimaginable utopia (Orrskog 1992:23). We come closer to sustainable development when we reduce materials and energy flows and attempt to return residual products to nature. Achieving the above requirements means that we are approaching a city which is greener, smaller-scaled and demands less traffic. A pre-condition for the principles of sustainable development to be achieved is a substantial increase in the awareness of the inhabitants.

3) Characteristics of Human Settlements

Typical of northern housing is a very loose structure, low buildings, and long distances between centres. Tradition in building was very strong up until World War II, when it was broken. Most Finnish towns were founded in the 17th and 18th centuries at the Swedish kings' command. The making of a town plan was part of the order. The basic town plan stayed the same from one century to the next; the popular Renaissance grid-plan (Tarumaa 1991:9). The proportions of the city, for instance, street widths and the height of the buildings bordering them, showed clear variation during different periods, as did the roof shapes and the facades, but the basic scale of the town remained the same. This grid-plan has turned out to be an ecologically successful solution. Although the straight streets were sensitive to certain wind directions, the enclosing of blocks with buildings and fences guaranteed an excellent microclimate within such blocks. The block comprised four to six sites, including in addition to accommodation other facilities, so causing the residents to spend their outdoor time in the inner yard and not in the streets as in southern climates. The small block size contributed to the formation of the town's small-scale granular form, which helped to create a favourable microclimate. The low building and wide streets made it possible to take advantage of the warming effect of the sun. The main building material was wood, which, as a renewable material follows the principles of sustainable development, and gave the town a warm, uniform and harmonious feeling (Nikula 1990:6).

The northern towns were small in population and size. For instance, in the great fire of Oulu in 1822, when almost the whole town was burnt down, about 3,000 inhabitants lost their homes. About 330 buildings were destroyed in this fire (Lilius 1985:30).

The right-angled grid-plan, small enclosing blocks, open courtyard space for communal use, and the unheated porch between outdoors and indoors, all follow the basic divisional hierarchy of town spaces into public, semi-public, semi-private and private. This clear basic structure, abandoned by functionalism and finally destroyed by modernism, has been shown to give its inhabitants the essential feeling of security which is the basis of natural human behaviour in different urban spaces. The mutual interdependence of city structure and feeling of safety has lately been found to be a planning factor of utmost importance (Newman 1973).

This "wooden town" was the planning model up till the beginning of this century. This is when the new European town ideals start to have an effect, the first of them being Camillo Sitte's romantic medieval ideals. Urban building was however rather limited until the 1960s, when the real city migration took place. Compared to the population and the numbers of migrants, this movement was at a world peak in its intensity (Auvinen 1981:14). This fleeing from the countryside also shattered the peaceful development of the towns. The residential areas built in line with dormitory suburb theory and realized in the functionalistic open building style, completely destroyed the previous town structure. Clarence Perry's original idea of the suburb (Hurme 1978:60) did not materialize in the northern countries, but the suburb was separated from the existing town structure as a separate entity surrounded by nature. Thus was born the "forest city" (Tarumaa 1982:47). Due to modernism the last principles of sustainable development disappeared from town planning.

Northern villages were consistent, fixed structures until the surveying operation undertaken at the beginning of the 18th century and called in Finnish "Isojako" (= the general parcelling out of land) changed the situation completely (Manty 1988:135). The purpose of the Isojako was to rejoin the separate plots of land which over the years had been split and were situated far from each other. This led to buildings being put up on the newly merged farms. Thus the traditional compact village milieu disappeared and the building of the characteristic scattered village, typical in northern areas, began. Even today the same scattered village structure predominates, apart from in those centres of habitation which have developed into urban areas. The scatteredness is increased further by the existence in Finland of the common right to build, which means that every building site owner outside of urban areas will get building permission for a dwelling providing that certain conditions are fulfilled (Building Act 1958).

PUBLIC PARTICIPATION

The sustainable development-oriented planning process is usually understood in such a way that the residents' opportunities to play an influential
role are good; they start as early as when the aims of the plan are discussed,
and participation in the planning is active throughout the whole process.

One of the main goals in town planning is to control the whole process;
first in planning and then in building. In the interest of this overall control a
hierarchical planning system has been developed, which begins with
regional planning, and continues through master planning down to town
plans and the individual block level. The aims of this comprehensive planning system also carry over to the level of detail—the realisation itself. This
planning method, hierarchically guided from the top, applied to the post-
war rebuilding period and the 1960s urbanization manoeuvre when
dynamic development and territorial growth were typical for communities
(Pakarinen 1992). The time-scale from planning to build was, however,
long. It was soon noticed that the comprehensive plan aims were already
out-dated before their realization began. In practice, alongside this instrumental or goal-oriented planning, there developed a type of planning,
based on a small steps policy, called incremental planning (Friedman and
Hudoon 1974:8–9). The new planning aimed at a certain flexibility, so that
it was possible during the planning to react to new demands coming from
outside. The aims were not defined too precisely at the beginning, so that
later it was possible to increase specificity. The traditional hierarchy, however, was retained in the planning practice, and also the inhabitants' and
other outside parties' participation in the process, occurred after the aims
had been established, when the planning was already in progress. In this
way the inhabitants' participation in the planning was also directed from
above.

The spreading of the postmodern ideology at the end of the 1970s also
meant the reappraisal of the inhabitants' role in the planning process. Faced
with growing uncertainty in technocratic and rational planning, search
began for new options from residents' ideas, and from other options than
the planners' viewpoint. One of the first attempts in Finland was a research
by the Oulu department of architecture called "The village in northern Finland" (1984). The main task of the research was to find a new planning tool
based on the inhabitants' point of view and not necessarily following official planning formats. The residents' participation in the planning began in
the definition of the aims, the evaluation of the planning needs of the area,
and the necessity and desirability of different steps. In practice, "village
planning" means the meshing of urban planning and building design. Current official plans are difficult to read, so the town planner's aims concerning both operations and the quality of the environment will not reach the

building designer. It is a question of a major communication failure between planners (Tarumaa 1982).

This new planning method has become known as communicative planning. In it the planning is based on a dialogue between different partners, all the way from setting the aims, and highlights constant open discussion thereafter. As a result of this kind of planning it is not however a town plan but rather a strategic plan. A strategic plan can be for instance a vision of the whole; it is a tool for discussion between all the planning levels and all positions (Keim 1994:2).

By the means of which planning method can we reach the best possible result for the environment? The variety of tasks in urban planning speaks for the use of different planning methods. Detailed technical solutions demand rational handling, while many basic solutions at the beginning of the planning require compromise and pluralism. A very unstable and complicated situation can be resolved only through incremental decision-making (Sulkava 1992:114).

For successful ecological planning it is essential that it be seen in a wide enough context. Prerequisites for this planning method are communicative planning and a new kind of general understanding of everything that affects the environment and those using the environment. Without the users' knowledge of the necessity of this new way of thinking we cannot achieve the change of general routines, which is a prerequisite for the reduction of burdens on the environment (Pakarinen 1992:129).

THREE CASE STUDIES

1) An Ecologically Sound Habitat—Case Rovaniemi

In this project alternative models have been developed for a new residential area, which are based on different planning ideologies. The task was preceded by a broad written analysis of different planning ideologies. In the final model, the ideologies known as winter-city problems and ecology-based planning have been combined. Although ecological planning is not so conservative in several respects than winter-city ideology in present-day planning methods, what they both have in common is a strong stress on a climatically aware solution. For this model the most suitable site has been sought within the area on the basis of the above-mentioned principles. In accordance with the analysis, however, the existing city structure should be condensed before any expansion is considered.

Rovaniemi is a town of about 30,000 inhabitants, situated a few kilometres south of the Arctic Circle, in latitude 66°33'. The town is the centre of Lapland. In Rovaniemi's climate, the average temperature over the year is 0°C, and the duration of the thermal growing season is about

(a)

(b)

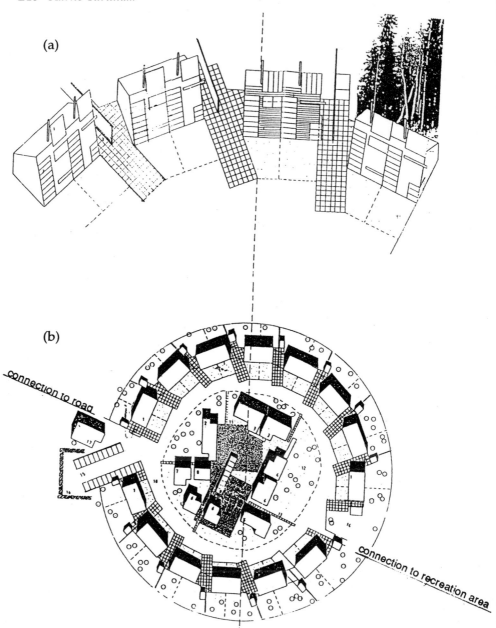

Fig. 1. Experimental block: Schematic layout. (a): 1. Solar panels; 2. Large windows to the south; 3. Parking; 4. Front courtyard; and 5. Forest courtyard. (b): 1. Semi-datached house; 2. Kindergarten; 3. Collective housing; 4. Rented house; 5. Rented house; 6. One family house; 7. One family house; 8. Common facilities; 9. Green house; 10. Area of collective gardening; 11. Block square; 12. Natural forest; 13. Wooden bridge; 14. Playing area; 15. Parking; 16. Edge of evergreen trees; 17. Collection of waste treatment and 18. Courtyard road

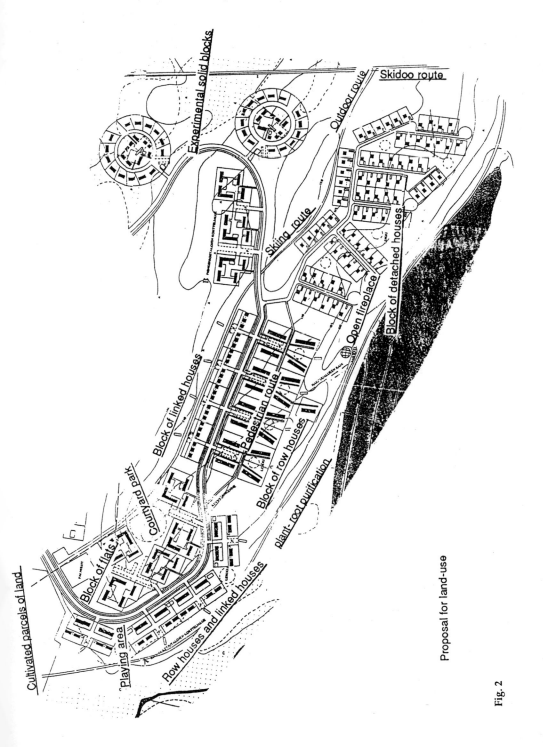

Proposal for land-use

Fig. 2

120–140 days. Permanent snow cover lasts from the beginning of November until mid-May, and the average snow cover is about 70 cm (Outila 1993:42). During the Second World War the whole town was completely burnt. The new town plan was made by the architect Alvar Aalto, He did not follow the old grid system which was traditional for wooden towns, but developed a new town plan which had its source in nature—called the Reindeer Antler Plan. The name comes from the tree-like town-structure, reminiscent of a reindeer's antler (Rautsi 1988:53). This tree-like model was generally respected and considered appropriate to a modern town structure until C. Alexander (1966) destroyed it in his famous article "The City is not a Tree".

The town is making a component master plan for the year 2010, in connection with which a decision has been made that the city will expand to the south. Because of the range of possibilities for the use of the area, there was a wish to examine the issue on the basis of different land-use ideologies. The size of the planning area is about 12 km^2, with about 2,300 new inhabitants (Outila 1993:44). The research work was completed as a final dissertation in Oulu University's department of architecture. One of the main themes was to find out what kind of possibilities there were in the southern extension area to carry out the principles of sustainable development in future town planning. The starting points for this research were ecology-based planning, winter city ideology and a techno-futuristic town model. In this connection we shall take a closer look at the first two of these.

Before the land-use plan for the area, a nature and environment analysis was made (Puotiniemi 1993), according to which it is quite easy to distinguish different landscape types. Topographically the area is hilly, forested landscape, with a lake in the middle. The valleys between the hills are mainly swampy. Based on the environmental research, the areas closest to the present-day town are technically cheap to build. At the same time the image of the landscape is improved by replanting partly-cut forest areas. The areas do not break up the town structure any more than is necessary, and furthermore the best nature areas will be retained as recreation areas for the local inhabitants. Negative points to be mentioned in the chosen areas are the loss of beautiful lake views and the lack of enriching effects in the water area. In evaluating the possibilities of the planning area and applying the different ideologies to it, the planner reached a solution where both the ecological and the winter-city model could co-exist. As town models for each of these two ideologies were developed, their physical forms approached each other so much and their solutions became so similar that the planner joined the two into an ecology-based winter city model.

When we compare ecological planning recommendations and winter city planning principles, we find a great similarity. Both stress the necessity of planning based on climate-awareness and decreasing greatly the use of energy. But there are differences, too. The ecological model tries to find new energy resources and does not accept the use of unrenewable natural resources. The winter city planning ideology lays emphasis on decreased energy use but also accepts the use of present-day energy resources in more effective ways. From the waste disposal perspective, the winter city is willing to accept present waste processing practices providing that the technical solutions are good and conform to the law and statutes. Ecological planning, on the other hand, tries to find new ways, with the underlying principle of returning all waste to natural circulation. In terms of traffic, both solutions require the development of public transportation and light traffic, but in the winter city the use of private cars does not receive such a negative response as in ecology-based planning. The determining factors in the situating of new accommodation in the area are, in ecology-based winter cities:

- maximal use of south-facing orientation in the interests of decreased energy consumption and the microclimate
- protection from the strong northwest winds
- the possibilities available for using the enclosing block model around open spaces in the area
- the density of the city structure
- minimizing the lengths of the streets
- the planning of snow dumping areas, their use and visual integration into the fragile areas of the cityscape
- planning for the use of motorsleighs and provision of space to keep them
- good light traffic connections to recreational routes, ski and motorsleigh tracks
- analysis and adoption of new street profiles suited to winter use
- optimal use of plants in microclimate planning.

In the chosen area the bulk of the new accommodation is situated on a south-facing slope. In the building area notice has been taken of the factors generally associated with ecological planning, such as the free downward flow of cold air, the use of forest for wind protection, the preservation of the natural water flows of the terrain, the use of plant-root purification in sewage-treatment, and maximized use of solar panels. In traffic arrangements, the idea of the usual network has been abandoned in favour of one centralized route serving the area. In the northern part of the new area solar energy cannot be exploited as effectively as in the south-facing area. In this area, new block forms offering a good basis for communal living, have been examined. Because the number of residents in a block is small, the maintenance of services demands from the residents a new, more social response to the community. The accommodation, that seeks to create a traditional village milieu, is enclosed within nature, the seat of its own mosaic culture. The pattern for the block is reminiscent of the old Lappish housing form.

The final conclusions of the planner are that the area should not, however, be the prioritized direction of expansion. Concentrating on the town centre in Rovaniemi is a better solution because:

• the functioning of town centre amenities can be revived
• the scattered townscape will become more compact and people will be close to the already existing services
• the need to travel between home and work will decrease
• the ever-decreasing family-size speaks for apartment block and row house types of accommodation (Outila 1993:51).

2) Environmental Impact Assessment (EIA) and Architect-Case Pudasjärvi

This case deals with master plan analysis in connection with Environmental Impact Assessment (EIA), and the architect's role in EIA-oriented research work. The project deals with the aims of EIA. Although the peat power station causes environmental problems, its realization could also bring new activity to an area otherwise poor in this respect. The question is whether we can accept ecologically questionable solutions for the sake of people's welfare.

Pudasjärvi is a small centre of population which is situated about 80 km to the northeast of the City of Oulu. The area has suffered great losses through migration, and the population is constantly decreasing and ageing. The main occupations are agriculture and forestry, about 24%, and the public sector, about 23%. Continuous unemployment is a nightmare for business life. At the beginning of 1994 there was about 30 per cent unemployment— about 1,500 people. A particular feature of the local nature is that about 70 per cent of the area of the whole community is swamp land. The total number of inhabitants is 10,800 (Lindroos 1994 : 20–21).

The local and area authorities have for several years campaigned for the building of a peat power station. The building of the plant would decrease the expected 15 per cent reduction in the population figure by the year 2010, the employment situation would be improved by the creation of 400–600 new jobs, and with the improved employment figures it would be possible to maintain the basic council services. Despite the financial benefits, some local people have resisted the project; they are concerned about both preserving the reindeer population and environmental damage caused by the plant.

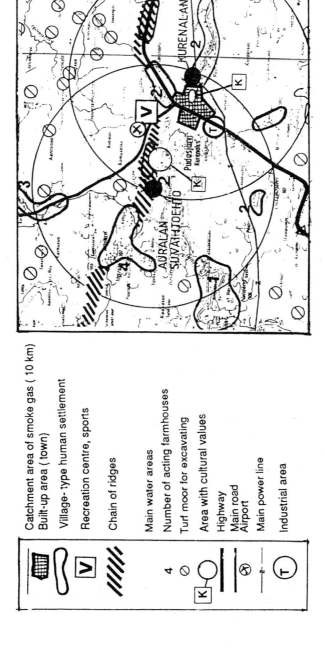

Fig. 3

Catchment area of smoke gas (10 km)
Built-up area (town)
Village- type human settlement

Recreation centre, sports

Chain of ridges

Main water areas
Number of acting farmhouses
Turf moor for excavating
Area with cultural values

Highway
Main road
Airport

Main power line

Industrial area

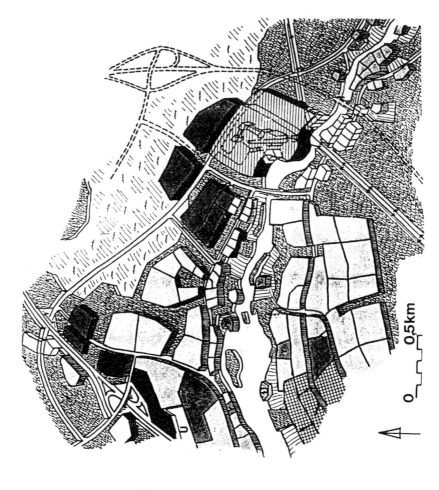

Illustration and structure of the land-use

 Existing built-up area

New built-up area

Disturbed settlement,
the activities must be changed
or disappear

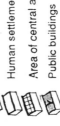 The plant area with its expansions

Human settlement

Area of central activities

Public buildings

Industry

Industry with no environmental
impacts

New activities made possible
by heat loss of the plant

 Open landscape

 Area of recreation and sport

0,5km

0

Fig. 4

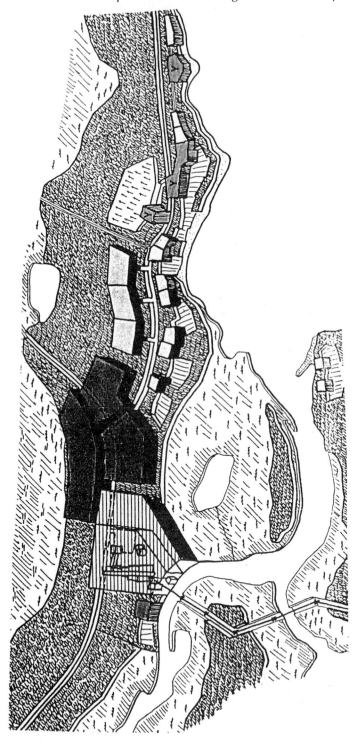

Fig. 5

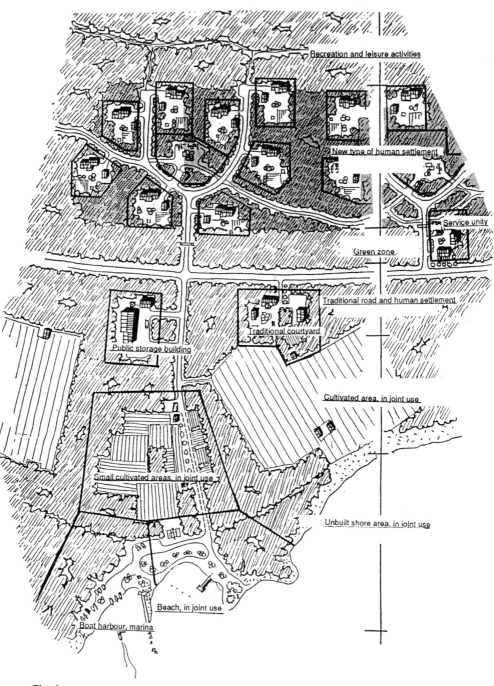

Fig. 6

The law of Environmental Impact Assessment did not come into force until September 1994 (EIA 1994, 468), but the law has preliminarily been applied widely in projects of this type, so that the residents could be informed of the advantages and disadvantages. Environmental impact assessment based on the law generally takes the form of a collection of positive and negative effects of the project on the natural environment.

In order to promote the project, environmental impact assessments were carried out in 1993, which considered both the building of the plant and the use of the peat swamps. Analysing the "zero option", in other words leaving the plant unbuilt, was not however included in the EIA process, which included instead a land-use survey at the master plan level. According to the findings, the worst environmental effects would be increasing traffic, dust problems caused by the peat, and the problem of re-use of the swamps after production. The ministry of trade and industry and the council authorities have together chosen two alternative locations on techno-economic grounds. The one located closer to the centre would have negative effects on the day-care centre, the school, housing and recreation.

In this work the aims of EIA have been expanded. An exploration of the positive possibilities could also be a part of them. Although the building of the plant is not in itself desirable, it would provide the opportunities for new operations. The town planning analysis of the power plant starts from these possibilities and their land-use solutions.

This work's relationship to EIA is that in addition to the EIA, a choice between options is made and finally a new master plan is made as a basis for building. The master planning analysis is a 1994 Oulu University department of architecture final dissertation (Lindroos 1994).

The point of departure in the general planning analysis is the two chosen locations. In the analysis of these locations it becomes clear that in terms of techno-economics or of environmental impact there are no significant differences. So the choice between the alternatives is to be made primarily on the basis of the master plan effects.

For both of the possible locations of the power plant a structure model for land-use at the master plan level was made. The disadvantages of the solution proposed by the council and situated close to the village centre are the traffic noise caused by peat transport, the power plant's own operational noise, and difficult traffic solutions. The demolition of existing buildings. and the disturbances caused by the plant to the day-care centre and other services are causes of great resistance among the inhabitants.

Also the potential for location of innovative new operations near the plant using waste energy is more economical in the second alternative. This other option is situated further out from the centre, about 5 km from it. Here the disadvantages are smaller and the possibilities for enlivening new operations are good. The great size of the plant, different from the rest of the built environment, also points to, in terms of landscaping, its situation at the edge of the urban area.

The master plan town model proposes the projected land-use up until the year 2020. Central aims of the plan are, in addition to taking account of environmental impact, the development and unification of the traditional village with the new style of dwelling models, the structural joining of the built-up area and the power plant, the adjustment of the old historico-culturally valuable church area to the new situation, and finally, the development of new ideas for unbuilt common areas. The basic master plan solution based on these aims forms a ribbon-like belt of activity, in which the "pearls"—the units of different activities—are separated from each other. At the heart of the structure, around the old church, the ribbon divides not only into vertical sections but also into horizontal zones. The ribbon structure joins the power plant area and other land used in connection with it into the urban area.

New operations based on the multiple use of peat and the exploitation of residual heat from the plant are also accommodated within the industrial and production belt. The peat power station forms the nucleus of the structure. Functions dependent on the residual heat have been situated near the power plant, like greenhouse horticulture and a sports hall. New innovative functioning is represented by the "peat park" to the east, which is a variation on the idea of a technology park. The park, with its business area and research centre, forms a centre for the multiplicity of peat use and expertise. Peat research, teaching, and product development for a range of peat products, manufacturing and local sales will take place here. Physically the area forms a harmonious, village-like whole, in which a special high street for retailing the products forms its functional heart.

The area around the church represents the oldest village settlement. The traditional village settlement with later structural additions, and the new-style village settlement, each form their own belt in the ridge area. In planning, the smallest structural unit in the old village settlement is a single courtyard, whereas the new form of settlement is based on cells comprising 8 to 10 dwellings. The more compact dwelling form is separated from the central road by a green belt so that the old road in the historico-culturally valuable church area will retain its traditional appearance. In the new building process, the quarries which have central locations in the vicinity of the church will be neatened and landscaped. Also, areas in public and communal agricultural use, and public use of land adjacent to water, are shown in the plan. In spite of the traditional dispersion of dwellings, the land-use is effective enough to avoid unreasonably high expenses causes by distance.

The church area settlement is linked to the centre by the new light traffic route through the nearby recreation centre. The recreation area closest to the centre is expanded with new amenities through the optimization and re-use of the landscaped quarry areas. The new travel accommodation for visitors in the area can be used during the building of the power plant as accommodation for workers.

The aim in EIA is not just unifying the planning procedure, but also preventing negative environmental effects. If we think about land-use planning this is not enough; we should guide the planning procedure toward a more objective-oriented direction. This would also decrease the suspicion and antipathy toward EIA, and furthermore promote the multiplicity of the analysis:

a) The architect's part in EIA analysis is to evaluate the effects on land-use and the community. To do this one needs creative planning and a broad overview.

b) The architect's role in land-use related EIA analysis is to work as a specialist in his/her own field by pointing out the effects of the project on the environment, for instance by making alternative land-use models to illustrate the effects (Lindroos 1994:80).

3) Communicative Strategy—Case Sotkamo

This case presents an experiment following the new planning idea, where, through the participation of the residents and landowners, the aims are to find a solution to a deadlock situation which will both expand the urban area and generally develop the environment. The problem consists of large farms where livelihood practices are changing and as a result causing changes to the environment, along with the administration's desire to enlarge the urban area and improve its efficiency. The results of the analysis in this case are unofficial plans generated by the residents and researchers and acceptable to both, which in the course of the planning process the authorities too approved. Present planning procedures are not at all effective in such cases. In order for justifiable plans, such as this one which was found to be highly appropriate, to be used more widely, posts giving priority to environmental issues should be created for area architects throughout the country.

Sotkamo is a small town with about 11,000 inhabitants situated in northeast Finland. The main occupations are in farming and forestry as well as in the public service sector. The urban centre is an area surrounded by lakes, and its topography can be characterized as having high hills and steep slopes ending in sandy shores. In some contexts, Sotkamo is said to be one of the most beautifully located villages in the country. The area has all the prerequisites for the enjoyment of outdoor pursuits, and has thus

The future of the Cities ?????

Fig. 7

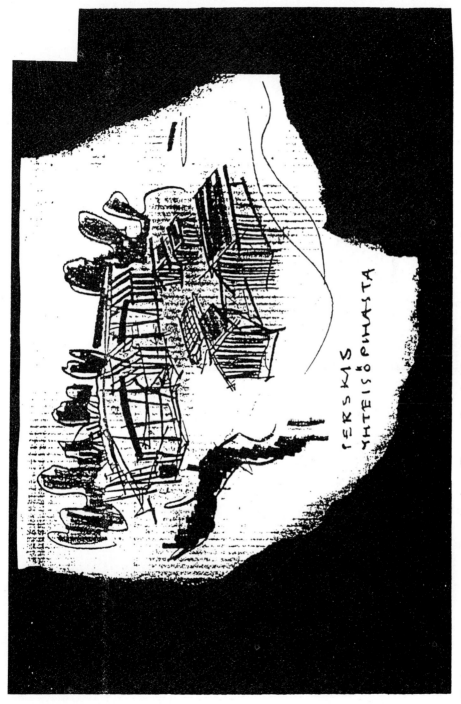

Perspective sketch of the community yard

Fig. 8

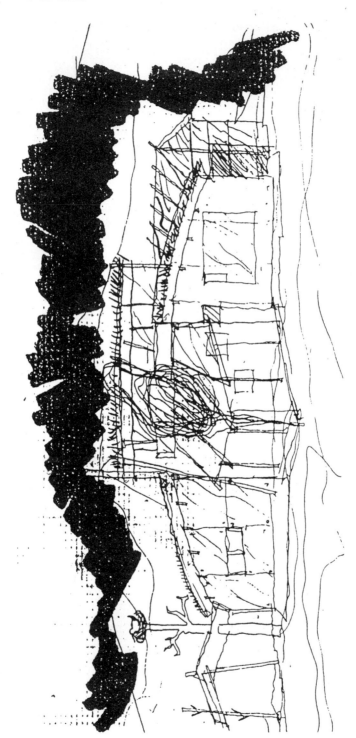

A house with its grass roof and trees rising up through the pergola

Fig. 9

become the country's most notable cross-country ski resort (Kyntoviilu 1992:51–55).

The beautiful hill landscape imposes great demands on the planning of the built environment. There have been arguments for years over traffic planning in the area. Expansion of the urban area has also been proposed on several occasions but up until now the inhabitants have always dismissed all the projects to make new plans. All the potential areas for expansion are primarily agricultural. Dispersed northern village settlements comprise working farms with their open field areas. Lack of trust between the authorities and the inhabitants is very real. The inhabitants doubt their chances of influencing land-use planning decisions. Planners are worried about the state of the environment and are trying to find new methods and planning tools for guiding construction.

In the research reported here, land-use was analyzed farm by farm. The aim was to find ways in which a solution satisfactory to all parties could be found. It became clear right at the start that there were no ready-made patterns to solve this problem, but that they would have to be developed during the work.

Attempts were made to find planning targets from among the chosen areas on a voluntary basis. Voluntariness proved to play a significant role in the development of the planning ideas. Twenty-seven farms, which for the most part made up fixed but not very compactly built villages, came forward as volunteers in this experiment. The farms' sizes ranged from 50 to 350 hectares. The analysis work itself started with the examination of each of the farms and negotiation with its occupant over the anticipated future land-use. Some of the farmers already had clear ideas for development, while others expected the researchers to tell them what they could do. The most important task of the first visit was, however, to find a common language, and through that a certain kind of trust relationship between the land-owners and the researchers. In most cases this succeeded. Thus a solution was reached in several difficult questions through negotiation in an open atmosphere, when the planners' and the landowners' interests were on completely different levels. It also belonged to the strategy of the plan that changes and corrections could still be made right up to the end (Kyntoviilu 1992).

The planning meetings took place on site, i.e., on the farms. Thus the landscapes became familiar to the planners in different seasons. There was always one council representative present at the planning meetings. Some of the local officials reacted with great suspicion to the project. The suspicions were on the one hand that all the shore areas would be filled with holiday accommodation, and on the other hand that the outcome would be too dispersed and absolutely inefficient land-use. The council representatives present at the planning meetings became very much more positive when it became clear that the afore-mentioned matters did not become predominant aims. The farmers and the researchers however, always had the power to make proposals and decisions. The prejudices felt by the other officials were dispelled at least partially by a joint seminar arranged for all interested parties. In addition, numerous meetings were arranged with the authorities, at which none of the plans was changed but the village as a whole was examined in terms of, among other things, ecological and environment-consciousness aspects.

The planning process part became more important during the making of the plans for each individual farm. The farmers and planners processed their ideas together for a year. The farm plans thus produced did not conform to official plan format—firstly because we wanted to avoid the impression of bureaucracy, and secondly because with farmers sitting at the planning table, what emerged was both their own symbols and their own planning language. The plan was broken down into the following divisions:

1) An environmental analysis affecting the whole village, containing suggestions for improvements, proposals for unbuilt zones, the content of new construction, and building recommendations. The environmental analysis also gave guidelines for environmental-political livelihood practices.

2) From the village level the plan moved in to focus on the individual farm. The farm plan itself contained an introduction, in which the most significant ideas were explained.

3) The history of the farm gave the basis and background for developing new functions, which were explained in detail.

4) Lastly there was the written description of the plan. In general, this description dealt with livelihood practices, planning guidelines for the nucleus of the farm, planning recommendations for the new farm-dwelling, and similar recommendations for holiday accommodation. The analysis of the environmental effect of field farming was one division of the description, as was the analysis of the landscape value of forested land. Also the other new livelihood-related activities were dealt with. The description included a drawn map-type plan, and a collection of special drawings which gave detailed suggestions for each procedure.

Because in each case the plan made was for only one farm, the new operations vary, from dwelling to holiday accommodation, different kinds of business activities and even bio-agriculture. The planner's task is to place the functions without incurring negative effects and to preserve a certain overview of the whole. At the end the researchers returned the plan in person to the farms, and checked it through once more with the farmers to avoid any possible misunderstandings at this point.

In planning projects of this kind, the normal boundaries between town planning, building design, landscape design and care of the environment are removed. Sometimes it seems that the other planner's qualities were of greater value than expertise in architecture and town planning. More important than knowledge of different "isms" was the ability to quickly see the possibilities and needs, and to build the ideas developed together into a solution.

The farm plans were based on the interaction of the farm's livelihood and land-use. Normally the architect comes into the picture when we know what to plan. In this project the land-use planning started from the changing of the farm's livelihood and the building activities for different purposes after that. The planning method is labour-intensive and cannot be done within the authorities' normal resources, but the function of the area architect in a wider form could be a good starting point for this kind of planning. Based on this research it seems clear that with active grass-roots level actions we can retain residents' trust in planning. This of course does not mean that one would accept inhabitants' unjustified building demands; the plans must follow the principles of sustainable development also in other respects. Because the local authorities have played a part in the planning, they could not very easily disregard them, although they are not official town plans (Kyntoviilu 1992:133).

SUMMARY

The definition of Sustainable Development was written into Finnish Building Law 17.8.1990/696, the first and most important paragraph of the law. The content, briefly translated, is that an area is to be planned in a way that saves natural resources and supports the sustainable development of the environment. The term is surely clear to all, but everyone chooses where to lay his/her own emphasis. Among architects and planners, the stress is strongly on the side of the ecological aspect, but also the social factors and inhabitants' greater participation in planning than in the past is felt to be important.

I presented Case Pudasjärvi at the Bauhaus seminar. In the seminar, problems of the case were discussed. There was little interest in the architect's role as a part of EIA. But there was lively discussion over the question of whether environmentally poor solutions can be made in the name of "humanity", in other words to ensure the income of people in their own home area, or in the name of the preservation of a whole community in an area. A final conclusion can be crystallized thus; that ecological issues in building are so important that bad solutions must not be made, but at the same time the authorities must make strategic plans for society in circumstances which are not based on continuous growth, nor even on maintenance of the present situation (Bauhaus Seminar 1994).

REFERENCES

Alexander, C. 1966. The city is not a tree. In: Arkkitehti 7–8/ 1966:120–126 Helsinki. The Finnish Association of Architects.

Auvinen, R. 1981. Asuminen ja ihmisen kasvu (Living and man's growth). Helsinki: Centre for Urban and Regional Studies, Helsinki University of Technology, B36.

Börve, A.B. 1990: If you can't beat them—join them! In: *Nature Adapted Design.* Winter Cities Forum 1990, Proceedings. Edmonton, Canada: International Winter Cities Committee.

Friedman, John and Hudson, Barclay. 1974. Knowledge and action. A guide to planning theory. *Journal of the American Institute of Planners,* 40:1:2–16.

Green Paper on the Urban Environment. 1990. Communication from the Commission to the Council and Parliament Brussels: Commission of the European Communities.

Hakanen, M. 1993. Kestävän kehityksen periaatteet asumisen ja yhdyskunnan suunnittelussa (The Principles of Sustainable Development in Community Planning and in Dwelling). Final report. Helsinki University of Technology, Faculty of Architecture, Research Institute for the Built Environment, B 23, Espoo.

Hautamäki, L. 1989. Harsh Areas in Finland. In: *Habitat International,* 13:2:77–85. Oxford, UK: Pergamon Press.

Hurme, R. 1978: Aspects on the history of the neighbourhood concept. In: *Studies in Art History* 4:57–66. Karkkila: The Society for Art History in Finland.

Keim, K.D. 1994: Local Potentials and Strategic Planning. Tampere seminarium 22–25.9.1994, Manuscript.

Kyntoviilu. 1992: Tilakohtaisen maankäyton suunnittelutyon loppuraportti (A Study of New-Type Planning Methods, Final Report). Edit. Sari Niemi-Nousmaa and Nina Väistö, directed by Aarne Tarumaa, ass. prof., University of Oulu, Department of Architecture, B 13.

Lahti, P. and I. Harmaajärvi. 1992. Urban Form and Sustainable Development. International Experiences. Ministry of the Environment, Government Printing Centre, Helsinki.

Lilius, H. 1985. The Finnish Wooden Town. Andreas Nyborg A/S, Rungsted Kyst, Denmark.

Lindroos, H. 1994. Pudasjärven turvevoimalan ympäristovaikutusten arviointi, Yleiskaavallinen tarkastelu (The Environmental Impact Assessment of Pudasjärvi Power Plant, The Master Plan study). Dissertation Work, conducted by Aarne Tarumaa, ass. prof., University of Oulu, Department of Architecture.

Mänty, J. 1988. The Winter Factor in Finnish Urbanism. Pages 133–158 in: Cities Designed for Winter: edit. Jorma Mänty and Norman Pressman (eds.), Helsinki: Building Book Ltd.

Naisbitt, J. and P. Aburdene. 1990. Megatrends 2000: Ten New Directions for the 1990s. Denmark: Licht & Licht Agency.

Newman, O. 1973. Defensible Space. Crime Prevention through Urban Design. New York: Macmillan Publishing Co.

Nikula, R. 1990: Good Nature, Evil City. Pages 4–20 in: Finnish Town Planning and Architecture: Helsinki: Museum of Finnish Architecture and Ministry of the Environment.

Orrskog, L. 1992. In: *Urban Form and Sustainable Development. International Experiences.* P. Lahti and I. Harmaajärvi (eds.). Ministry of the Environment, Government Printing Centre, Helsinki.

Outila, T. 1993. Printtivaaran maankäyttömallit (The Town Planning Models of Printtivaara). The Dissertion Work, conducted by Aarne Tarumaa, ass. prof., University of Oulu, Department of Architecture.

Pakarinen, T. 1992. Kohti moniarvoista yhdyskuntasuunnittelua (Towards multiconscious townplanning). in: Kunta, kuntalainen ja ympäristö:118–134, edit. Seppo Aura and Pekka Siitonen, Government Printing Centre, Helsinki.

Pakarinen, T. and Kokko, K. 1993. Urban Ecology—Research and Implication. Ministry of the Environment, Physical Planning and Building Department, Helsinki.

Pohjoissuomalainen kylä, osa 2.1984 (The Village in Northern Finland, vol. 2). University of Oulu, Department of Architecture, A 8.

Pressman, N. 1988. The Need for New Approaches. in: Cities Designed for Winter, edit. Jorma Mänty and Norman Pressman, Building Book Ltd., Helsinki.

Puotiniemi, P. 1993. Printtivaaran luonto ja maankäyttö (Nature and Land-Use in the Printtivaara area), Rovaniemi.

Rakennuslaki 16.8.1958/370 (Building Act). Version 469/1994

Rautsi, J. 1988. Alvar Aalto's urban plans 1940–1970. In: *Urban Reflections*, DATUTOP 13: 43–64. Tampere.

Sulkava, R.J. 1992. Intressiristiriidat kunnan toiminnassa (Conflicts in the facilities of a community). Pages 103–117 in: Kunta, kuntalainen ja ympäristö: Seppo Aura and Pekka Siitonen (eds.), Helsinki: Government Printing Centre.

Sustainable Development and the Future of the Cities 1994. Seminar in Bauhaus, Dessau 27.8.–3.9.

Tarumaa, A. 1991. The Renaissance Town Plan. Seminarium in Hailuoto, arranged by the Faculty of Literature, University of Oulu, 22–23.4. Manuscript.

Tarumaa, A. 1982. Asuntoalue ja liikenne (The living area and traffic). University of Oulu, Department of Architecture, A 4.

Laki ympäristovaikutusten arviointimenettelystä (YVA) 10.6.1994/468 (Act of Environmental Impact Assessment).

Zrudlo, L. 1988: The Design of Climate-adapted Arctic Settlements. pages 85–109 in: *Cities Designed for Winte.r.* J. Mänty and N. Pressman (eds.). Helsinki: Building Book Ltd.

Katowice—Economic Structure and Sustainable Development

Irena Jedrzejczyk and *Inge Osthoff*

INTRODUCTION

This study presents the results of an empirical research project on the economic structure of old-industrial regions in Central and Eastern Europe, following the example of Silesia in Poland. The prime focus of the research was to create a scientific basis for working out a strategy of sustainable development for the Voivodship (province) of Katowice.

In particular, the research aimed at: (1) recognition of the economic structure of the region, (2) identification of ecological problems connected with the structure, and (3) investigation of the types of social problems that may arise from eventual changes in the structure.

The study is based on the following proposition: Restructuring of the economy in the region is the foundation of sustainable development in Upper Silesia. This requires the development of completely new labour-intensive industries that will be both energy- and material-saving.

SILESIA IS ONE OF THE MOST CONTAMINATED REGIONS IN POLAND AND IN EUROPE

Silesia is one of the most contaminated regions in Poland and in Europe. In 1993 from its territory 476,000 tons sulphur dioxide (SO_2), 176,000 tons nitrogen dioxide (NO_2) and 278,000 tons of industrial dusts were emitted. A high water requirement—1545 dm^3/km^2 in 1993—resulted in an enormous amount of domestic and industrial sewage—a total of 685 billion m^3.

Only 34.6 per cent of the liquid wastes were purified properly. In 1993 Silesia produced 76,295 thousand tons of industrial waste. The amount of industrial waste stored reached 114,772 $tons/km^2$ and the amount of domestic litter was 1,069 m^3/km^2.

On the territory of the voivodship three zones of environmental hazard have been defined: (1) Rybnik region, (2) Upper Silesia zone, and (3) Myszkow and Zawiercie towns and their surroundings.

The balance of nature has been completely destroyed in those regions. There is an incessant concentration of dusts, sulphur and nitrogen oxides as well as a concentration of heavy metals exceeding admissible levels many times (lead, cadmium, zinc), and volatile hydrocarbons (see also Table 1).

Table 1: Ecological Data about Ecological Disastrous Zones in the Katowice Voivodship—Comparison 1982 and 1992

	Rybnik		Upper Silesia		Mysz.-Zaw	
	1982	1992	1982	1992	1982	1992
General						
area km^2	1038	1025	3134	2982	204	284
population tsd.	592	592	2935	2929	96	109
population density p/km^2	570	578	937	982	471	384
Water						
water requirement						
– industrial dam^3/km^2	52	44	163	96	79	29
– municipal dam^3/km^2	50	43	153	116	45	25
industrial/municipal sewage						
– total dam^3/ km^2	62	54	289	210	80	38
– biochemical cleaning %	33.1	49.5	9.7	26.6	43.3	89.9
– uncleaned sewage %	27.8	12.1	45.3	29.1	9.1	3.7
Air						
dust emissions						
– total t/ km^2	59	18	141	36	164	11
– degree of purity %	96.7	98.5	90.9	96.5	41.9	94.9
gaseous emissions						
– total t/km^2	211	122	461	205	100	23
– degree of purity %	x	6.9	10.3	26.1	0.4	2.0
SO_2-emissions t/km^2	171	72	193	99	23	10
Solid waste						
total vol. industrial waste tsd t/km^2	168	366	97	131	10	14
deposition %	46	46	26	26	48	68
Forest						
exposed area %	x	100	97.8	99.9	x	x

In each of these regions not only the air, but water and soil are also contaminated. The contamination of the environment implies negative effects for the people living there. In Poland the rates of illnesses such as cancer, respiratory diseases and heart-circulatory disturbance are significantly higher than the average. In particular, children are affected. There is a higher rate of premature birth, stillborn and children born with mental or physical disabilities. Furthermore, the contamination of the environment negatively affects the economic development, i.e., in some years the cost of the environmental degradation mounted up to 10 per cent of the GNP.

THE MOST CHARACTERISTIC FEATURE OF THE ECONOMIC STRUCTURE OF THE REGION IS A DISTINCT UNDERDEVELOPMENT OF SERVICES

The environmental degradation of Silesia is caused by its high urbanization and industrialization and by its outdated economic structure, antiquated technologies and negligence in building facilities for protection of the environment.

Katowice voivodship covers an area of 6,650 km^2, which is almost 2 per cent of Poland's territory. However, it is populated by 4,007,000 inhabitants, which is 10.5 per cent of the population of Poland. There are forty-nine towns and cities here, with a total of 3,494,000 people, which means that 87.2 per cent inhabitants of the region live in urban areas Some of the cities have the highest population density in Poland: Swietochlowice 4,654, Chorzow 3,879, Sieminanowice Slaskie 3,245 Czeladz 2,212 people/km^2. Certain branches of industry dominate the economic structure of the region (Table 2). Professions comprise 45 per cent of jobs in the sector, followed by trade 10.9 per cent, building industry 9.6 per cent, agriculture 8.6 per cent and transport 3.8 per cent (Table 2). The most characteristic feature of the economic structure of the region is a distinct underdevelopment of the tertiary sector (services). The industry is dominated by the energy production and material-consuming branches. There are 62 coal mines and 16 iron steel companies situated in the region, producing 98 per cent of Poland's coal output (150 to 200 million tons of coal a year), 32 per cent of coke, 54 per cent of raw steel, 46 per cent of rolled steel, 100 per cent of zinc and lead, as well as 27 per cent of electric energy. Much of this production is due to a self-supplying cycle within these industries themselves. The mining industry generates a demand for steel and an outdated technology in metallurgy creates a huge demand for energy. Similarly, production in the machine-building industry is stimulated by the needs of the mining industry. Due to the antiquated technologies, the industry branches are responsible for a huge amount of pollution. For example, the production of the 62 coal mines also implies the accumulation of million tons of coal waste stored on heaps and 1.5–2 million tons of saline discharges are sent to the rivers.

Table 2: Economic Data of the Katowice Voivodship

(1)   The importance of the Katowice voivodship for the national economy
  – 98% of coal output
  – 32 % of coke production
  – 54% of raw steel production
  – 46% of rolled steel production
  – 100% of zinc production
  – 100% of zinc production
  – 100% of lead production
  – 27% of electric energy production

(2)   The industry structure of the Katowice voivodship
  – coal mines
  – energy
  – metallurgy
  – chemical
  – building
  – industry of consumer goods
  – others

(3)   Employment after fields of the economy 1992 (tsd.)

– total	1.589	(100.0%)
– parts:		
industry	708	(44.5%)
building	154	(9.6%)
agriculture	136	(8.6%)
transport	60	(3.8%)
trade	173	(10.9%)
school system	95	(6.0%)
health care system	88	(5.5%)

(4)   Development of unemployment 1991–1993

	Katowice voivodship			Poland		
	1991	1992	1993	1991	1992	1993
unemployment (tsd)	116	148	172	2155	2509	2890
rate of unemployment (%)	6.4	8.6	9.7	11.4	13.6	15.7

BARRIERS IN RESTRUCTURING THE ECONOMY THROUGH REGIONAL STRATEGIES OF SUSTAINABLE DEVELOPMENT

An appeasement of ecological problems and a diminuition of pollution in the last few years—i.e., the emissions of dust dropped from 96 to 16 t/km^2 and the emissions of sulphur dioxide lowered from 143 to 55 t/km^2 compared with 1980 (Table 3)—occurred mainly for two reasons: (1) The

Table 3: Ecological data of the Katowice voivodship 1980 and 1992

	Katowice voivodship		Poland	
	1980	1992	1980	1992
General				
area km^2	6650	6650	312683	312685
population tsd.	3734	4006	35735	38418
population density p/km^2	561	603	114	123
Water				
water requirement				
– total dam^3/km^2	178.7	154.5	45.4	40.2
– total hm^3	1188.4	1027.7	14183.6	12569.6
– industrial hm^3	499	386.4	10137.6	8362.2
– municipal hm^3	654	592.2	2722.6	2838.1
industrial/municipal sewage				
– total dam^3/km^2	144.5	103	15	11.1
– total hm^3	960.9	685	4861.3	3461.3
– cleaned sewage %	75.3	72.1	57.7	71.3
– part of biological cleaning %	11.5	34.6	15.2	32.5
– uncleaned sewage %	24.7	27.9	42.3	28.7
Air				
dust emissions				
– total t/km^2	96	16	8	2
– degree of purity %	94.9	97.0	94.7	96.8
gaseous emissions				
– total t/km^2	267	111	16	10
– degree of purity %	x	19.5	11.4	21.4
–SO$_2$-emissions t/km^2	143	55	9	6
Solid waste				
total industrial waste vol. t/km^2	56128	114722	2924	5704
waste vol. on municipal dumps m^3/km^2	963	1069	124	131
waste volume per year t	37325.4	76293.2	914202.7	1783609.5
part of deportion %	46.9	46.9	34.6	34.6
Forest				
wooded area tsd. ha	184.5	187.3	8622.7	8717.6
area exp. to emissions tsd. ha	139.6	162.9	382.4	146.4

development of the environmental infrastructure has been a major factor. The environmental actions rose due to more investments as well as for financial incentives. This includes tax reduction to avoid environmental threats and/or the increase of fees and fines for environmental polluting practices. Furthermore, the controls of the supervising administration were expanded and strengthened and even the quality of control has as a result of new environmental monitoring systems. (2) The reduction in the industrial production was another factor because of loosening markets and the poor quality of the products. This development resulted in a lower energy input. On the other hand , the price increase for prime energy such as coal led to a reduction of energy input as well.

Although the ecological degradation could be lessened to a certain degree, the ecological situation of the region has to be continually improved. In brief, the following actions should be undertaken:

- If investments for modernizing the mines and companies or for the installation of end-of-the-pipe-technologies are not profitable, the company should be closed.
- New technologies for exploitation of coal and the production of energy and industrial goods should be installed.
- The installation of the new technologies will lead to more productivity and efficiency in the sectors.
- In order to improve the quality of coal, new technologies like coal-washing methods should be introduced.
- The subsitution of coal with clean energy sources like oil and gas should occur.
- The prices for coal and even electricity and heat should be increased significantly.
- Financial incentives like tax reductions should be introduced in order to encourage firms and households to save energy (i.e. the substitution of energy sources; actions for heat resistance; improving the technical equipment like valves for radiators).
- The process could be supported through foreign cooperation using the knowledge of the partners.
- The environmental standards should be intensified. This is not only to be seen under ecological point of views; it is even to attain the EU-norms.
- The actions involved in environmental protection laws should be strictly followed.
- The use of fees and fines should be completely regionalized.

The realization of the proposals are connected with problems which should be briefly named:

- As long as the cost of production in the energy sector will be significantly lower than the price for imported coal, Poland will rely upon hard coal, which means that Katowice voivodship will rely upon coal.
- The substitution of the coal with clean energy sources in short terms is not possible. Due to the immense foreign debt, the import of oil and gas cannot be financed. The domestic production of oil and gas is much too low. For these reasons the state will continue to rely upon coal in the near future.

- Whatever regional interests may be, the energy policy is determinded by Warszaw. In particular, companies of the energy sector are state-owned; although a privatization has been discussed. There are significant administrative obstacles, investors are not ready to take over the obsolete companies and even if privatization would be possible, the savings to the public would probably be low.
- Due to the outdated technologies and age of the mines and companies investments of modernizing or for the installation of end-of-the-pipe-technologies are unprofitable under cost-benefits aspects.
- Financing for these programmes is one of the biggest problems, low-cost solutions are needed.
- After 1990 the price increase for clean energy sources was much higher than for hard coal. This was a disincentive for substitution.
- Closing of coal mines or industrial companies will be met with resistance from current management. They will be afraid of losing their economic and political influence.
- The support through foreign cooperations is hindered. It is important to encourage investments and to reduce obstacles.

The voivodship can only decide about 50 per cent of the fees and fines; 50 per cent has to be paid to the national fund for environmental protection. In the case of fees and fines for SO_2- and NOX-emissions as well as for the discharge of saline waters, the national fund for environmental protection receives 100 per cent of the money. But the point is that the voivodship receives only 10 per cent of the money back.

Another problem is that the fees and fines are often not paid by the firms, because of their lack of money.

It has to be taken into account that the reduction of emissions will lead to more industrial waste.

The modernisation of firms and production technologies as well as the stricter application of the environmental standards will increase the cost of production. This implies a decline of the energy and industrial production. Threat of unemployment seems to be the biggest obstacle here. The industry gives jobs to 700 thousand people; mines and steel companies are big establishments employing from a few to several thousand workers. After 1989, the decline of industry caused the rate of unemployment to rise steadily. For this reason and because of unsure or absence of social insurance system the planned restructuring changes will not find the support among the hundreds of people working in the named sectors. They will fear to lose their jobs. Nor will they find the support of the managers from big mining, energy and metallurgical companies. They will be afraid of losing their economic and political influence.

In the future, the restructuring of the economy in the Katowice voivod-ship must take into account the environmental and social consequences. As long as the companies are state-owned, Warszaw has to do more, which in-cludes more investments—párticularly environmental protection invest-ments. In the case of privatized firms or pieces of firms, the federal government must implement an incentive programme, i.e., tax reduction for firms which contribute to the improvement of the environment. Beyond that Warszaw must establish a social insurance system in order to ease the effects of unemployment on the worker, i.e, through financial support.

On the other hand, the responsibility for the restructuring of the economy should be to the voivodship and local administration, because they know better what actions will be necessary for their region. However, regardless of the economic juncture, stable improvement of the condition of the environment and the avoidance of social problems can only be achieved by changes within the economic structure of the region. If the responsibility is given to the voivodship administration the new build-up regional and expert planning has to work out programmes to cover what is needed and to work out and use legal, administrative and economic instruments, con-sidering ecological and social implications. For this reason it will be impor-tant to increase the environmental and social awareness of administration staff in order to set the "right" decisions.

If the modernization and automatization of old industries is possible it should be undertaken under economic terms if ecological aspects are taken into account. In the case of a possible modernization and automatization during the phase of restruction and later on by the utilization of the new technologies, qualified workers will be needed. Building up new innova-tive industries like environmental protection industries will only occur if ecological claims are fullfilled. For these new branches qualified workers and experts are needed. Small and middle enterprises are also needed for the production of industrial and consumer goods. Building up the craft sec-tor (installations, building, mechanics) is an important task. Broadening and renewal of the technical infrastructure, e.g., communication systems, transport, should be encouraged. Another important factor is the health-care system, which is underdeveloped taking into account the bad health conditions of the people living there. Fullfilling the tasks of building up small and middle enterprises, the craft sector, the renewal of the technical infrastructure and the health care service, qualified workers and experts are needed. Therefore, education in schools, universities and the training in the firms or in other organizations has to be intensified. For this reason, the building system should be reorganized and/or built up.

CONCLUSION

Diversification of the economy is the key. It is necessary to state that a change of economic structure in the old-industrial regions in Central and Eastern Europe is the most important factor of sustainable development of these regions. However, the risk of unemployment and feeling of fear caused by it are the most difficult obstacles that have to be faced. The first stated objective of the sustainable development strategy is to diversify the economy. Broadening the economic base is very important to these regions because their dependence on a single industry makes them extremely vulnerable.

The Messages of Folk Architecture

Jadranka Veselic-Bruvo

INTRODUCTION

The art of building is as old as human society. From ancient times human society has been witnessing the eternal struggle for survival on native soil, striving to subdue and tailor this art to one's needs while concurrently contending to adapt to that same soil through a creative effort of building a home. A house evolved as an existential category, a result of protecting ones home and hearth, while with respect of construction and aesthetic principles it was the most logical form. The development of the house pervaded by the characteristics of the ambience in which it was built followed the evolution of man and human society, reflecting his needs and capabilities. In its framework of space and time, folk architecture reflects and expresses the entire conceptual and emotional capabilities of human society. It is defined by two groups of factors: natural conditions and social implications. The first group includes the geological texture of soil, terrain configuration, climate, vegetation and available building material. The second group encompasses historical events, migrations, level of welfare and ethnic characteristics of population, organization of family and social group.

The physical conditions of the environment are endangered to the maximum. However, the struggle for survival should be accompanied by devotion to humanity of space and elevating the living space on a creatively higher level, fighting against automatism, technicism and capitulation to practice. When living in a firm bond with nature it is difficult to learn its laws and find the balance of living and one's place in it. The relation between man and nature generally ends as a merciless exploitation of the basic elements—water, air, flora and fauna, in order to enjoy the luxuries the development of civilization has made accessible. This is in contradiction with the eternal human need to directly perceive nature and understand its sense. The return to the sources of natural balance as opposed to self-sufficiency of artificially-created ambiences is the only avenue to, and the way of survival. The examples of balance are not encountered in the metropoles of the world, but in native ambience, in messages emitted by folk architecture that undoubtedly speaks of organic unity with the landscape, of human criteria, comprehension of natural building materials and relationship with nature. This spatial perfection has during the time been created by nameless peasantry who have always lived in harmony with nature. Shaping the living premises for the most vital needs (cooking, eating, gathering, leisure and love, hygiene) has not only resulted in the creation of purposeful space but also in the establishment of aesthetic principles and creative action in space.

The essential principles of the logic of life have resulted in the formation, both spontaneous and planned, of several different rural groups. The peasant, the folk builder, generally isolated from any external influence, has lived in immediate contact with nature and built economically, applying a number of ideas rooted deeply in his/her conscience as inherited building experience. These are the natural conditions on the one hand, and the human imagination based on the imminent principles of artistic creation, on the other. The feeling for rhythm, symmetry, harmony, proportion and scale has rendered the balance and beauty governing the idyllic rural landscape.

The Pannonian region has been characterized by planned building since the times of Mary Therese. The house, as a result of the most logical and most purposeful organization of a farming household, is located on the very building line with the gable turned towards the street. By the rhythm of gables the folk builder contests the monotony of the Pannonian plain.

The Mediterranean region with its mild climate and many days of sunshine is typical for the life in the open—in a yard or on a street. The need for protection against cold winds (bora) and summer heat prompted the formation of a cluster of either single household or complete hamlets. Mildly sloping roofs are the consequence of minimum snow loads, projection of eaves is small because not even the larger ones would protect the house walls against the wind-borne rain. The light and warm colours of stone are complementary with the blue of the skies and the sea. The edge and surface are the carriers of the dynamic game of light and shade under the hot Mediterranean sun. The hostile climate and abundance of precipitations in the central mountain region have dictated the life in confinement. Here, each house lives its introverted life in the intimacy of the warm hearth. The solid mass of the dark roof is architecturally most prominent, and its strictly defined volume often softens vivid house front. A miraculous harmony of volume and shape in a brown shade of lumber has been achieved.

Middle of the nineteenth century was the time of breaking ties with tradition, of the disintegration of rural structures under the influence of the

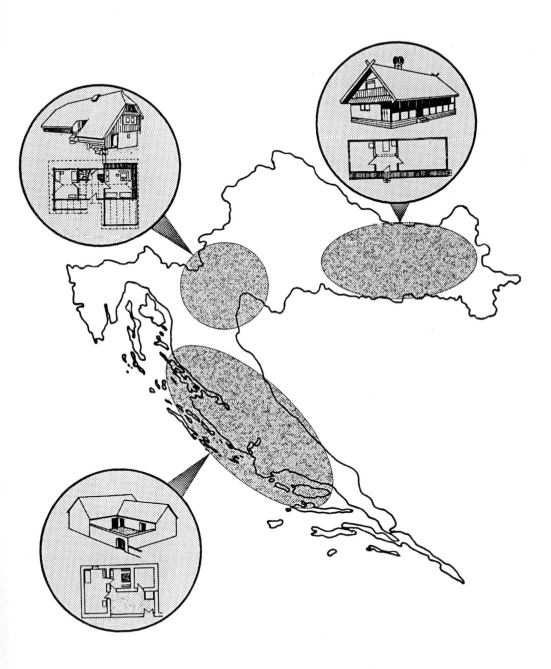

industrial revolution, and the social trends it caused. Connecting of ever larger spaces enabled the use of industrially-produced building material and the application of new quickly learned and insufficiently tested experience, while the feeling of belonging to one's limited local space was being lost. Forced urbanization and industrialization after the Second World War, which was supposed to take us into the happy future while everything traditional was considered retrograde and outdated, brought neglect of agriculture and country, causing further dissolution of rural regions and their social structure, degradation of traditional lifestyle and economy, thus causing change in the rural landscape. These were the times of wrong and unjust policy towards the country, peasants and agriculture. The collective consciousness grew to cause even the rural population to feel ashamed of its tradition. The state was interested in, and the profession controlled only the development of cities, while minor settlements were left to their own fate. Such a situation adversely affected smaller settlements. The castles and timber-framed manors were used to the verge, and then left to wreck. Traditional houses and street fences were mercilessly knocked down. The quality of the new constructions was incomparable with the earlier. Thus, the settlements lost their native attributes and their identity, namely their image.

The cultural monument's protection services started validation of the traditional building craft as an important part of a complete cultural heritage. This move was comparatively late, and had no serious support from the social system. It was therefore not possible to stop further degradation and impose better protection of the remaining valuable buildings and structures. These have been forgotten by the architects, abandoned by the younger generations that have migrated to the cities and are most often despised by those who presently live in them.

The rural society increasingly sought the models for their houses in suburbs which is the closest urban group to the peasantry. Unfortunately, the models have as a rule been bad.

In the sixties and seventies the migratory workers returning from the countries of their work started building, often using the patterns of the questionable "European ready-made architecture", which further destroyed the Croatian rural heritage, its homogeneity and original building forms. During this process, in some regions of Croatia the last preserved rural clusters of folk architecture were destroyed.

The reconstruction of rural clusters, which most directly present the achieved level of the architectural and building culture of the Croatian people in certain regions, must be accompanied by the simultaneous initiation of the new construction of the rural area based on the tradition and currently vital principles of rural building art, with all the comforts that the modern farming households should have. Such building revival supports the spiritual revival of the country and its population. The basic issue is to be capable of differentiating between the important and unimportant, to preserve the important and discard the unimportant and obsolete, to introduce the modern elements and build the new on that basis.

It is possible to preserve the regional characteristics by using modern building techniques in rural areas and by using all positive heritage of the traditional building craft: maximum respect of characteristic historical allotment and its organization, specific layout of the structure, preservation of route, cross-section, building and street lines of the old road communications and finally protection and remedy of the remaining structures of the traditional building craft.

Therefore, in the Pannonian region the traditional allotment should be enforced, the traditional location of the house on the lot should be kept and the character of the street preserved. The street (gable) frontispiece of the Slavonian house carries its identity. The street frontispieces, although similar, have their own peculiarities, and charm. In Dalmatia, the cluster should be preserved as an essential unit of the rural image, since it is the only element that provides for quality (private) life in the open. The stone wall has sufficient thermal characteristics that must be maintained in case industrial materials are used for building.

The fact is that new brick structures have changed the traditional orientation and layout of building on the lot, and that mainly narrow lots house the buildings with a wider frontispiece turned towards the street—the giant structures. The settlements are undergoing changes caused by the new unplanned and aggressively oversized infrastructure systems or by the lack of any traces of old architecture and the association with the former land organization and concept of a settlement and its traditional structure. The basic principles of folk architecture correspond with the principles of modern architecture:

• rational sizing and functional organization of space tailored to human needs,
• limited use and shaping of building material,
• structural construction system,
• harmonically determined concept of space, and
• organic unity with the environment.

EXAMPLE OF FOLK ARCHITECTURE IN CROATIA: THE TUROPOLJE TIMBER BUILDING

The Southeast part of the City of Zagreb between the Sava and Kupa Rivers is covered with the arable Turopolje plane or the Zagreb Field and the low hills of Vukomericke Gorice or Vrhovje (the highest hill is Zeridovka, 255 m a.s.l.). Turopolje was named after the primeval tur cattle (European bison) which lived in the immense forests and marshes of Turopolje until the 17th century. The Vukomericke gorice were named after the tiny village of Vukomeric, which again was named after Vukomer from the 14th century tribe of Vukote. The centre of this region is the Velika Gorica settlement. The basic architectural characteristic of this region, regarding the forest capital, was timber building. As regards the history of art, Turopolje was the focus of the creative church building which has the common roots with the secular rural architecture—the same materials and elements are used, with the same rustic way of finishing. Still, while building a church, the folk builder had a chance to express his freedom and originality remaining true to the ancient carpenter craft and with detailed knowledge of the material.

In this region the people have since the ancient days lived in large family cooperatives, and the oldest known record of the common property of several brothers comes from 1343. By the end of the nineteenth century, and particularly after the First World War, the dissolution of the cooperatives started. The cooperatives included a larger number of families. They had a common house and estate which was jointly cultivated. The cooperative was headed by the master who managed the estate and represented the cooperative, but his authorities were restrained by the obligation to act in consensus with all adult male members of the cooperative. The kitchen was managed by the mistress, with the help of the young daughters-in-law. In large cooperatives one woman was exclusively in charge of bread-baking, one man was in charge of the oxen, and another took care of the horses. In the evening, at dinner around the large table placed in the corner of the house, the men would discuss the activities of the next day. While eating, the men would sit on benches while the women would eat at their feet.

The cooperative houses were three-part buildings with a large room in which the members of the family lived, a smaller room which was the repository for trunks, and a kitchen without a ceiling, with an open fire. Such houses had a four-eave roofing with straw cover and very often with a tiny hall.

In Posavina and in the eastern part of Turopolje the timber houses called "cardak" (blockhouse) were found. They had a perfectly carved outdoor staircase and porch. The farm premises were on the ground floor, and the first-floor premises were the living quarters.

The old timber houses looked like "lonely sculptures", and the family cooperative life in them was functionally organized. Harmony was reached between the humans and the other living creatures around. The search for beauty led the people to decorate their home, which is most frequently evident from the cuts in the beam passing horizontally through the ceiling centre on the floor which is almost always as long as the house. The carved

ˇCardak"—East Turopolje, village Mraclin   [Picture 1]

date is the year of building, adaptation or any other significant date related to the house or the family cooperative, and it is found in the segment which passes through the main room on the floor; the year is often accompanied by a rosette or some other decoration. Decorations are more visible on the external part of the house—the window jambs and trims may often have a decorative rim, while the door was painted or decorated with inlays arranged into a mosaic. The most frequent decoration is on the gable frontispiece up on the floor. Sometimes, these are the gable timber-ending decorations, the decoration above and between the windows shaped as a decorative frieze with geometrical or vegetation motifs, sometimes the name of the master of the house is written, or of the carpenter, and the year of construction. More often, the railing of the staircase leading to the upper floor is and the pillars supporting the staircase roof and porch are also decorated.

The nobility had been building large timber-framed castles, the manors. The ground floor premises were for farming purposes, the brewery and the chamber, and the first floor had five large rooms—the

[Picture 2]

[Picture 3]

[Picture 4]

Window decoration   Entrance decoration

largest was placed in the middle, furnished with an enormous table, and used as a dining room; the adjacent room was a sitting room with classical furniture, and the remaining three were the bedrooms. The roof was covered with shingle. The most beautiful and the best preserved mansion is that of the Modic-Bedekovic family in Donja Lomnica, built in 1806. The oldest preserved mansion was built in Vukovina in the middle of the 18th century on the old estate of the Viceroy Ga{par Alapi}, and nearby is the timber vicarage in Staro Cice from 1831.

Although the size changed, construction of the Turopolje house remained the same: timber planks with "Croatian corners".

The timber village chapels made of oak planks were built during the 17th, 18th and 19th centuries, after the Turkish devastation in the 16th century. The most attractive examples of the sacral timber architecture are the Sta. Barbara chapel in Velika Mlaka (17th century), St. George chapel in Lijevi Stefanki (1677), St. John the Baptist chapel in Busevac (1622), Holy Trinity chapel in Pokupski Gladovac (1874), St. Roko chapel in Cvetkovic Brdo (1888), St. John the Baptist in Lukinic Brdo (1909), St. Peter chapel in

"Croatian corner"   **St. George chapel, Lijevi Štefanki, 1677.**

Pokupsko Cerje (1932), the chapel of Wounded Jesus in Pleso (1757), and the chapel of St. Anthony in Gustelnica (1888).

Regardless of type and structure, all the chapels are timber-framed with oak planks, designed as uniform rectangular halls with five-side apse. The gable is protruding and supported by poles which simultaneously solves the entrance porch. The windows are placed on both sides of the entrance ending in semi-spherical or segment arch. The walls were bleached, and the split planks (sawn planks in younger buildings) tidily joined in a "German corner".

The bell towers were always covered with pyramid-shaped shingle roofs. The gable roof is covered with shingle or tiles and it mildly slopes to the polygonal apse. The foundation beams are laid on stone or brick underpinning. Sometimes, it was possible to open the sides of the small hall so that the chapel interior was visible and the people could attend the mass from the Allsthese buildings, from the rural housing architecture to the timber-framed manors and small chapels, plot fences, crosses in the crossroads, crosses on the grave-mounds were made by the local carpenters called "palirs" organized in the so called "palir guilds". Their tools were

Holy Trinity chapel, Pokupski Gladovec, 1874

Detail: entrance ceiling, St. Anthony chapel, Gustelnica, 1888

large axes for rough woodworking, and the small ones for finishing. They travelled from one village to another, working the wood and leaving behind the architectural creations which undoubtedly speak of organic unity with the landscape, respect of human criteria, use of physical properties of the material, harmony with the native Turopolje surroundings—THE BEAUTIES OF TUROPOLJE.

Ecological Urban Development: An Experiment in Active Learning

Bernd Hamm

INTRODUCTION

Since its inception in the early 1970s, the Faculty of Socio-economic Sciences of Trier University committed itself to three basic principles for its graduate studies programmes—interdisciplinarity, empirical orientation, and practical relevance. The major didactical tool for this is a compulsory one-year student's project. The experiment described here was developed in this context as the project in our programme on Urban and Regional Development. The experiment had several specific components and appreciated favourable conditions: (1) In the introductory course, we decided to design it as a two-year project, (2) This should continue to stretch into the students' diploma theses; (3) The project was not, as usual, fully pre-designed by the supervising professor, but began with a Futures Workshop to define its subject and methodology; (4) Being intended to be innovative in a number of respects, it received a generous grant from the responsible Land Ministry for Science and Continuing Education.

HOW THE PROJECT DEVELOPED

On an experimental basis, the course scheduled to introduce students to the sociological component of our Urban and Regional Development graduate programme was designed as a Futures Workshop, following the method which was developed by the late Robert Jungk. Essentially, this method starts with defining a problem and then unfolds in three phases: A thorough critique of the present situation, a discussion of what an ideal solution of the problem could be; and the development of projects so as to bring the unsatisfactory present closer to the ideal. The course brought together some 45 students of different major disciplines—management, economics, geography, sociology, political science. At its critical assessment phase, we discussed the widening gap between real world problems and increasingly fragmented specialization in the ivory tower of university studies, a reason for deep discontent among all participants. The major problem was perceived to be the rapidly sharpening crisis of threatened human survival on earth. The issue was dealt with in depth revealing that although the bottom line was seen as global environmental degradation, the problem had many facets including increasing socio-economic polarization within and between countries, increasing distribution fights, increasing violence, crime and deviant forms of behaviour, increasing migration from poor to rich areas, and decaying capacity of the polity to regulate emerging conflict. It also became clear that the driving forces for this crises are to be found in the global economic and political structure allowing the rich countries to be the major consumers of global natural resources.

The fantasy phase, then, continued with the issue of global sustainability. We developed some basic characteristics of a global society taking care of its natural resources, not overexploiting the non-renewable ones, preserve reproducibility and carefully use renewable ones, avoid high-risk technologies like nuclear power, and satisfy the basic needs of all humans. In such an "ideal" society, science must play a role different from what it plays now, i.e., from one centred on growth and competition neglecting the limitations of the planet, to one useful to re-orient our western model of consumption and our political, economic and social mechanisms of control and regulation towards global sustainable development. In this world, the rich countries would have to re-adjust their systems so as to bear their proportional share of the crisis and bring down their resource consumption dramatically. Most of what we understand as wealth is in reality unnecessary and wasteful consumption.

During the last phase, realization, it became clear that in the highly urbanized rich societies like ours, ecological urban development would be a path of re-orientation of primary importance. How could this be achieved? We also found that our project would not be well conceived if it would simply replicate the usual pattern of positivist methodology and retrospective data analysis. There must also be a change in the entire approach to reality, as well as in the social relationship in class.

The first semester (winter 1992/93) ended with a decision taken by sixteen students to engage in the new and obviously demanding project, while the others decided not to commit themselves to such an extent. The Project Group then, during the second semester (summer 1993), went into library work to find out in more detail about the nature and content of sustainable development, and how it could be formulated in more operational terms. A number of short-term papers were produced which centred around resource depletion in different types of societies, and model projects aiming at reducing such depletion in European cities. By July 1993, we found the work we envisaged to conduct should: (a) have a real practical impact in our own environment, and (b) use a methodology closely related to action research proposals prominent in social work in the early 1970s but rarely discussed now. It was still open whether or not such an opportunity could be found. Thus, the paper work would not be our primary objective. Among the projects we discussed were several in the Trier region affected by de-militarization and conversion into civilian land-uses.

On the basis of information collected, we decided that small groups of students should go out on excursions during the summer break to study on spot experiments made in different German cities up and down the country in resource-minimizing strategies. All these attempts were sectoral, some dealing with traffic and the restrictions for the private car in favour of public transit and bicycles, some with careful use of energies and special emphasis on renewable sources of energy, some with ecologically intelligent architecture in urban revitalization as well as in new housing construction areas. After an evaluation of these visits we made up our minds to go together on an excursion to visit the allegedly biggest, most comprehensive and most progressive project in regional innovation in Germany—the International Building Exhibition (IBE) Emscher Park, an area extending some eighty kilometres east-west in the northern Ruhr region, its most depressed part. This was done in November 1993.

The IBE is, in fact, not one project but rather a conglomeration of about eighty different projects. The entire programme uniting these projects set forward three general goals: ecology, employment, and participation in decision-making. It works with a special funding mechanism which sets projects evaluated and accepted by the IBE Board of Directors on top of the priorities in the land government, and therefore of all land ministeries and their respective budgets. Thus, IBE was advertised and project proposals invited—about 400 came in to be considered. Among the 80 finally accepted where urban renewal and revitalization projects, new construction, old industry museums, landscape and park architectures, women's projects, renewal of sewage systems, traffic-related ones etc. All this ended up in a "golden nuggett-strategy" with mostly small-scale pilot models scattered all over the depressed area. All projects were selected to emphasize user participation, ecologically sound use of resources, help to increase local employment, and encourage local innovation and mobilize endogeneous potential. The concept looked promising, to give exactly the sort of information we needed. We started our one-week excursion with an official presentation of the entire concept at IBE headquarters in Gelsenkirchen. After this, we visited a great number of these individual projects, talked with residents and users, discussed with city officials and critics, went to see planning and architecture shops as well as opponent groups whose project proposals had not been accepted.

The final result was, in part disillusioning, primarily due to three reasons: (1) The ecological goals were rarely fulfilled; this was partly due to the fact that the Ruhr area and its political organizations are widely dominated by the interests of the big energy suppliers; (2) Citizen participation was in fact reduced to merely symbolic aspects like decisions about the colour of the carpet or wall-paper, or the alternative of having more storage space versus a guest room in the appartment. (3) The endogeneous potential, i.e., the innovative spirit and creativity of the local population, seems to have been more frustrated than encouraged, the major reason being again the close interlinkages of the political machineries with local project proposers. The empirical reality was only rarely in line with the professional PR presentations of the programme. Some projects would very clearly have gained in quality, and some flops avoided, if the citizen's views had really been taken seriously.

It was during this excursion that we came to know that a small town in the vicinity of Trier (6,000 inhabitants) had been admonished by the district administration to begin with its development planning. The city council had entrusted a special development committee with the task to develop and submit general guidelines along which this planning should occur in the future. The committee was to be moderated by a professional planner. Its mandate should be fulfilled by the summer of 1995. As this looked exactly like the practical case we had in mind but not yet found, we contacted the mayor and became finally accepted to consult this committee. Our intentions and potential contribution to the process were seen in two aspects, i.e. citizen participation, and ecological urban development. All steps to be taken were carefully discussed with the committee which, on the other hand, accepted some of us as regular consulting participants to its meetings.

The students' group discussed the strategy that should be followed so as to make a significant contribution to the planning process. Convinced that ecological urban development would only become a permanent issue and pressure on the local politicians if it is organized as a learning process for all, we considered citizens' participation as a task of primary importance. Therefore, the first task was to make citizens know that development planning was about to be set in motion. Secondly, the Committee was our direct target group. Composed of members of the political parties represented on the city council, plus representatives of the major voluntary associations, they were all lay persons who had never been involved in a similar task. The moderator, geographer and planner by profession (and, by chance, one of the first graduates from my Trier University programme), organized its work in ten thematic sessions each of which was supposed to result in a list of development guidelines; at the end, all sectoral arguments were to be pooled together and evaluated against each other so that a comprehensive result could be expected. Our procedure being to a large extent dependent of what happened in the Committee could not be fully planned from the outset but rather developed step by step:

1) We wrote a little brochure to inform citizens about the beginning development process and how it was organized, to demonstrate that this is of importance to everyone in the community, and to show that there are alternatives—conventional versus ecological orientations. We added a few examples to give a clear impression that ecological planning is not simply an offspring of the fantasies of some students but a beginning reality in many places. We had about 2,500 copies of a brochure printed. On a sunny Saturday morning, when people could be expected to work in their gardens, we went to distribute the brochure to all households of the community. This provided quite a number of opportunities for first personal contact and talk. The action had been announced in the local newspaper, so some people were already aware of it. The brochure also contained a business-reply postcard so people could let us know if they were interested in becomes actively involved. All events organized and actions taken by us was addressed first to the committee, then to those citizens (some 30 who got personal invitations to all events) who had responded to our brochure, and finally to the general public.

2) We contacted all school heads in the town to encourage teachers in all schools and classes to have their pupils draw and paint pictures on their vision of an "ideal" city. About 450 pictures were collected with this effort. We organized an exhibition in the local cultural centre and in the local bank, with a formal opening by the mayor. A speech was given to the audience on global environmental problems and the relevance of local action. This was again announced and later covered in the newspaper. A planned futures workshop for members of the committee had to be postponed due to local elections, summer holidays, and other events.

3) The local association of business people invited us to present our views to their annual meeting. The resulting discussion was, as could be expected, partly sceptical, but ended by being generally supportive. The president of the association and member of the committee, himself an architect, could be convinced for an ecological perspective including an orientation more towards local self-sufficiency than towards supra-local and growth-oriented outlooks. This was supported by the general threat of having big chains take over small businesses, with a resulting increase in import-export relations.

4) We had an impression that our arguments were still considered somewhat exotic by a majority of committee members. So we organized a half-day workshop on ecological town development and invited some specialists—architects, landscape architects, retail specialists, traffic planners, local energy specialists—from other small towns to report on their respective experiences and on the possibilities they could perceive in the given situation. This event ended up with a strong plea for more citizen participation and for reconsideration of two zoning-plans which had been finished but not yet set in force. Increasingly, we could observe committee members use ecological arguments and point to our contribution.

5) Next, we organized a Futures Workshop for committee members and some others. They had almost two full days to discuss the future of the town and initiatives to be taken. It was only then that committee members became aware of the futures workshop methodology and learned to use it as something serious. Gradually, our group gained in credibility and support.

From the schedule of our students' project, we were rapidly approaching the final phase. Students were supposed to write their final report during the summer semester 1994 and, as their comprehensive exams were coming close, they had no more time to devote in the project. On the other hand, our involvement was such that we could not pull out at this point, as substantial results had still to be seen. We therefore formed a small group of five, including two part-time research assistants and two students who wanted to continue working with me. This was by the end of 1994.

6) Throughout the entire process, some of us had assisted in the work of the committee and participated in its meetings. Citizen participation remained a topic on the agenda and we were encouraged to continue to stress this point. Of more immediate importance was a discussion of traffic problems where the very topic of the committee's work, i.e., through-traffic crossing the downtown area, was being discussed. Among several options as solutions a new bypass road was planned. This problem had been under public debate for long and it seemed the solution was at hand. After some in-group discussions we found that a new road was likely to produce more private traffic rather than divert it from the built-up areas. We started slowly and carefully to argue that this bypass might not be necessary if consequent restrictions on private traffic could be imposed over the entire town: speed limits, dead-end and one-way streets, speed bumpers, trees and flowers to be planted, parking restrictions. It took several meetings to find people receptive to our arguments, but finally our proposal was included in the list of recommendations to be made to the city council. Any decision to be taken for or against a new bypass road could be postponed until the effects of traffic restrictions became clear. Under public pressure, the city

council decided to follow our proposal well before the committee report came on its table.

We also argued in favour of a thorough ecological review of the two zoning-plans. The workshop had been helpful to prepare the ground and motivate the committee to come back to issues which it did not expect to find on its table. The committee was finally so convinced that it recommended to the city council to take the decision immediately and thus stop the procedure of enacting the planned regulation. The Council approved. The next step was for the Town Council to engage two or three professional planners with experience in this sort of task for a committee meeting to review the zoning plans and to give advise on what the major legal instruments and fixpoints ought to be. After this and if necessary, a new plan could be commissioned. One of the students started work on her diploma thesis in which she brought together arguments in favour of, and practical experiences made with, ecological regulations in zoning plans. This was certainly one of the major achievements of our work.

Another important issue was public transportation. We arrived at the following situation: There is a railway-line touching the northern edge of the town, but although the long-distance line is very busy, the existing railway station has been out of use for years due to lack of demand from the town inhabitants. It was not difficult to understand that re-activation of the station was a compulsory part of any attempt at ecological urban development. The problem is that the station is cut off from the residential areas by a commercial zone, and is therefore outside walking distance for most residents. We have therefore proposed re-location of the commercial zone towards an empty area north of the railway tracks, together with zoning the space between the existing residential area and the railway station as a higher density residential area. We have just begun justifying this proposal and cannot tell what will be the outcome initial reactions have been negative because the proposal seems too utopian besides being too costly for most committee members.

7) Our next action was a proposal to school teachers to ask their pupils to write essays on the future prospects of their town. The authors of essays which appear especially creative will be invited to participate in another Futures Workshop. The goal could be to write a position statement for the committee on behalf of the young, and this might open avenues to invite positions statements from, or organize public hearings with, the old, women, handicapped or other groups which would usually have no voice. The committee already agreed that this could be the next step after it finished its first version and before submitting it to the city council.

8) In all action taken by us, and upon our suggestion as also that of the committee, extensive newspaper coverage was mandatory. Even if active

and visible participation by citizens was not overwhelmingly impressive it could be assumed that the general level of information was high. It remains to be seen what this will mean for the public debates of the city council when it comes to enact the basic principles for the future development of the town.

CONCLUSION AND EVALUATION

This was, of course, an experiment in active and community-related learning which we could not copy from an existing blueprint, which we could not foresee in its development, and in which we could invest only limited resources. What did we achieve, and where did we fail? Although the process is not yet finished, we could assist in informing and raising the awareness of the public, beginning with the young. We could convince the committee and the city council that wide citizen participation makes a difference and contributes to improving the planning process. And we could submit and organize arguments convincing enough to take decisions in the spheres of private traffic and zoning according to the ecological criteria. These are achievements we consider worth the effort. Despite the complexity of comprehensive ecological urban development, it is reasonable to concentrate on a few strategic elements. The side effects were of course that members of the committee did reflect on what "ecological" would mean, and used the argument on several other occasions.

Our experiment, as citizen participation in general, could only succeed under conditions where decision-makers were open to arguments. In very conflicting situations with clearly polarized positions of interest, especially in zero-sum situations, neither citizen participation nor contributions like ours would have been so openly welcomed and effective. It therefore makes sense to scan the scene more carefully for open or hidden agendas before any real involvement can be considered.

What we did not achieve, however, was mostly in the field of traditional university teaching and learning. Of course there had been many opportunities for the project leader to generalize and theorize the practical experiences made, and to contribute to a final report of higher (academic) quality. There was neither enough time nor enough interest for this. But as the entire process, in case it should be repeated, could be better organized, there might be improvements possible. On the other hand, this is what other courses and seminars in the graduate programme do achieve. Certainly, the learning by doing and direct community involvement was a new and unexpected experience for all of us. We learned to understand that it is not university folks who are bound to teach others but rather that our comparative advantage is in searching, scanning, filtering and concentrating information which would not be so easily accessible to the people involved.

We all lost a good deal of our usual arrogance and learned to listen to others with more respect and attention. We also learnt that institutional authority between professors and students is not a valid argument per se, and should not determine the social atmosphere in the working group. This, too, we consider a step towards sustainability.

Finally, direct university-community interaction needs other curricula and conditions to become really and permanently fruitful. We cannot ignore the structural differences between a university course and a real world planning process. A one-year students' project has a very limited frame of reference in which action-related research is difficult to integrate. It was to our advantage that we agreed to have one project run throughout the full two years of graduate studies. But even this has nothing to do with the time frames of real world action which may be longer, or shorter. A more flexible form of organization should be found—which would mean a revision of the entire graduate programme and the reduction of the workload in other forms of learning. We did not arrive at the coordinated set of diploma thesis on this panning problem which we hoped to achieve.

To our surprise, there was general openness for the sustainability argument in all members on the Committee, irrespective of their party or association affiliation. We even could gradually pull back and trust on the input given. It was not so much information given from our side but rather the encouragement to others that their partly intuitive, partly incomplete information may become a basis for taking stands. Thus, looking back, it was not so decisive that our own knowledge was far from perfect. It was rather the issues we raised and the questions we asked which were instrumental to set the process on the right tracks. There was surprisingly little difference among the Committee members, and political fighting was the exception rather than the rule.